What people have said about Selma James

"One of the most important figures in the new way of thinking in the 1970s and 1980s was Selma James. James's *Marx and Feminism* deserves to be considered one of the great feminist contributions to Marxist thought . . . not so much a rupture with Marxism as its necessary extension."
—*Monthly Review*

"An intellectually ambitious attempt to synthesize Marxism, feminism, and post-colonialism, not with the usual sellotaped hyphenations."
—Jenny Turner, *London Review of Books*

"Selma James is a treasure . . . one of the key political thinkers and activists of our times."
—Marcus Rediker, author of *The Slave Ship* (Penguin Books, 2008)

"In an era where women are encouraged to 'lean in' to capitalism and power, *Sex, Race, and Class* provides a much-needed reminder that housework and care work are work—and deserve to be recognized and compensated as such. James not only details women's campaigns that might otherwise be forgotten but provides a valuable blueprint for organizing towards a truly liberated society."
—Victoria Law, author of *Resistance Behind Bars: The Struggles of Incarcerated Women* (PM Press, 2012)

"When Selma James speaks, I listen. When she writes, I read. She has been a crucial part of my re-education for decades. She is one of the few public intellectuals who engages with issues and people all over the world yet still remains connected to the grassroots. The writings and ideas of Selma James are as relevant now as they have ever been. Her solidarity knows no borders, her compassion excludes no sufferer."
—Benjamin Zephaniah, poet, writer, lyricist, musician, and naughty boy

"Building from the brilliance of *Sex, Race, and Class*, this work powerfully addresses the recent and present struggles of those whose labour of caring protects the future. This is about how grassroots movements can challenge power, and change the world."
—Bonita Lawrence, Indigenous Studies, York U

"Since *A Woman's Place* (1952), Selma James has been giving us unique insights into the meaning of autonomy and the political potential of care work. This new anthology illuminates the significance of James's work for a revolutionary climate politics. A true gift from one of the most brilliant minds of our time."
—Stefania Barca, author of *Forces of Reproduction* (Cambridge University Press, 2020)

"Selma James is a force of nature in the flesh and on the page. She fearlessly grapples with complex ideas, but her writing remains crystal clear and compelling. Stop what you are doing and read her now!"
—Maya Oppenheim, women's correspondent, the *Independent*, UK

"Selma James's prose, at once theoretical and inspirational, has provided a renewed praxis to consider and work with. . . [P]utting motherhood on the political agenda rather than women in boardrooms made her politics at once meaningful and important."
—Amrita Shodhan, feministsindia.com

"Selma James is a living icon. Her groundbreaking Wages for Housework Campaign informs decades of feminist thought and activism. James's writings are needed now more than ever."
—Kristin Lawless, author of *Formerly Known as Food* (St. Martin's Press, 2018)

"An insightful and exceedingly intelligent political analyst."
—Dr. Gerald Horne, author of *The Dawning of the Apocalypse* (Monthly Review Press, 2020)

"Selma James has been living and writing about the intersections of race, class, and gender since long before the concept of intersectionality was introduced. . . . [Her] book is inspiring because of her ability to write plainly, incisively, and accessibly about complex ideas and complicated political moments."
—Paul Kivel, author of *You Call This a Democracy?* (Rowman & Littlefield, 2006)

"*Sex, Race, and Class* is a must-read for anyone who wants to understand and change the world from an exploitative culture based on women's work to one where we all are valued, and that includes men."
—Margaretta D'Arcy, Irish Republican, author and playwright, and anti-war campaigner

"Clarity and commitment to Haiti's revolutionary legacy. A sister after my own heart."
—Danny Glover, actor and activist

"Coming as I did from the working class into academia, Selma James has helped me to see how an academic can take direction from the grassroots movement and be useful to it. Her work should be in every library, on every reading list, a must-read for all of us trying to change the world!"
—Maggie Ronayne, National University of Ireland, Galway, and trade unionist

"Selma James is the champion and philosopher of the revolutionary subject that is the housewife. Her theory and practice are one."
—Qalandar Bux Memon, editor, *Naked Punch Review*

"It's time to acknowledge James's pathbreaking analysis: since 1972 she has reinterpreted the capitalist economy to show that it rests on the usually invisible unwaged caring work of women."
—Dr. Peggy Antrobus, feminist, author

"Reminds us that liberation cannot be handed down from above. A feminism that truly matters."
—Dr. Alissa Trotz, Women & Gender and Caribbean Studies, Toronto

"[R]eflects in concentrated form the history of the new society struggling to be born. In this respect, Selma James embodies in these essays the spirit of the revolutionary tradition at its most relevant."
—Dr. Robert A. Hill, literary executor of the estate of CLR James, University of California, Los Angeles, and director of the Marcus Garvey Papers Project

"In varied contexts and at many venues, including the UN, James's output over six decades shines with radical clarity on the economy, humanity, and society. . . . Hers is a gift of clarifying often knotty issues in words that people can grasp."
—Seth Sandronsky, *Z Magazine*

"This book is not only an intellectual tour de force, it is the best how to manual for organizing I have ever read. . . . The staggering breadth of James's writing takes your breath away . . . practical how-to feminism from one of the outstanding thinkers of our time."
—Cary Gee, *Tribune*

ISBN: 978–1–62963–838–6 (print)
ISBN: 978–1–62963–854–6 (ebook)

Library of Congress Control Number: 2020934741

Cover by John Yates / www.stealworks.com
Cover photograph © Peter Marshall
Interior design by briandesign

10 9 8 7 6 5 4 3 2 1

PM Press
PO Box 23912
Oakland, CA 94623
www.pmpress.org

Printed in the USA.

Our Time Is Now

Sex, Race, Class, and Caring for People and Plan

Selma James

Contents

Introduction

Margaret Prescod

This second volume of writings by Selma James, *Our Time Is Now*, deepens and develops the themes of the first selection published in 2012.[1] I am thankful for this opportunity to review the long road she and I have travelled together.

In 1974, I thought the author of *Sex, Race, and Class* was Black.[2] When friends told me she was not, I argued that a white woman could not have written a pamphlet that had such clarity about race and autonomy. Nearly fifty years ago, Selma James wrote about what today in academic circles is called "intersectionality."

In a women's study group in New York City that was the precursor to International Black Women for Wages for Housework (BWWFH), Audre Lorde, the distinguished poet, Andaiye from Guyana, and others of us would discuss how as Black women we could not cut ourselves up into parts—the part that was a woman, Black, low-income, lesbian, etc.—we were a whole and we faced the oppression and discrimination that came with each part. We could not choose one over the other. Uniquely, *Sex, Race, and Class* spoke to that.

When I was a young teacher in Ocean Hill-Brownsville, in Brooklyn, I sat in the aides' room during breaks and lunch; I could not stand to be with the teachers who were white and, for the most part, racist and disrespectful of their students. It was in this context that our group questioned what feminists were going on about: a job outside the home never meant liberation for us, now or historically.

Sex, Race, and Class started with those with the least. It assumed the women's movement was broader than white middle-class feminism. This made an opening for women like me, who did not see our own situation in what was being put forward as feminism, to be active on women's rights. It meant that what I had been doing with welfare mothers in the community and their children at school was part of the women's movement. Mainstream feminism had never acknowledged the Black women who not only held their families together, figuring out how to do the difficult job of raising their children with the fewest of resources, but were also the activists in their communities. Demanding money from the State rather than competing with men for a career was not considered feminist.

The perspective that *Sex, Race, and Class* put forward enabled those of us—Black women—who wanted to work with and in the Black community but were fed up with the sexism of organizations dominated by men to find our way, find our voice, find our autonomy.

Selma's writing brought a freshness, an easily understood and practical analysis. As a Black immigrant from the Global South—Barbados—I easily related to "A Woman's Place," even though it was written in 1952 Los Angeles. It wasn't bogged down in the academic formulations that so many political people get caught up in. The language was popular, straightforward, and it was full of home truths. As a fan of her husband, CLR James—from Trinidad—I was delighted to learn that he had encouraged her to write it.

"A Woman's Place" described and identified caring work as the nub; this was then developed in the 1970s classic she co-authored, *The Power of Women and the Subversion of the Community*.³

But it was *Sex, Race, and Class* that made the biggest impression on me—it inspired me to borrow money to travel to London to meet the woman who had written it and to see if indeed she was the real deal. Turns out she was.

The International Wages for Housework Campaign (WFH) Selma founded was not simply an analysis. It was a perspective and a demand. It didn't have a missionary approach about helping others—we were all in the struggle for our own liberation. That impressed me. WFH wanted to act, to campaign for money for mothers, for caregivers. Though we were not at what left analysts called "the point of production," we were workers!

The phrase "unwaged" work, which she coined, hit home to me. I grew up in a small rural village in a British colony. I saw how hard the women worked: the cooking, the cleaning, growing food, taking care of the children, making and washing the clothes, comforting everyone, trying for their families to have a life of dignity. But hard work did not equal a pay cheque, even when entire communities survived on this work. So focusing on unwaged workers, on campaigning for money for caregivers, starting with those with the least, in my village, as in New York City, made sense as a step in changing the world.

Raised in the movement of the 1930s that won social security and welfare, Selma brought her working-class experience, including time working in factories, into the WFH Campaign. (She does not have a university degree.) A member of the US organization headed by CLR,[4] she joined him in London, England, after he was deported under McCarthy. She did support work for the anti-colonial and anti-apartheid movements.[5] She was the first organizing secretary of the Campaign Against Racial Discrimination, and a key witness in the famous Mangrove trial, the first in Britain where Black defendants challenged police racism and won.[6]

From 1958 to 1962, the Jameses lived in Trinidad, spending months in Barbados and Jamaica, working for independence and federation of the English-speaking Caribbean. The lessons and skills learnt along the way were integral to Selma's work as international coordinator of the WFH Campaign and, from 2000, of the Global Women's Strike (GWS).

Meeting the Campaign inspired Wilmette Brown, who had been in the Black Panther Party and had lived and worked in Africa, and me to found Black Women for Wages for Housework (BWWFH) in 1975. We organized with welfare mothers and Black and Puerto Rican students in the SEEK program at City University of New York (CUNY), who were demanding stipends and book money and for their welfare checks not to be cut if they received either. We also organized with Black sex workers, and the founding of the New York Prostitutes Collective, which later became USPROS (US PROStitutes Collective), grew out of that.

Her pathbreaking piece "Sex, Race, Class . . . and Autonomy" relates the unique theoretical and practical process that led to the creation and development of autonomous organizations within the WFH Campaign, now best known as Global Women's Strike. Autonomy has been the key to keeping the Campaign and every organization in it focused on attacking racism and every form of discrimination in every struggle. It has been the basis of forty-five years of continuous effective organizing. It lifts the perspective of Wages for Housework from an academic exercise to a concrete way of organizing internationally, despite and against the divisions among us. With Black Lives Matter bursting out nationally and internationally, autonomy and how to work together across sectors is pushing forward onto everyone's agenda. This piece is useful now for now.

Soon after BWWFH was founded, there were problems with the New York WFH Committee, which was white. They accused us of being "too pushy," disagreed with our focus on mothers who were on welfare, and refused to work with us. The WFH groups in England, Canada, and the US stood strongly with us, defending Black women's right to autonomy, making sure that we had the support and resources we needed to carry out our campaigning. The New York Committee dissolved. Mariarosa Dalla Costa, who led the WFH groups in Italy, told Selma that we Black women were "presumptuous," and the international, which was coordinated from London, broke relations with Italy.

So there was a split on race. Perhaps we should have written about it at the time, but we didn't see the point of putting our resources into a public fight that would have distracted from the organizing we were learning to do.

We carried on with our successful campaign to ensure that mothers were able to keep both their welfare payments and their student grants without reduction. We formed the Queens College Women's Action Group on the campus where I was working and launched the "No Cuts Just Bucks" petition. We were also able to win the first childcare program at CUNY for students, faculty, and staff.[7]

In preparation for the first congressionally mandated conference on women in Houston, Texas, in 1977, we formed the Coalition of Grassroots Women. It included women like Beulah Sanders, a former president of the National Welfare Rights Organization, who got delegates elected to conference. We took our BWWFH newsletter *Safire* and strategized with London by phone[8]—Selma reminded us that we were not lobbyists but movement people trying to get a job done. We succeeded in getting the National Women's Conference to pass the pathbreaking resolution that welfare should be called a wage. The press release announcing this victory is included in this volume. It was drafted by Selma after we called her—we were exhausted! She read it to us by phone the next morning, and we were able to issue it.

The Houston resolution was never implemented, but Phoebe Jones, who jointly coordinates the US network with me, has made the case that it helped to hold off federally mandated welfare work requirements for two decades.

By the end of the 1980s, mainstream feminism had dug in, heralding that any job outside the home was where true liberation lay. The right to welfare was being chipped away, and Black welfare mothers, undefended with few exceptions, were being targeted by both Republicans and Democrats.

The Soviet Union was breaking up, and the anti-nuclear movement was exploding. In the UK, the WFH Campaign and BWWFH were witch-hunted for refusing to be with either the Eastern or the Western blocs—insisting instead on organizing at Greenham Common Women's Peace Camp with Yellow Gate, which was stubbornly non-aligned and anti-racist.[9]

Many an organization would have folded as the media trashed the WFH leadership in the UK. But Selma was not fazed. She'd been through the

McCarthy witch-hunt, she knew what to do to keep the Campaign focused and unafraid—we not only survived, we came out of this period stronger.

I moved to the West Coast for personal reasons, and in the mid-1980s I founded the Black Coalition Fighting Back Serial Murders out of outrage after seeing a TV announcement that eleven Black women were victims of a serial murderer in South LA. Selma, though in London, was a phone call or letter away and a constant source of encouragement—we always prioritized money for long distance calls to keep the network together.

As the point of reference for the international campaign, Selma worked closely with the late Clotil Walcott, founder of the National Union of Domestic Employees in Trinidad and Tobago, and the late Andaiye, who had returned to Guyana and was a founder of Red Thread, a women's organization. She made sure Clotil, a fantastic grassroots organizer, would have the global platform she deserved. In "Andaiye: The Uses of Autonomy," Selma reviews how applying the Campaign's perspective gave Andaiye new insights into Guyanese history.

During the UN Decade for Women and follow-up conferences we took our perspective to the UN. Our fifty-seven-strong multiracial delegation to Beijing (1995) from countries of both the Global North and the Global South reflected the network we had built. Working closely with Andaiye, who was a member of the CARICOM delegation,[10] we successfully combined grassroots campaigning with lobbying in the halls of power. The pieces published in the "Time Off for Women" section give an idea of the organizing in this period.

The section culminates with "An Income to Care for People and Planet," with Nina López, which brought together human reproduction and the reproduction of the natural world as one whole—greater than the sum of its parts. A crucial campaigning development.

In "Revisiting the Works of CLR James," Selma's observations and insights about two CLR classics, one on the Haitian Revolution and one on cricket, and her interview about their life and work together are particularly valuable and have lessons for organizing.

As she often says, it is not enough to lift up those who made the revolution in Haiti over two centuries ago, we must stand with their descendants—the Black Jacobins of today who are struggling to defend that revolution—not only in words but in action. So when, in 2003, I connected with the distinguished and dedicated Haitian Pierre Labossière (the year before the US-backed coup against Haiti's first democratically elected president, the beloved Jean-Bertrand Aristide),[11] Selma proposed that the whole GWS network support the Haitian grassroots. As she points out, the Haitian movement, though the most pivotal to the abolition of slavery in the Americas, is the most neglected—we all owe a great debt to Haitians and must pay it.

In 2011, Selma and I were invited to Haiti to welcome Aristide, his wife and colleague Mildred Trouillot, and their children back from exile. In "The Black Jacobins, Past and Present," Selma speaks about her admiration and respect for the extraordinary work of the Aristides and for the courage and resilience of the grassroots.

Andaiye and I mobilized for the Caribbean to oppose the coup. The GWS, although unfunded, helped to send us to Haiti to meet with activists on the ground. I have been back several times, both for Women of Colour in the Global Women's Strike (WoC/GWS) and as a journalist to report on the fraudulent elections and the massacres by UN forces and by the various US-selected presidents installed after Aristide.[12] One of Selma's articles with Nina López compares Jean-Bertrand Aristide with Venezuelan President Hugo Chávez and Tanzania's first President Julius Nyerere.

Selma refers to Nyerere's "Arusha Declaration" as one of Africa's great contributions to world politics.[13] Her introduction to *Ujamaa: The Hidden Story of Tanzania's Socialist Villages*, republished here, recounts the movement for African socialism promoted by Nyerere's anti-imperialist anti-capitalist leadership, his unique acknowledgement of how hard women worked, and the greed for power of his party colleagues that ultimately defeated him and the movement.[14] Personal ambition, as a political force from which we must protect our movements, is a constant preoccupation that our network was trained to recognize and reject whenever and wherever it appears.

When the Poor People's Campaign—A National Call for Moral Revival emerged in the US, and we immediately began to work with it, we learnt that they called their movement structure "fusion"—whoever comes into the work brings their own issues and experience and enhances and develops the whole, from the bottom up. This is very close to the way the WFH/GWS (on a much smaller scale) has always organized. It is an exciting development of how sectors can come together.

My touchstone is always my village, my parents who taught me to be proud of who I am and where I come from, my grandmother whose hard low-waged work as an immigrant to the US helped us to survive, and my daughter. Growing up I wanted to be part of changing the world so no child should ever be hungry as I often had been. Working with Selma has been the most formative political relationship in my adult life. It has helped to bring the dream of that young village girl to fruition.

Thank you, Selma. And congratulations for your ninety years on your earth walk.

Love and power,
Margaret
August 2020

Notes

1   Selma James, *Sex, Race, and Class: The Perspective of Winning—A Selection of Writings 1952–2011* (Oakland: PM Press, 2012).
2   Originally published in *Race Today*, January 1974; see Selma James, "Sex, Race and Class," accessed September 18, 2020, https://la.utexas.edu/users/hcleaver/sexraceclass.html.
3   Mariarosa Dalla Costa and Selma James, *The Power of Women and the Subversion of the Community* (Bristol, UK: Falling Wall Press, 1975).
4   The Johnson-Forest Tendency; see "Beyond Boundaries—A Talk with Selma James on Her Political Activities and Years with CLR James," 155–74, this volume.
5   George Padmore and Dorothy Pizer were family friends, and Ethel de Keyser, who headed the Anti-Apartheid Movement, was Selma's close friend.
6   See reference in "The Organizational Strategy of Autonomy," 204–15, this volume.
7   Years later, there was a CUNY-wide strike for childcare.
8   London helped with layout and printing money.
9   Margaretta D'Arcy from Ireland, who lived at Yellow Gate part-time, wrote an account of the dispute; see Margaretta D'Arcy, "Power to the Sisters!" in John Arden and Margaretta D'Arcy, *Awkward Corners* (Grantham, UK: Methuen, 1988), 229–39. Those aligned with the Soviet Union tried to prevent the book from being released, but eventually it was.
10 The Caribbean Community is a grouping of twenty countries for economic integration, foreign policy coordination, human and social development, and security; see "Who We Are," Caricom, accessed November 22, 2020, https://caricom.org/our-community/who-we-are.
11 Pierre Labossière is a member of the Haiti Action Committee in Oakland, California.
12 See "Special Report: Massacres in Haiti," Pacifica's Margaret Prescod, Real News Network, April 14, 2019, accessed September 18, 2020, https://tinyurl.com/y3v85rm8.
13 Julius Nyerere, "The Arusha Declaration," February 5, 1967, accessed September 18, 2020, https://www.marxists.org/subject/africa/nyerere/1967/arusha-declaration.htm.
14 Selma James, "Introduction," in Ralph Ibbott, *Ujamaa: The Hidden Story of Tanzania's Socialist Villages* (London: Crossroads Books, 2014).

From Wages for Housework to a
Care Income
(1977–2020)

Houston: Equality Begins with Money

(1977)

This press release was issued after we won the historic resolution described below at the first congressionally mandated National Women's Conference in the US, attended by twenty thousand women. Aid to Families with Dependent Children was the first wage that single mothers had won from the State, but it was not recognized as a wage. Such payments in any country have always been a focus for organizing for the Wages for Housework (WFH) Campaign. When it was passed, I got a call in London with the great news asking me to draft a press release, which I read to Margaret Prescod over the phone the next morning.

At the International Women's Year National Women's Conference (November 18–21, 1977) in Houston, Texas, the Wages for Housework Campaign announced itself as a national and international force.

Margaret Prescod-Roberts of Black Women for Wages for Housework (US), a delegate from New York State, led the Wages for Housework contingent which came from many states, as well as from Canada and Britain. We were determined that the conference should go on record against Carter's Welfare Reform "Program for Better Jobs and Income" now before Congress. We were determined that welfare, the wages some women have won, would not be lost at Houston.

Many other individuals and organizations came to Houston to fight the welfare women's cause, among them three delegates who were leaders of the great women's movement for welfare in the 1960s—Frankie Mae Jeter, Beulah Sanders, and Johnnie Tillmon.

The question we all faced was how, on behalf of all the women who could not afford to be at Houston, to refuse Carter's welfare "reform," which the official resolution in the proposed National Plan of Action endorsed.

On the agenda in alphabetical order, welfare was, as usual, at the bottom. Money for women, either on welfare or in low-paying jobs, single or married, lesbian or straight—and always one man away from welfare—was scheduled to come last, the anti-climax after the "feminist" issues.

But welfare isn't just "another feminist issue." It's every woman's insurance policy against complete dependence and starvation.

Pro-Plan, the ruling coalition of the conference, discouraged any departure from the official resolutions, all of which they backed. They claimed that Pro-Life, the anti-abortion coalition, would use debate on any issue as the occasion to block the three resolutions which Pro-Plan considered crucial: the ERA,[1] abortion rights, and lesbian rights. But they were wrong.

Another coalition emerged.

The "Pro-Money Coalition," which included disabled women, Black, Hispanic, and Native American women, lesbian women, prostitute women, and homemakers—placed, replaced, and "displaced"—made welfare, the money we have already won, the focus for all other issues. The power to refuse rape, battering, and low-paying jobs—and to win childcare, education, custody, and lesbian rights, as well as the choice to have or not to have children, depends on our access to money. Money is the power to live our own lives and make our own plans.

As we discussed in our own groups, caucused with each other, and lobbied the delegates, the Wages for Housework Campaign demonstrated that together we have the power to change the agenda, refuse Carter's reform, keep the money we have already won, and demand more. Pro-Money was able to win over both Pro-Plan and Pro-Life.

As the substitute resolution on welfare was being presented, a banner carried by Black and Hispanic women demanding "No Cuts—Just Bucks" moved through the coliseum. And from the bleachers Black and white women of all ages and from every region chanted together: "Every mother is a working mother." Not even the Ku Klux Klan, which was openly present in the Mississippi delegation, could deny that!

The substitute welfare resolution, which was overwhelmingly passed, states:

> The elimination of poverty must be a priority for all those working for equal rights for women.
>
> We support increased federal funding for income transfer payments (e.g., Social Security, SSI, AFDC).[2] Congress should approve a federal floor

under payments to provide an adequate standard of living based on each state's cost of living. And just as with other workers, homemakers receiving income transfer payments should be afforded the dignity of having that payment called a wage, not welfare.

We oppose the Carter Administration proposal for welfare reform (HR 9030), which, among other things, eliminates food stamps, threatens to eliminate CETA training and CETA jobs paying more than minimum wage,[3] and does not guarantee adequate day care. We oppose proposals for "workfare," where welfare mothers would be forced to "work off" their grants, which is work without wages, without fringe benefits or bargaining rights, and without dignity.

We strongly support a welfare reform program developed from ongoing consultation with persons who will be impacted.

"The women from the bottom of America fought for a place on the agenda and won," said Margaret Prescod-Roberts. "We were what was happening at Houston. The other women, some of them on their way to the top of US government and industry, saw that. They dropped their own resolution and backed ours.

"The next battles are first for implementation and second to extend the victory of wages for women everywhere who work for free or for peanuts."

Notes

1   Reference to the Equal Rights Amendment to the US Constitution banning discrimination based on sex. Passed by the Senate in 1972, it has still to be ratified by all US states.
2   Supplemental Security Income (SSI) and Aid to Families with Dependent Children (AFDC).
3   Comprehensive Employment and Training Act 1973.

Time Off for Women (1985–1990)

In 1985, at the UN Women's Conference in Nairobi, after we won the UN resolution to count women's unremunerated work, the press from a number of countries came to us and asked what we were going to do about it. We said, "Well, we'll have some international actions," and they said, "Do you mean a strike?" and I said, "Well, some kind of stoppage. And since October 24 is the tenth anniversary of the Iceland Women's Day Off, we'll do it then." They headlined: "Women Strike!" But we were more modest. We called it Time Off for Women, inviting women to make their work visible by not doing it, taking whatever time off they could. We sent a message to Iceland which was read to the thousands of women who had gathered to celebrate their tenth anniversary. We said: "Iceland women opened the UN Decade. The women of the world are closing it together." We heard there was a great cheer!

For many years, Time Off events took place in a number of countries every October 24. From the letters we got back, sometimes weeks after (computers were just coming in), we figured that women in about sixty countries took some time off or some collective action.

Leading up to Time Off Day, we issued weekly updates, some of which are published here with my 1985 speech in London. This was before email and computer layout programmes so we used bold letters to vary the script. The originals used the British format day-month-year.

October 24, 1985, Time Off for Women

I just wanted to remind people, or let those people know who came in later, that the day was organized as a result of the Wages for Housework Campaign having lobbied at the final conference of the UN Decade for Women for the UN to agree that all of women's work, waged and unwaged, in the home, in the community, on the land, in agriculture, everywhere, that all of that work finally be counted in the GNP of every country;[1] and that there are women in many countries who today are in one way or another taking Time Off.

Now I have a taxi waiting for me because Yorkshire Television is going to have us on, and we don't miss one opportunity to go on the media—we're media greedy—because that is the way to get the information to women. One of the things I've learnt in organizing this day is that when we called Time Off for Women there wasn't a woman who didn't think she was entitled to Time Off, but she thought it wasn't real—until she saw it in the media. When she saw it in the media, she said, "It's real, it's happening, I can actually think of taking Time Off for myself or with my neighbours or even come to see what other women are doing." So though I haven't a lot of time—you have, I hope, the whole day. What an enormous thing, a whole day.

I wanted to speak before I have to go. The first speaker today was a full-time housewife and a young woman, and I also identify myself and feel deeply in my soul that I am a housewife, because much of my life I have been a full-time housewife. Now, they tell full-time housewives a lot of things that are not true. They tell you that you don't work; they tell you that you work very hard. They don't value you, and then they tell you that they don't pay you because you are invaluable. They tell you that you are a specialist in this work, that nobody else can do it. And then they tell you, worse, that nobody else *is* doing it. And that is the most pernicious lie of all.

You are doing that work, but other women who are not full-time house-wives are also doing it, and they don't want you to know, because they want to keep you separate from the rest. They tell you that if you mix with the others, you will lose your dignity, lose your power, lose your respectability. Our respectability was never worth anything anyway. We never had too much power. And our experience is that only when we acknowledge that all women are doing this work in varying degrees do they afford us the dignity of taking any notice that *we* are doing it.

So we're getting together. This day has been a big opportunity for us to get together. And I think that I'm not the only housewife here who's saying to herself, "We are the housewives; we are the women who our husbands have warned us against." They told us that we shouldn't be with women like us. They said we should stay home by ourselves. We are breaking with a great many barriers, lies, distortions, and what the media calls "the real housewives." It's something they make up, and they tell you that if you don't organize, that if you stay at home, that if you do whatever they say, you're real. But once you leave, you're not real. You're not a real housewife, you're not a real mother, you're not a real grandmother, you're not a real neighbour, you're not an "ordinary" woman anymore—and therefore you don't count. When you were at home, and you did nothing about your situation, and they didn't count you, then you counted. See, that's how they do it.

It's time now, today, that we begin to acknowledge that we are every woman, each of us, carrying the burdens of the world, two-thirds of the world's work, and that in the course of acknowledging that burden and making governments acknowledge that burden, we are in the process of lifting that burden, finally, once and for all, off our shoulders.

Just one other thing. In organizing the event I took a lot of the international phone calls. The Flemish woman from Belgium was really keen, and there were two things that she conveyed which many women conveyed—but the Flemish woman felt it so deeply that she spelled everything out, even though it was expensive on the international telephone.

First of all, she said, "The feminists don't want our work to be counted. They don't want to acknowledge housewives." Now, there are many women here who consider ourselves feminists, but we're not that kind of feminist; we're not the kind of feminist who thinks that only the career woman is the ideal—maybe they think Margaret Thatcher is the ideal, she's a career woman, and she certainly doesn't like housewives.

The second thing that she said was. "We understand that you work with prostitutes, and that you work with lesbians." I said, "Yes, we do." And she said, "Well, you know the Flemish women are very Catholic, and they don't work with prostitutes or lesbians." I said to myself, "They may not *know* they work with prostitutes or with lesbians." I said to her, "That's fine. The important thing is to win, and we must all come out and take Time Off together." She just breathed a sigh of relief and said, "Yes!" by which she meant—at least this is how I understood her—"I wanted to see if you were going to tell me that *I* had to work with prostitutes, and *I* had to work with lesbians." And since I didn't tell her what to do, only that she could take some Time Off in her own life, she was quite willing for *me* to work with prostitutes and lesbians.

I think that's how a lot of women are. They have come to the women's movement to liberate themselves from the burden of work, from the burden of slavery, and from the burden of poverty. They've come into the women's movement to work with whichever women also want to relieve themselves of the burden of work and slavery and poverty, and as we grow and join together, we will win.

. . .

Final Update Before the First-Ever "Time Off for Women," October 24, 1985

Dear Sisters,

Since the last update on October 8, we know that **Belgium**, **Egypt**, (**Northern**) **Ireland**, **Norway** and **Switzerland** will also be taking **Time Off** on **October 24**. And more cities in **Britain**, including in **Wales** and **Scotland**, have joined us.

Messages of support enclosed. Dora Russell sent £20. Doris Lessing sent £20 (approximately $26) but no message—but the money talks! Other messages are promised, and Anna Bowman, chair of Camden's Women's Committee has issued a press release in support.

We now know of women who heard about **Time Off** by word of mouth and are planning to invade their town centres on **Oct 24** with brooms, mops, and petitions—the kind of event that can be done with a minimum of preparation and yet have a great impact.

With women in about two dozen cities in the UK and almost two dozen countries taking **Time Off** together, this will be a historic occasion in the movement of all women and of all workers. In the course of organizing the international network which is bringing to birth this global event aiming to make all women's work visible, the work that has already become visible is women's massive organizing. There are literally millions of women in all kinds of organizations from **Kenya** to the **Dutch** countryside, from **Norway** to **Trinidad**, and from **Montréal** to **Cairo**. It is clear that the movement of women is more massive than anyone knows and capable of moving quickly and imaginatively, overlooking differences among us and concentrating on what we have in common. There are even indications that women are planning to have total strikes on **Oct 24**, 1986!

Please note that the **Time Off for Women** banner is held up with a broom on one side and a hoe on the other. Many women whose unpaid work extends out of the home and into the fields (they are often called farmers' wives) are taking **Time Off** on **Oct 24**. We are demanding that governments count *all* women's work. This is the opportunity for those of us in cities to demand that our own work be counted and at the same time demand that the work of those of us in the countryside in the Third World and in rural areas in the metropolis also be counted. This is the first time, in fact, that city women and country women, that Third World women and metropolitan women, have had the same demand and are making that demand together. One housewives' association in Europe was aware and respected that the Wages for Housework Campaign "works with lesbians and works with prostitutes," and their membership, "being very Catholic," did not. But they had no objection to taking joint action. In fact, on the issue of counting women's work, many women are ready to bypass what usually divides them from other women and, thus, also bypass the limitations on their organizing and on their power. We hope everyone who is taking action on **Oct 24** will be open to (almost) any support they are offered, since counting women's work can cause a re-evaluation in many women's minds about many issues.

Also bear in mind that there's more to this "housework thing" than has met the media eye up to now. Especially in the economic crisis, the work of women is multiplying. With less money, housework gets harder. With more unemployment, "tension management" becomes a full-time job. With hospital closures, patients who are still ill are sent home—for us to care for. With nursery cuts, mothers work harder with longer hours. With fewer meals on wheels and less home help, it is women at home or "after work" who take up the slack—not only mothers, but daughters, sisters, nieces, aunts, neighbours, friends. If our kids are Black, there is too often a whole lot of work dealing with the police, and having to deal with racist attacks on ourselves and our families is another mountain of invisible work. Remember too that women do a lot of work to keep churches going, to keep community groups and tenants' associations going, PTAs ticking over[2]—and so on. All this work, which keeps the world going, is uncounted and invisible. Women count—governments must count women's work.

We enclose the press release, the messages of support so far (these are messages of support for *your* event too), and a badge in case you haven't seen it. All of these can help you with the press and what to say to them and to represent the international network of action for counting women's work of which you are part.

Good luck, and have a good **Time Off**. Love and power to the sisters internationally.

Selma

Messages of Support for TOFW 1985
received as of Monday 21st October (in alphabetical order)
Tony Benn, MP—Just a line to wish you success on October 24, when the "Time Off for Women" movement is holding its events in London. I strongly support this. . .

Mary Cane, Deputy Mayor of Camden—Congratulations for your impact on the UN End of Decade for Women Conference. We women must pursue recognition for all our work with unswerving persistence. All strength and love for the future of all women working together. Best wishes.

Glyn Ford, MEP—It's about time men recognized that women contribute to their wealth and well-being. Congratulations on your victory in the United Nations, and I hope that Governments will follow their lead.

Bruce Kent—Congratulations and best wishes on this important occasion.

Alf Lomas, MEP—As you know, I am always interested in your work, and you can count on my full support. I would like to send a message of support to the Open Day and congratulate you on all your efforts and achievements. I hope that following your success at the UN, you will now see some positive results. Best wishes.

Dora Russell—I enclose a donation of £20 (approximately $26). It is unlikely that I will be able to come to the meeting at Conway Hall. I hope it will be successful, but I also hope that it will be based on the whole question of women's unpaid work, including that in the fields and underpayment in factories.

Ansel Wong, Principal Race Relations Adviser, Greater London Council—Congratulations on your recent victory in Nairobi. . . . It is crucial to the struggle of women that their contribution to the world economy, whether it be remunerated or unremunerated, be recognized. That this demand should now come from a UN Conference can only lend it increased strength. We wish you every success on October 24, when women all over the world will be taking Time Off to make their national governments recognize the significance of their contribution. In Struggle.

. . .

October 17: Update of Activities for Time Off 1986—excerpt

And if you feel **Time Off for Women** can't accomplish much, remember the following two facts of history: Robert Wedderburn was the son of a Jamaican slave mother and a Scots slaveholding father who became a known preacher and organizer among working-class people in England. He was the first Black activist to send revolutionary propaganda to the West Indies from Britain, and his message to the people who were enslaved was to **go on strike annually for one hour**. The second fact is from the *Guardian* of December 31, 1985: In a letter, Colin Bibby, a teacher, talks about how he participated in the Great Teachers Strike (which was in fact about all the unwaged work teachers do which is never counted). He says, "Every month I take half a day's strike action in twenty-minute blocks and the combined effect closes the school for a week." Can you imagine what would happen if all women did that? We would close more than a school. Therefore, I say unto you: **take as much Time Off as you can!**

. . .

UPDATE of Activities Time Off 1990 (TO90)

"[U]nless] the Government adequately funds community care, women will continue to be exploited as the unwaged, unnoticed workforce making good the deficiencies in statutory provision."—Melanie Philips, commentary, recent *Guardian*

It took five years of **Time Off** (the first was **Oct 24**, 1985) to get such a clear media statement of how government policy depends on women's unwaged work. Congratulations to us all on the effectiveness of our work—our **Time Off** work!

Since 1986, we've asked councils to acknowledge their dependence on women's work by giving women **Time Off** with free leisure services; every year some say yes. In a few places, it's become tradition. For **TO90**, **Bury**, **Newham**, **Rochdale**, **Southwark**, and **Tameside** Councils offer free/low cost leisure services, some for a week, with sports like golf and horse riding—not usually available to the likes of us! **Aberdeen** put **TO90** together with One World Week in a fair/workshops, plus women's disco. In **Dundee's** main shopping centre, a two-week photo exhibit on women's unwaged and waged work in the Soviet Union. **Lothian** will run workshops for Council employees. **Tayside** will have three days of women's oral history seminars. **Peterborough** Town Hall: women's open day with workshops, exhibition, and international costume/craft fair.

Another change since 1985 is that women, increasingly aware of how much unwaged work we do, are demanding more of what's ours. TOGS, the Belgian housewives' organization which has taken **Time Off** since 1985, and which calls **TO-Day** "International Housewives Day," will hold a **TO90** speak-out in the main railway station in **Brussels**; from there to the minister of labour, and then hopefully to the prime minister, demanding wages for educational and caring work in the family. They're also hot on the trail of Belgian MEPs to press for support of the European resolution that the value of women's unwaged work be included in the EEC's GNPs.

So are the Italian housewives of OIKIA in **Verona**, **Naples**, and **Bari**. And, on **Oct 27**, they will be petitioning in Verona for implementation of any parliamentary initiatives such as this, all over the world.

In **Ireland**, Women in Media has asked the Council on the Status of Women to support the EEC resolution. On **Oct 27**, Margaretta D'Arcy and other women will lobby MEP Mark Killilea to get his support. Her Women's Radio, on the air from Nov 1–7, will have the theme, "Free Airwaves, Free Women: Women Count—Count Women's Work Radio Week"!

The **Greek** Non-Aligned Women's Movement are expecting **TO90** national media.

In **Barcelona**, **Spain**, the National Autonomous Union of Family Administrators (housewives) are organizing fifty thousand women to march to the Spanish government in **Madrid** in June 1991. . . . They will be protesting that housework isn't legally recognized as work, and they want money. More news to follow. Meanwhile, a Bristol woman teaching English to teenagers in **Barcelona** is creating a *Who Works for Me?* (*¿Quien trabaja para mí?*) exhibition with her class all **TO90** week.

North American women will be celebrating **TO90** in **Los Angeles**, **Philadelphia**, and **San Francisco**, with events centring on sport, alternative health, and fundraising. LA WFH launched **TO90** at the prestigious Huntington Library in a packed workshop on "Unwaged Work: The Nub of the Double Day—A Programme for All Working Women: In the Academy, in Service Industries, in Business and in the Home, etc." They're now preparing to meet with congresspeople to frame a bill to count women's work for the 1991 session of Congress. Then begins the hard work of organizing the Wages for Housework International Conference in Philadelphia, October 1991. (*Are you looking for money to get you there?*) **Montréal** Wages for Housework and Payday will interview French-speaking London women for community radio.

This year **TO90** in **Trinidad and Tobago** contends with the state of emergency which bans all outdoor meetings and any political activity and imposes a curfew, but they're doing better than ever. **Oct 18**: they celebrated Diwali, the Hindu festival of light; **Oct 19**: they attended an all-Caribbean women's meeting; **Oct 21**: Social Evening—women from African, Asian, and mixed descent communities, North and South Trinidad, didn't wait for the evening but were in and out all day. They played the tape of MP Mildred Gordon's speech when she presented the Ten-Minute Rule Bill on counting women's work in the House of Commons; **Oct 24**: press conference. This is the first year they had a couple of donations from local industry which they can sell as fundraisers. *And* they're circulating a letter to their PM, calling on him to implement the **T&T** National Policy to count women's work!

In the **UK**, all kinds of groups have distributed **TO90** leaflets, including women's centres. **York** Women's Centre will petition on **Oct 27**. On **TO-Day**, students at Froebel College **South London**, will petition in the refectory. Women in all **Oxford** colleges will attend a **TO-Day** picnic in Radcliffe Square, city centre. For at least the past three years, **Bristol** Poly and **Cardiff** University Students Unions have given **women employees a day's paid Time Off**, in recognition of their unwaged work. **Warwick** University women have leafletted all halls of residence. Trainees and staff at **Camden** Training Centre will stop work an hour early to have a cup of tea before joining us at the Commons SPEAK-OUT.

As well as petitioning in all the market towns and displaying a banner in front of the Town Hall, the **TO90 Tameside** group held a free showing of *Shirley Valentine*, award-winning film about a housewife who changes her life by taking **TIME OFF**, and had a great jumble sale; the People's Centre in **Denton** has a **TO90** night out with local entertainers and a DJ; **TO90** has won Council transport—a minibus—to the House of Commons SPEAK-OUT.[3] **Bristol TO90** is also bringing a minibus to the HofC SPEAK-OUT.

Who Works for Me? the anti-sexist, anti-racist children's art exhibition is **TO90**'s successful ongoing project: **Bristol** had its first showing at All Hallows Community Education Centre—women's unwaged campaigning had won the reopening of this great community resource. *Who Works for Me?* is also on show at London's **St Pancras** Library for two weeks and at **East Ham** and **Bury** Town Halls in **TO90** week.

TO90 got a flying start, first with a July **TIME OFF** demonstration in **Nicosia, Cyprus**, which we only heard about from a visitor to our centre. Then, on **Oct 2**, in **Blackpool**, **UK**, a Labour Party Conference fringe meeting: "Count Women's Work—Legislation Now!" Speakers: MPs Mildred Gordon and Tony Benn; MEP Stan Newens; Sam Weinstein, Utility Workers Union of America; Claire Glasman, WinVisible; and Wilmette Brown, Black Women for Wages for Housework; Anne Neale, Wages Due Lesbians, chaired. The meeting of sixty people made clear that "carers" also means mothers, and that the work of people with disabilities caring for themselves must count!

When **Ashton** Labour Party activist Chris Clark met Neil Kinnock, Labour leader, arranged by *Labour Party News*, she asked if women "as carers . . . can expect a wage from the next Labour government for the work we do?" He said he agreed in principle but the country couldn't afford it! (This at a time when £2 million [approximately $3.5 million] a day are being thrown into the Gulf, with Labour Party support.)

WFH women have petitioned regularly in **Bristol** and, with Payday men, all over **London**. New this year is Payday's statement explaining why it's in men's interest to sign the "Women Count—Count Women's Work" petition—counting women's unwaged work uncovers everyone's unwaged work! Since Payday men have been petitioning with us, we notice more men are keen to sign—being asked by other men is an encouragement to some; it puts others on the spot.

There were many memorable comments from women who signed, but maybe the one that summed it all up was from the Black woman who urged her teenage daughter to: "Sign it! You don't want to be a slave all your life." Amen, and power to the sisters. Have a Good **TO-Day**!

See you at the SPEAK-OUT in the Commons!

Notes

1   Gross National Product.
2   Parent Teacher Associations.
3   UK Parliament.

Articles in the Media (2012-2020)

In October 2010, the UK *Guardian* invited me to contribute to their "Comment" pages. What follows are some of those articles, as well as articles for other publications. Earlier ones appeared in *Sex, Race, and Class: The Perspective of Winning.*

How Women's Work Has Been Pushed Up the US Political Agenda (2012)

Hilary Rosen's "stay at home" mum jibe has led to recognition that all mothers are entitled to welfare for their work—a worthy US import.

Guardian, April 25, 2012

You can't predict when a breakthrough will come your way, and from what quarter.

For forty years some of us have been campaigning to convince governments that carers, beginning with mothers, are marginal neither to the economy nor to political life.

Women reproduce the human race (and, thus, the whole workforce), and are everywhere its primary carers from womb to tomb. Yet we were told even by leading feminists that caring was work in a care home but not in our home, and that childcare was a job like any other—but not if done in families. We were also told that children and their "working mothers" would benefit from daily separation even at the earliest age, even when they hated it, and even that we were backward if we wanted to be with them. Children could not continue to be the priority of a liberated woman any more than they were men's priority. (Nobody noticed that then they would then become nobody's priority.)

But now, virtually overnight, the carer's case has become high profile in—wait for it—the US election campaign.

Pro-Democratic pundit Hilary Rosen aimed to discredit Republican candidate Mitt Romney when she said that his wife Ann, multimillionaire mother of five sons, "had worked a day in her life."

Women were furious, first that the Democrat Rosen had demeaned mothers, and, second, that the Republican Romney had the nerve to claim that she did all the work of raising her brood herself. She publicly denied the existence of that army of cleaners, nannies, maids, and gardeners that every domestic worker for the well-to-do can describe in detail. Thus, the long-smouldering debate about the value of "stay-at-home moms" versus mothers who take on the double day broke cover at the centre of the US election campaign.

What the debate came down to was: Should women who were not millionaires have the choice to raise their own kids? The poorest women could not; they could be made to work outside the home without wages in order to qualify for welfare. (This is Workfare, now in the UK as well.) And since good childcare was hard to find, as well as unaffordable (ditto in the UK), this often means that to get welfare to feed and house their kids, mothers had first to neglect them.

Millions of other women will tell you how physically and emotionally exhausted they are by their double and, with the economic crisis and increasingly low-paid temp jobs, even triple day. They are profoundly aware of how much they and their children are paying for the jobs they must go out to, to survive and/or for a semblance of financial independence. And they're furious.

The match that ignited the tinder, however, was the projected voting figures.

Pew Research Centre for the People and the Press have claimed that 95 per cent of Black people will vote for Obama, and only 2 per cent for Romney; 67 per cent of Latinos will vote for Obama and only 27 per cent for Romney; while 60 per cent of white men will vote for Romney and 34 per cent for Obama. However, white women's projected vote is 49 per cent for Romney to 44 per cent for Obama: the white female vote is far less racially divided, and thus both candidates know they must be responsive to women's issues. No wonder Mitt Romney rushed to our defence: "All moms are working moms," this devout Mormon uncharacteristically said.

Not to be outdone, President Obama told us: "Here's what I know, that there's no tougher job than being a mom. . ." and gave the example of his wife Michelle and the labours of his own single mother. Ms. Obama added: "Every mother works hard."

This "minor" issue—how mothers are to spend their lives and how our children are to be cared for—had already emerged. Last December, Democratic Representative Gwen Moore tabled the Rise Out of Poverty Act entitling single mothers of children under three once again to get welfare without taking a Workfare job. The Rise Act was to begin to address the desperate poverty, homelessness, and destitution of hundreds of thousands of women and children (and, of course, disproportionately families of colour) in the richest country in the world.

Women were already mobilizing in support when the present battle was joined, and a further bill emerged that Rep. Moore and other Democrats in Congress are backing.

On 18 April, Democrat Rep. Pete Stark introduced the Women's Option to Raise Kids (WORK) Act, "which would recognize that all parents who stay home to raise young children are in fact doing important and legitimate work." Rep. Stark went on to say that "Mitt Romney [had been] . . . forcing low-income mothers into the workforce before he decided 'all moms are working moms.' . . . I think we should take Romney at his most recent word and change our federal laws to recognize the importance and legitimacy of raising young children. That's why I've introduced the WORK Act to provide low-income parents the option of staying home to raise young children without being pushed into poverty."

The class divide is crystal clear. Also clear is the connection between women's unwaged work, poverty, and our lack of choice.

Thus, it was that a slur on a US multimillionaire mother led to recognition that all mothers are entitled to welfare for their work, enabling them to rise above poverty and to raise their own children if they chose to. And since "welfare reform" in the UK from Thatcher onwards has followed the US model, can we now campaign for the importing of this new enlightenment, this new feminism, from across the Atlantic?

What if Women Want to Look After Their Children Themselves, Liz Truss? (2013)

Elsewhere in Europe, there is a better understanding of the importance of supporting women's own provision of childcare.

Guardian, January 30, 2013

It is extraordinary that the government is only now turning its attention to childcare. Given its record of rising child poverty (3.5 million children, including about half of children from Black or Pakistani households; police in Islington distributing food vouchers to kids shoplifting bread), we can't assume that mothers' and children's well-being will be the aim. Rather, childcare is a means of getting mothers, especially those on benefit, out to work.

So I'm shocked but not surprised by Elizabeth Truss's proposal for more "industrialized" childcare—raising low wages by raising productivity: one adult to cater for the needs of six toddlers.[1] Not too many seem convinced that any adult can do that without constant crisis or worse.

Just as unbelievable is that an education in English and maths is a training for caring. In fact, loving care, which any sensible mother might have told them is the central need of children, was not even mentioned by the minister. We know from the experience of raising the educational qualifications for nurses that caring has not been enhanced by a university degree; quite the opposite. I've heard nurses complain that their supervisors demand they spend less time chatting with patients and get on with the bandaging or the injection or the pill-dispensing.

There's also an assumption that a basic function of childcare is lifting the child to the first rung of the education ladder. But what children learn in childcare is how to be with others. Catering to their needs enables them to more easily relate. If the staff levels are too low, children will have to compete with others for affection and attention. That is not what we want our children to learn.

The government plans are in response not only to the crisis of unaffordable childcare that many sectors of women have complained about, but also a rise in the need for childcare. More women are going out to work—or at least looking for work in a dread job climate—because of desperate financial need. For example, in 1999, income support for single mothers began to be phased out. Since then, thousands of women have been thrown on to the job market. When this particular cut (based on Tony Blair's characterization of mothers caring at home as "workless") was imposed by New Labour, there was no accompanying policy for caring for the children of mothers forced out to work.

Beneath this major and, many think, destructive change in social values is the assumption that women are better off if they leave their children for waged work. What work, for what wages, and at what cost? Shouldn't we ask? The obvious class facts remain largely unstated. As Alison Wolf writes: "A majority [of women] do jobs . . . concentrated in heavily feminized occupations such as retailing, cleaning and clerical work. Their average earnings per hour and over a lifetime are well below those of males."[2]

Many women have a different view to the government of when their children are too young to be with strangers full-time: 88 per cent of mothers with young children who have full-time jobs would rather work part-time or be full-time carers, according to a Mumsnet survey. A case in point is childminders—often mothers who want to raise their own children and finance this by sharing the work of raising other people's children.

We have to remember that women forced to take whatever job is available will be forced also to take whatever childcare is available which they can afford. Most of us are just not in a position to defend our children from being among the "too many" that the childcare worker has to deal with. Polly Toynbee's description of toddlers "strapped into high chairs in front of the TV" is already a reality for many.[3] Mothers know it and are helpless and often riddled with guilt in the face of it.

When a decade ago a *Guardian* journalist desperate that she had little time for her children and worried that her own interests contradicted theirs asked, "Is more childcare really what we and our children need?"[4] she was asking a key question.

And since the government appears to favour European examples, let's give some. In Finland and Norway, parents are entitled to a universal cash-for-care benefit if they care for young children at home rather than use publicly funded day-care. In Norway, 68 per cent of parents with under-threes welcomed this as freedom of choice even when they didn't apply themselves. In Finland, more than 50 per cent of mothers with children under three apply for the benefit.

This begins to recognize and respect the caring relationship between parent (usually the mother) and child. Important enough to fund.

Notes

1 Elizabeth Truss was the Conservative government's education minister when she made this proposal; "Childcare Reforms Defended by Minister Elizabeth Truss" (video), *Guardian*, January 29, 2013, accessed September 27, 2020, https://www.theguardian.com/money/video/2013/jan/29/childcare-reforms-elizabeth-truss-video.

2 Alison Wolf, "Working Girls," Prospect, April 23, 2006, accessed September 20, 2020, https://www.prospectmagazine.co.uk/magazine/rise-of-professional-women-decline-female-altriusm.

3 Polly Toynbee, "How Do You Fit Six Toddlers into a Buggy? Ask Liz Truss," *Guardian*, January 29, 2013, accessed September 27, 2020, https://www.theguardian.com/commentisfree/2013/jan/29/hofit-six-toddlers-in-bugy-truss-childcare.

4 Becky Gardiner, "Guilt Complex," *Guardian*, November 15, 2003, https://www.theguardian.com/politics/2003/nov/15/gender.schools.

From Welfare to Wages, Women Fight Back against the Uncaring Market (2013)

The Welfare State is the latest victim of the market's corruption of all it touches. Fighting like hell is the only option.

Guardian, May 1, 2013

It's almost unbearable to wake up to a world in which the Welfare State that has defended us from the worst excesses of the market is being destroyed. The only way to hold on to the last vestiges of entitlement, and even reverse defeats, is to fight like hell.

Bereaved but determined families pursuing those who neglected vulnerable patients in Staffordshire had to do a massive piece of organizing before the deaths of hundreds were looked into. (Other suspect hospitals are emerging.)

Parents of children needing heart surgery organized against closure of the Leeds heart unit and won a court judgment. Then they had to struggle to prevent that judgment from being circumvented. But they did it.

Attacks on people with disabilities were unthinkable. Now suicides and premature deaths of sick and disabled people targeted by the work capability assessment and other cuts are described by campaigners as "genocide by the back door."

Single-mother families and large families were protected. Now children in low-income families have become "extra," targeted even before birth by adoption targets or, once born, by exclusion from schooling and social housing. ASBOs and heavy sentences await the inevitable rebellion and protest, including against rising racism.[1]

How did it get to be so threatening to so many?

When the women's movement began in the 1970s, women were the carers. Working-class women also did waged jobs, but the well-being of children and others remained the primary concern. Women formed the movement not to eliminate caring but the dependence, isolation, servitude, invisibility, and almost universal discrimination that a wage-dominated (i.e., male-dominated) society imposed on the unwaged carer.

The women's movement faced a choice. It could embrace the market: careers for some and low-paid jobs for most. Or it could find another way to live: demanding that the work of reproducing the human race was recognized as central to all priorities. Getting wages from the State for this work, carers would help reshape all social relationships: reorganizing work to incorporate men into caring and women into—everything

Feminism largely chose the market. This enabled governments to demean rather than recognize caring. "Workless," according to New Labour, mothers are now urged to "do the right thing"—go out to work irrespective of workload, childcare, the needs of those who depend on us.

Cuts in social services and public-sector jobs attack women—three-quarters of public employees. Government aims to push women into the private sector, which pays—especially women—less and demands more. This lowers wages generally, imposing working conditions previously unthinkable. Already more families with adults in jobs are in poverty than families where adults are unemployed. When government says it wants "work to pay," it means driving claimants below the lowest paid: from poverty to destitution, unable to refuse £1 or £2 [approximately $1.50 or $3.00] an hour (many immigrants face this)

The market, which we are urged to love, honour, and obey (Marx said it was a fetish), has corrupted all it touches, including the life of the planet. When recently a scientist warned of imminent destruction from climate change, we were told it would be "impractical" to try to stop it. Incredibly, the media did not gasp at this suicidal greed.

Many people say this is not the society they want to live in. But how can we confront all that needs changing?

First, we must acknowledge the thousands already refusing hospital and library closures, cuts in benefits and legal aid, factory farming (concentration camps for animals), a poisonous food industry, toxic pharmaceuticals, media-police corruption, sale of playing fields, tax havens, warmongering, criminalization of protest...Campaigns share one vital tenet: our entitlement to what we are struggling to reclaim.

Our problem is not only that we have allowed cuts—and perhaps the unkindest cut has been of the universality of child benefit, the money that recognizes society's responsibility for children. Our problem is that it has seemed foolish and impractical to dare to challenge the market when no major party is on our side.

With a three-way coalition against us, this has got to be a DIY job. On May 1, International Workers' Day, the Global Women's Strike will launch the petition "Invest in a Caring Society: A living wage for mothers and other carers"—aiming to "redirect economic and social policies towards people and the planet and away from the uncaring market." A challenge to the market by women, the carers, can only strengthen all those already fighting like hell.

Notes

1   Anti-Social Behaviour Orders are a civil offence introduced by the Blair government. Breaking the order is a criminal offence and can result in a fine, eviction, or even prison.

When Women Disappoint (2014)

Recent debate has focused on whether infighting distracts from fighting inequality. But haven't feminists always argued about priorities?

Guardian, March 7, 2014

It was Harriet Harman, feminist and civil liberties activist, who announced, as frontbench spokeswoman of New Labour, that one-parent benefit was to be abolished. It was her sister frontbencher Yvette Cooper who announced welfare reform, taking income support from—again—single mothers, including those fleeing domestic violence.[1] No prominent feminist has joined or supported protests by women with disabilities, or women of colour, or homeless women. Polly Toynbee's defence of the Welfare State has not been supported. Those of us trying to change the world for women, and therefore for everyone, don't expect any help from the *Daily Mail*, so we don't complain when we don't get it. But we do expect it, or at least we used to, from feminists who claim that women, especially those of us under attack, are their priority. When they disappoint, we're furious. Ambition seems to be their priority, and their sisterhood reserved for women like themselves.

One of the fiercest debates provoked by the founding of the Wages for Housework Campaign in the 1970s was on welfare. We said it was single mothers' right to payment by the State for their caring work. The refusal of feminists to acknowledge that work enabled Tony Blair to call mothers "workless" and made way for welfare reform's definition of a good mother: she goes out to a job, even below the minimum wage, with whatever childcare she can afford. We knew what was at stake, and we put a marker: for grassroots women, for caring, for a living wage.

Just as fierce was the attack on women making a living through sex work. And when police recently raided flats in Soho, London, where women were working safely, and dragged some into the street in their underwear, there was not a word from known feminists.[2] There is a new division among women, between the 13 per cent who are professionals, managers, etc., and the rest of us down at the grassroots. They are at best an instrument of the other side; at worst they are the other side.

Notes

1 See "The Grassroots Labour Movement That Shook Britain," 175–201, this volume.
2 The English Collective of Prostitutes worked with the women to defend them from prosecution and deportation, as well as campaigning together with the local community to protect their workplaces from developers. The police claimed to have raided to rescue victims of trafficking, though none were found.

Child Benefit Has Been Changing Lives for 70 Years. Let's Not Forget the Woman Behind It (2016)

Eleanor Rathbone's idea that mothers should be paid for the work of bearing and raising children was radical in its time—and inspires to this day.

Guardian, August 6, 2016

Universal family allowance, now known as child benefit and no longer universal, was paid for the first time 70 years ago today. It was primarily the work of Eleanor Rathbone.[1]

When suffrage was won, many who had fought hard for it left the movement to pursue the careers they had previously been denied. But for Rathbone, suffrage was a preliminary goal in the quest to change the situation and status of "the sweated woman worker, the unhappily married wife, and the poor law widow."

She was from a wealthy and unusual ship-owning family in Liverpool, which had earlier refused to transport slaves. Her father had sought Florence Nightingale's advice to improve healthcare in the workhouse, and in the process of carrying out her instructions had founded district nursing.

Eleanor Rathbone continued in this tradition: she campaigned for money for war widows, against slum housing and the casualization of dock labour; she helped Spanish refugees who had fought Franco and Jews escaping Hitler. Few social justice issues escaped her concern and that of her lifelong companion and supporter, Scottish social worker Elizabeth Macadam.

As a feminist, Rathbone's first commitment was to working-class housewives overlooked because their work of reproducing the human race brought neither recognition nor reward. In 1918, her family endowment committee published Equal Pay and the Family: a proposal for the national endowment of motherhood. It argued for the introduction of family allowances to give mothers financial independence and a route to pay equity. Men, considered the head of the household, were entitled to a family wage. The wife's dependence justified lower pay for any woman who went out to work. Once mothers had money of their own, the committee argued, all women's status and power would rise, both within the family and outside.

In 1924, Rathbone made the full case for the endowment of motherhood in *The Disinherited Family*:[2]

> Nothing can justify the subordination of one group of producers—the mothers—to the rest, and their deprivation of all share of their own in the wealth of a community which depends on them for its very existence.

Some prominent women in the Labour Party and the unions, with the exception of the miners' union, were opposed, while Labour's women's sections and the Co-operative Women's Guild—working-class housewives, some of whom also had waged jobs—were passionately in favour.

Rathbone's ally Maude Royden, of the Women's International League for Peace and Freedom, said:

> Our object will not be to enable mothers to earn their living, but to ensure that, since they have earned it, they should get it. . . . The one really fundamental difference between men and women is (again) a "difference," it is certainly not an inferiority. For women to try to reduce it to a trifle when it is really so great a thing is an acceptance of masculine standards too dishonouring and too artificial to endure.

In 1929, Rathbone, now an independent MP, took her campaign to Parliament. She convinced Lord Beveridge, on whose 1942 report the post-war Welfare State was based, to recognize the work of the housewife with "family allowances in cash." He later commented that it was "a new idea" that "part of the total national income . . . should be assigned to those individual citizens who were undertaking the rearing of the citizens of the future." It became the first measure of the Welfare State. Rathbone was disappointed. The small amount, paid only for the second and subsequent children, denied mothers the independence they'd earned.

When Edward Heath,[3] in 1972, tried to incorporate family allowance into the father's wage, the Wages for Housework Campaign pulled a national network together to prevent it happening. Women everywhere referred to it as "the only money I can call my own." It was sometimes the frontline against rape in marriage and husbands who spent housekeeping money in the pub—women could take the children to their mother's once they had a family allowance book to feed them so they weren't such a drain on her slender resources. It also fed the children when the father was on strike.

We don't know how many women keep their dignity intact with what is now called child benefit, but the principle remains: if you are a carer (of children or others) you are entitled to financial recognition by society for that fundamental work, and it is the height of sexism to be rewarded with poverty and dependence.

Unwaged carers alone save the State £132 billion [approximately $178bn] a year—the cost of a second NHS in England.[4] A basic income is now widely discussed. If we can consider paying people who are not working, surely we can pay mothers and other carers, women and men, a living wage for the work they do.

Rathbone has been neglected since, and much of feminism has been reduced to breaking the glass ceiling. But caring and carers have not gone away, and Eleanor is an inspiration for all of us campaigning for a more humane society.

Notes

1   Eleanor Rathbone (May 12, 1872–January 2, 1946) was an independent Member of Parliament who determinedly campaigned for money and rights for women.

2   The book was republished with an introductory essay by Suzie Fleming; Eleanor Rathbone, *The Disinherited Family* (Bristol: Falling Wall Press, 1986 [1924]). Copies are available from Crossroads Books and Crossroads Women's Centre in Philadelphia and London, England.

3   Edward Heath was the Conservative prime minister from 1970 to 1974.

4   The National Health Service was established in 1948 to provide everyone in the UK with free healthcare at the point of delivery. Figures are from "Unpaid Carers Save the UK £132 Billion a Year—the Cost of a Second NHS" (press release), Carers UK, November 12, 2015, accessed September 19, 2020, https://tinyurl.com/w6v255d.

What Women Want 2.0: Equal Pay (2018)

I was asked to comment on the results of a survey of what women wanted for International Women's Day 2018. I had to choose what a woman wanted and write in support of her preference. This is the quote I chose.

"[I want] wages for housework. Equal pay. Safety from violence and bullying."

Equal pay was a defining theme in the responses to the What Women Want 2.0 survey, showing that, despite commitments from companies and government, little progress has been made.

But change is coming. Women are making headlines by confronting employers who take advantage, sexually and with gross pay differentials! Even women who rose from the ranks are speaking out, acknowledging that they are not immune from sexist discrimination; they are making a way for the rest of us to be heard—finally.

Pay is social power; it determines how we live, with whom, and on what terms. I once worked in a tobacco warehouse when women on the assembly line were about to get equal pay with men who shifted stock. In our excitement, one woman proclaimed: "From now on I'm paying half the mortgage, and that'll change everything between us!"

Of course, women want jobs we enjoy, but most of us go out to work because we have to.

Wages measure the value of our time—which happens to be our life. When our wages are lower than men's, we are disrespected and undermined. In the UK, the pay gap hovers around 19.2 per cent.[1]

Inequality of income is inseparable from the unpaid caring work most women do at home, especially if we are mothers. In 2006, Baroness Alison Wolf showed how different sectors of women are affected by this. She compared women's incomes with the incomes of their male partners over a lifetime.[2] A woman graduate born in 1970, with two children, can expect lifetime earnings that are 88 per cent of her male partner; 57 per cent for women with middle-level qualifications; 34 per cent for women without formal qualifications.

These income gaps reflect part-time work and career breaks for the 80 per cent of UK women who are mothers. Thus, the cost of caring for children and others is less income, a hidden discrimination depriving women of de facto equal pay—like an employment tax on motherhood on top of childcare costs. This falls most heavily on low-income women, the majority. But even non-mothers are expected to put up with less—the lower "mothers' pay" sets the standard. Employers know what they can get away with in terms of discrimination, not only on grounds of gender but also of race, age, disability, and immigration status.

A century ago, suffragette MP Eleanor Rathbone was outraged that mothers who made society were denied "any share in its wealth."[3] She spent her life campaigning for Family Allowance, introduced in 1946, the first act of the Welfare State. She wanted this income to give mothers a level playing field to negotiate equal pay. In 1968, the strike of the Ford Dagenham women established "comparable worth"—equal pay for work of equal value—and won us the 1970 Equal Pay Act. But jobs like caring, cooking, cleaning remained "women's work"—undervalued and underpaid. Then the austerity cuts, 86 per cent of which fell on women,[4] created an employers' market, and women's power to refuse even barbaric zero-hours contracts almost evaporated.

Now the struggle has resumed, everywhere, and it increasingly focuses on caring. In Ireland, an employment tribunal ruled that "caring responsibilities" had been used to discriminate against women academics.[5] In Germany, thousands of metal workers downed tools for a twenty-eight-hour workweek if they needed to care for children or ageing parents. "We want employers to recognize that traditional gender roles in modern families are changing, and we want workers to have the chance to do work that is important to society," said a union spokesperson.[6]

Paid time to care is on the agenda. Just when new technology threatens to massively cut jobs, the status of caring is rising. We might reconsider Virginia Woolf's call for "a living wage for mothers,"[7] updated to include all carers and all genders. What an opportunity!

Notes

1   ONS Digital, "What is the Gender Pay Gap," February 12, 2016, Office of National Statistics, accessed September 20, 2020, https://visual.ons.gov.uk/what-is-the-gender-pay-gap.

2   Alison Wolf, "Working Girls," Prospect, April 23, 2006, accessed September 20, 2020, https://www.prospectmagazine.co.uk/magazine/rise-of-professional-women-decline-female-altriusm.

3   Eleanor Rathbone, The Disinherited Family (Bristol: Falling Wall Press, 1986 [1924]).

4   Women's Budget Group, The Impact on Women of the 2016 Budget (London: UK Women's Budget Group, 2016), accessed September 20, 2020, http://wbg.org.uk/wp-content/uploads/2016/11/WBG_2016Budget_FINAL_Apr16-1.pdf.

5   "I cannot escape the conclusion that the majority of female applicants drawing attention to their caring responsibilities outside the workplace disadvantaged them against the male applicants"; Orlaith Mannion, Equality Officer, The Equality Tribunal, Micheline Sheehy Skeffington vs. National University of Ireland, Galway, November 13, 2014; copy on file with the author.

6   Philip Oltermann, "German Workers Strike for Right to Two-Year, 28-Hour Working Week," Guardian, January 8, 2018, accessed September 20, 2020, https://tinyurl.com/y3yq9tme.

7   Virginia Woolf, Three Guineas, (Surrey, UK: Hogarth Press, 1938), 128; also see "An Income to Care for People and Planet," note 5, 60–77, this volume.

Decades After Iceland's "Day Off," Our Women's Strike Is Stronger Than Ever

(2018)

The Global Women's Strike has evolved into a worldwide protest with myriad demands.

Guardian, March 8, 2018

On the first day of the UN Decade for Women in 1975, the women of Iceland took the day off to demonstrate the importance of all their work, waged and unwaged, in the countryside and the city. Almost all women who were physically able came out of their homes, offices, and factories, and even female television presenters were replaced on the screen by men holding children. Some 90 per cent of women took part. They called it a day off, but we at the International Wages for Housework Campaign called it a strike, and took as our slogan their placard which said: "When women stop, everything stops."

Iceland was not international, but it was of international significance. What moved them to strike had to be moving in the souls of women everywhere; the question was: When would it manifest itself?

In 1985, at the final conference of the UN decade in Nairobi, we had won the UN decision that unremunerated work at home, on the land, and in the community should be measured and valued.[1] We called Time Off for Women for 24 October and a number of countries joined us. But we could not sustain international action.

It was not until 1999 that Margaretta D'Arcy, a writer, anti-war and Irish Republican activist, called for a national strike of women in Ireland to mark the new millennium on 8 March 2000 and asked the Wages for Housework Campaign to support her call. I wrote to the National Women's Council of Ireland, telling them that if they called the Irish women out on strike, we would make it global. They didn't, but we did. We launched the Global Women's

Strike with Margaretta and women from a number of other countries at the UN, in New York, in 1999. In most of the 60 countries where women went on strike it was a celebration, not a mobilization. But we were making a variety of demands. The first was: "Payment for all caring work—in wages, pensions, land, and other resources." What was more valuable than raising children and caring for others, we asked. "Invest in life and welfare, not military budgets and prisons."

The more women went out to work, the harder it was to also be a carer, and what was most galling was the lower pay for doing a double day. Caring and pay equity have risen on the political agenda, as well as other injustices that women face, beginning with rape and domestic violence often going unpunished.

Two years ago, two important movements manifested themselves. In Poland women went on strike to stop anti-abortion legislation. They succeeded in getting the government to back down. In Argentina, following police inaction after the rape and murder of a number of women, hundreds of thousands took to the streets with the slogan *Ni una menos* (not one less). Their call for an end to femicide swept across Latin America and beyond. This spoke to a pervasive injustice—in the UK, for example, two women a week are killed by partners or ex-partners. As a result of Poland and Argentina coming together, the International Women's Strike was formed last year and coordinated by Polish women. It was agreed that each group would determine their own demands. There were regular four-hour Skype calls (with English and Spanish translation) with women from more than 30 countries exchanging information about what they would be doing. In some countries, hundreds of thousands downed tools for some part of the day, had rallies, and banged pots; in others, the events were smaller.

Today, the idea of women massively withdrawing labour, waged and unwaged, is not a reality yet. The actions now are often overtly anti-racist and anti–every discrimination, anti-poverty, anti-war, anti-deportation, and anti-imperialist, including in Trump's US. They are always anti-violence. In Peru, the strike slogan is: "If our lives have no value, produce and reproduce without us!" Every sector brings its own concerns. Peruvian domestic workers are launching their petition: "A living wage for caring work—in your own home and other people's."

But how can you strike if you can't risk being sacked or endangering those you care for? This has always been the dilemma, especially of the carer on whom vulnerable people depend. In countries such as Spain, where there is general recognition of the strike's validity and even union backing, it's easier for women to walk out for at least part of the day—hundreds of thousands are expected to do just that.

In the UK, where such support is not yet forthcoming, women can still publicize our situation and what we want changed in call-ins and letters to the press, returning from lunch even 10 minutes late, banging pots in the streets or at the window, as women in Spain did against the 2003 Iraq war.

The Global Women's Strike is putting the family courts on trial for unjustly taking children from their mothers in a speak-out in the shadow of parliament; cleaners are demonstrating for a living wage; there is a sex work strike for decriminalization in Soho; and a picket of Unilever in support of the Sisters of Rohingya's call for disinvestment from Myanmar to end the rape and genocide there.

In Germany, another possibility to improve women's lives has opened up, which we are bringing to the strike. Some 3.4 million members of the IG Metall union are winning the right to a 28– (instead of 35–)hour week for at least two years in order to care for children and elderly parents. This is what we can win when striking and care come together.

Notes

1   Nairobi Forward-Looking Strategies for the Advancement of Women, United Nations, July 26, 1985, accessed September 20, 2020, http://www.un-documents.net/nflsaw. htm; also see Selma James, *Sex, Race, and Class: The Perspective of Winning—A Selection of Writings, 1952–2011* (Oakland: PM Press, 2012), 203.

The Crucial Work That Women Do Is Often Overlooked (2020)

Women's caring role in society means we end up doing a "double day," whether we like it or not.

Morning Star, March 6, 2020

When the women's liberation movement began in 1970, groups sprang up all over London and all over Britain. You would have a meeting and establish some of the things you wanted to discuss, but at the next meeting there were twice as many women, and you had to go over the same ground again. So the newcomers were told, "Form your own group," and the number of groups doubled and trebled.

A lot of women wanted to destroy all the hierarchies in society—not only of gender but of race, nationality, age, disability, sexuality . . . but especially of class. We were almost all white, but we were not all middle-class.

I had been involved in the anti-imperialist movement in the Caribbean and, back in Britain, in the anti-racist movement (we were a mixed-race family). I naturally brought that to women's liberation. Some women embraced anti-racism, but some treated it as an alien force competitive with feminism. They had not yet registered that most of the women in the world are not white; the number of people of colour in Britain, though growing, was still relatively small.

I also brought women's liberation to the anti-racist movement and fought it out with the men there; the women found their own voice.[1] At that moment in time it was difficult for most people—in any movement—to conceive of identifying as more than one sector. But some of us thought that we were all more than one sector, and that we shouldn't have to cut off any part of our identity to fit into any movement.

As women we identified first of all as those who did caring work for everyone but were the poorer and subordinate sex because we got not a bean for doing it. We had concluded that this unwaged work was central to the low status of women in every sphere and every country. We produced and cared for all the workers of the world, and thus gave birth to and maintained every economy. In much of the world this included growing the food we fed our families. We were often asked by husbands in so-called advanced countries: "What did you do all day?" as we put the meal on the table, while tending a crying child. We women worked very hard doing what wasn't considered work.

To redress this basic exploitation, we formed the International Wages for Housework Campaign (WFH). In 1975, WFH in London opened our first women's centre—a little squat which ultimately became today's Crossroads Women's Centre in Kentish Town.

It's one thing to campaign for unwaged work to be waged by governments, it's quite another for various sectors of women to organize together with this perspective and at the same time make their own particular case—as women of colour, as lesbian women, as sex workers, as women with disabilities, as single mothers, as rape survivors, as immigrants, as asylum seekers. . .

It was that autonomous but mutually supportive way of campaigning that enabled us to come together in a women's centre (there is more than one Crossroad Centre in the world), and even in an international network which includes domestic workers, farmers, factory workers, students, teachers, nurses, claimants. . . Since 2000, WFH has coordinated the Global Women's Strike in a number of countries. This International Women's Day is different in a number of ways. The women's strikes which have been taking place around the world on March 8 have focused on rape, domestic violence and the murder of women, and the demand to end the impunity men are being given by the State. Caring work has featured as never before.

Caring has even entered university syllabuses. This is not only because women are insisting that this massive contribution be finally recognized, but because we've gone out to work, doing a double day whether we like it or not. That was the only route to financial independence, or even family survival, once benefits were cut.

Now we face a climate emergency which threatens the whole of society and, in fact, the whole world. Strangely enough, it was this crisis which opened the way to updating WFH. The Green New Deal for Europe, of which we are a dedicated part, is proposing a care income paid to all who do caring work for people and the natural world, whatever our gender. At last protecting people and protecting Mother Earth are equated and elevated above the uncaring market. This is light years ahead of a basic income which hides the crucial work that women do, leaves intact the sexist division of labour and the domination of the market, and can even be used to abolish benefits. And it is certainly more respectful of caring relationships than parking dependent loved ones with "professionals" in order to "liberate" us, as some women economists urge.

We know enough about capitalism to worry that a "greening" of Europe means a new level of exploitation and environmental destruction of the Global South—i.e., where is lithium for electric car batteries coming from, and who is mining it? They will try to sell and celebrate this "development"— which makes international accountability and organizing even more urgent.

The new and massively growing movement to save the earth is having to confront every prejudice which has divided us. Fighting for climate justice is our chance and our need. This Sunday the Crossroads Women's Centre will open its doors to women and to every gender, welcoming all to meet the 15 organizations based there and what they try to accomplish through collective self-help.

The open day features workshops, films, exhibitions, music and refreshments. It runs from 12 noon–5pm.

Note

1   In their introduction to the 1975 publication of *Sex, Race, and Class*, Barbara Beese and Mala Dhondy wrote: "'Black Power' gave us social power as Black people. It also gave us a voice and focussed attention on that voice. We drew the attention of the white women's movement for the first time, through the platforms that 'Black Power' gave us. The women's movement began to take a look at our particular situation but had no basis on which to integrate our experience. As Black women in our own collective we have no choice to make between the two movements—we are products of both and not in opposition to either. Our existence poses no division in the class. It poses instead the potential for a linkage of its power"; *Sex, Race, and Class* (1975), republished as a pamphlet jointly by *Race Today* and Falling Wall Press (1975), 8.

Norway: Equal—At What Price? Working Life and Family Life from an Ethnic Minority Perspective (2013)

I was invited to speak at the MiRA Centre conference on "Gender Equality, Family Life, Care Work and Paid Work."

November 15, 2013

Thank you very much for inviting us here. We're happy to note what's happening to our neighbours—after all Norway is practically next door. But we're happy for another reason as well: the rates of breastfeeding in Norway are very high. We want to know how you did it!

In addition, it is plain that thinking on whether women should get paid for our caring work is very advanced here. We want to learn what you have found out in that debate. I speak from time to time in a number of countries, and I want to tell them. It's quite urgent for them to know that it's one thing to discuss wages for housework from morning to night when the actual money is not at stake, but it's another thing when the money is at stake.[1] That's a level of reality which we have not experienced. Therefore, we come here, Nina López and I, to learn.

What I want to do, because you are already so clever (laughter) and so well-informed, is perhaps to give the framework that we use, which you can then evaluate on the basis of all that you know. So I want to go into what the women's movement began by thinking, what we found out, what actually happened, and what we have now concluded we want. That's fundamentally the framework that I hope will be useful to you with your wide understanding.

We began organizing as women in the late 1960s and 1970s, and we said we wanted to change everything; please remember that, because now sometimes we don't want to change everything. Not sometimes; quite often. We began by wanting to change everything, and many said how we are going to do it is by getting women in positions of power, and they will help us once they are there. We are going to leave the confines of the home, and we are going to live a life fully in the society. We are going to look at all the institutions of society and point out the sexism, and many of us said also the racism, of those institutions. And we will change that, and we will change men, and we will change women, and we will change children, and we will change everything. Okay.

What some of us began to discuss and worry about was why women were in the subordinate position in the first place, because if you want to change something, you better find out what it is you are changing and why. And what we understood, and I certainly understood from personal experience, is that I, as a young mother, was locked at home wanting to go out, restrained financially, always worrying about the bills, serving a man who went out to work and came back every night and gave me the money; but it wasn't enough, and it certainly wasn't enough for me to consider my own needs. And what I understood was from my own experience and the experience of millions of women in the United States, and later in the UK. But I also had the advantage of having lived in the English-speaking Caribbean, where I had been part of the anti-colonial and federation movement. So I saw women in different positions from those I had known around me, for example, in London. I saw women who had to grow the food before they cooked it. And I saw women who cooked in a coal pot outside on a charcoal fire rather than on a piped gas cooker inside. I just turned the knob, pushed it, and the flame came; that was a very different life. So when I spoke about housework I was thinking of different *kinds* of women and the housework they did, a number of situations in which women were caring. The sister [who spoke earlier] said: power, equality, and freedom, but to me it is fundamentally power. I take power to be money first of all in this society. In a capitalist society, money is power, and if you don't have money, you don't have power, and that's how it is, and I challenge anyone to give another point of view. There are all kinds of powers that women have that we sometimes use to wheedle money out of somebody—yes—but it's the money we are after.

So the real basic division of power between women and men was that the men got paid when they worked, and the women, we did not get paid for "our" work because the work was "ours." We may not have wanted it to be ours. We may have wanted to share it. We may have wanted to duck out of it. But it was ours, and it was expected of us, and we were not cruel enough to ignore the needs of people who were dependent upon us and the care we gave them.

Having made that discovery I thought a long time about what to do about it. Going out to work was one option which was proposed when we complained.

But I had done that work—I was not a professional, I was a working-class girl, which meant I could type, I could clean houses, I could work on an assembly line, I could waitress. . . jobs like that. And there was a way in which women in the women's movement were speaking about work which was unrecognizable to me. They thought of work as some kind of liberation. I thought of work as slavery, but it had the advantage that it got me out of the home. So I was torn about it. I was certainly not in one mind about it, and I felt, and increasingly the women around me felt, that we had a right to wages for the work that we were doing, so we could get more labour-saving equipment in our homes if we wanted to. We could have more power in relation to men. We would not be financially dependent.

I remember when we women were expected to be financially dependent. That is not so much the ethos today. Thank goodness for that. We've won something. We are entitled to money of our own. But the cost I think is too high.

So we saw that women all over the world were unwaged for the caring work that we all did—also for most of the agricultural work we did. In fact, a lot of men were unwaged on an international level. The whole question of work in Europe was tied up with wages. Well, for any discussion on work on an international level, that was insufficient because millions and millions of people were working unwaged, women and also men. And if we thought of working-class people as only those who were waged, it was not only sexist, it was also racist, because we were leaving out those of us who were unwaged, not only most women but millions of men from the Global South.

I'm not in the left, but I am of the left. Almost all of that left was presuming that only those who had wages could change the world, and here we were, the unwaged armies of workers, demanding that the world change. And we saw that in the sixties, seventies and eighties those who were unwaged were making all kinds of revolutions and anti-imperialist struggles, one small one with which I was myself involved. So that it was impossible to pin the changing of history only on those of us who were waged; we were all involved in that process of change, of getting power, freedom and equality.

Now when I raised the question of wages for housework, there was a really big debate. I think you know about that debate. I think you've had it here. Fundamentally, there were two points of view put forward by those who were against us getting wages for housework. One of them was that we should fight instead for (some) women to get positions of power, and the other was that we had to raise the consciousness of women by encouraging them to go out to work. Fundamentally, they said we had to get the consciousness of women to the level of men. Yes, some women said that you had to raise women's consciousness, that if they were housewives, they didn't have too much upstairs. That's what they said, really, although they used very much nicer language to say it.

Some of us didn't believe that. Our view was that women had an understanding of the world which men did not. They were civilized by caring work. They were civilized by putting others' interest before their own. That is a civilizing experience, which, however, should not be a women-only experience. Men need it desperately. They need the civilizing of sharing the caring work that women are always doing. It's not that we needed our consciousness raised. We needed our bank account raised, and then we would be able to make much better choices and dictate the terms of our relationships.

Now what were women doing? We were going out to work. We were involved in the anti-war movement. I wonder if you in Norway know the Greenham Common Women's Peace Camp, which was a tremendous experience for thousands and thousands of women in the UK fighting against US nuclear missiles on this common land. It was built on the strength of women who were entitled to benefits and who were ready to devote themselves to the anti-war movement. Women were seen at that moment as really contributing to the society. You know the nonsense that you are not working if you are a housewife; women were changing this view by challenging the greatest power in the world and saying, "No, take your cruise missiles home. We have to worry about our children and grandchildren and ourselves and each other."

Women were doing justice work, because when you raise children you still take responsibility for their welfare when they grow up. You still want to be sure they are okay. So if they are stopped or beaten by the police or unfairly imprisoned—if anything happens to your child, though they're thirty, they're forty, they're fifty years old, they are still your child. And we see that all of the justice campaigns for men were manned by women. Women were the spearheads of all kinds of individual justice campaigns. You have a lot to say about immigrant women, which I was really interested in hearing. The following is a passage from an introduction to a book about immigrant women written in 1982.

> How much work do women do to make immigration possible, to make possible the rebuilding of the community in a new town, city, country; among other races; speaking other languages; with different food, dress, customs, education, religions, hierarchies? What is the hidden

cost—hidden because women pay it and are not paid for doing it—when the family and community have to confront and survive the economic and social consequences of racism, while the woman on whom such survival depends may be under attack as a woman even from within her own community?[2]

The kind of caring work that in every area of our lives is done by women who are enabling, who are protecting, who are preventing, who are making it possible for all of us not only to survive but to find some happiness—that work is hidden. It's hidden because we live in a capitalist society where the reproduction of the human race is not the priority. Production of things for sale is the priority, but the reproduction of the human race is not. Therefore, the kind of work that women are doing is mainly hidden. We who speak of it often don't really consider the extent of it, even the extent of the work that we ourselves are doing. And if there is one thing I would like you to remember from today, it's that women from the Global Women's Strike who came from England talked about the reproduction of the human race as the priority of the economy, or, rather, that it should be, that it must be.

Now what happened? What happened was that women did get posts. It was a struggle but women did get positions of power. We had Condoleezza Rice—sorry, but we did (laughter)—and others like her in the parliaments and the governments of the world, and in the management of oil companies—Rice had been one—and in the management of tobacco companies, and all of these organizations which when we began we had contempt for. And when we asked those women, "Well, what about us? What about doing things for us?" they said, "You must give me a chance." They said, "I've just come here, and I have to face sexism, and instead of getting support from you, I'm getting demands from you." And some of us shut up, but some of us didn't. We said, "You are there for a purpose. We sent you there for a purpose, and you are not helping us enough or at all."

Now, of course, there were exceptions to that; there were women who fought for us in any area where they had influence. But not many. I have to say that. Also, we saw that the powers that be were ready to integrate management racially and in terms of sexuality; they were ready to incorporate people with disabilities and any sectors which had formed movements that exerted pressure. You know, there are two or three wheelchair users in the UK Parliament, and we are happy that that is the case. We are not sorry to see the integration, but we are angry to see that little or nothing has changed for most of us. Sometimes it's got worse for us, yet we are asked to rejoice at their prominence. Well, Henry in Norway may be Hank in England, but it's the same persona. Secondly, the hierarchy which Henry tops, that has remained. We didn't want that hierarchy to survive; we were committed to undermining it, so there would be nobody at the bottom, because there would be no bottom.

That's the kind of society we had envisaged. But with austerity, which we have felt very hard in the UK and in a lot of other countries, with that austerity, women have been undermined, and, sister, you never said a truer word than that mothers are undermined. It's as though if you want to take care of your children yourself and not go out to work, you are a "beggar at the gate" and have to think of a better way of organizing your life.

Now I don't agree with that. We can't agree that caring should not be prioritized. I don't agree for another reason that was raised this morning. Another brilliant woman said, "What about the fathers?" In the UK, they work the longest hours in Europe. What has that to do with men sharing? How can we continue to think in terms of long working days when we want to be with other people and with each other in circumstances that we, not employers, dictate? But also, we see the effect of the work that we have been forced to do, that those of us who are immigrants are suffering, and we are not the only ones.

You know, what has happened to the ecology is unbearable, and not too long ago we heard an interview with a politician who was asked, "Look, the scientists have now agreed there is man-made global warming and what do you think can be done about it?" And he said, "Well, it's not practical to do anything." "Excuse me, are you saying it's not practical to act for survival?" Such people are suicidally greedy, and they are in charge of our world. And we women have to say something about priorities, as opposed to accepting the priorities that they offer and in fact impose.

We want to work less. That is, we want to do less waged work, but we also want to decide the kind of work that should happen in society. We need to demand that for our own survival and for the survival of the rest of the human race. We want men to work less, I think we can convince them of that! I think that a lot of young men are interested in knowing their children before they graduate from secondary school; that children should spend some time with them; that men should learn to care, that we can begin to reverse the tendencies in the society so that caring becomes the priority. One immediate result of that would be that if they want a new weapon we have to decide if the society can afford it and if we want weapons at all. But the society must afford caring. And it must make the caring relationship the central aim of the economy.

I want to say something about not only what we are entitled to but what we have done. I think that we as women have been making tremendous struggles in all kinds of spheres, making it clear that we can demand more and can get more, and these struggles have been hidden from each other. What women do doesn't really matter. In a lot of ways. And that's because the work women do is not counted in the same way as the work men do. And, in any case, men do not get a good deal either, and sometimes they don't even know it, because they are in charge of us.

I want to tell you about one or two things which you may not know about. One of the great struggles in Africa has been over subsistence farming versus growing cash crops. I think that a number of women here will know that. Women have been the traditional farmers. Some years ago, the figure was that 80 per cent of the food consumed in Africa is grown by women unwaged—80 per cent—and yet this work is not included in economic statistics. What is the economy? Something else. We have to think about that. We have to worry about how the economy is being presented to us when who is and is not growing the food, preparing the food, eating the food is left out of what is considered the economy.

In this struggle women have fought like tigers in order to keep the piece of land on which they can feed themselves and their children, and the men have been offered money if the land is given over to cash crops. The men have had a lot more power than the women and, therefore, very often the cash crops have been grown. Women in Kenya were told that the coffee trees that had replaced their subsistence crops were to be protected, and anyone who cut them down would be sentenced to seven years in prison. The women collectively cut them down—they got no years in prison, because there were too many women who acted together, and nobody would have eaten for seven years if they had gone to prison![3] (Laughter)

But they cut them down and planted their food crops. Now I think that's tremendously important, and I am very sorry that when something like that happens, not only nobody tells us about it, but when we do find out there are not thousands of women in industrial countries saying, "We support our sisters." We lack and must gain a far more international understanding of our fate. We are not only helping them; we are helping ourselves. If they don't move up, we in Europe move down. That's what's happening to wages in the industrial world. We are moving towards the Chinese level—well, we'd better start organizing with the Chinese! Beginning with whom? Chinese women, that's where we start.

So this kind of struggle that women have waged, that has been hidden and that has not been supported here, is the kind of struggle we want to know more about.

Recently, a woman has written a book about the result of only a few women moving up, and I'll end with that.[4]

The class line among women has deepened, and she estimates that about 87 per cent of women are outside of the upward move, so 13 per cent of women have moved up into management, into positions of authority and power. What she says is quite devastating. She says they don't think like women any more, because they live more like men. Often, they don't have children; but if they do, there are a lot of immigrant women to take care of them. You know, that's how it is. And they don't want to worry about us down here who are the overwhelming majority of the world's people and of the world's poor. And we have to change all that.

What do we do to change it? First of all, we acknowledge it, and, second, we look at what women have shown themselves to want and to be capable of achieving. I want to hear about Norwegian women, or, rather, women in Norway, but I have to tell you about women in the UK.

Those who are mothers mostly do not want to work full-time. They want to work part-time outside the home or not at all. That demand is not respected in the women's movement generally or in feminism certainly, although now organizations and networks are beginning to form to say precisely that. Our organization has always stood for women having the choice of going out, or working at home full-time, or combining the two, or working less outside for the same wage that we got when we worked full-time. (Applause) Wages for caring work means that it should always be paid in addition to whatever other waged work we do. We have an international petition which says, "A living wage for mothers and other carers," because every worker should get a living wage, including mothers and all other carers.

We have formulated this petition with the help of women in our network in both industrial and non-industrial countries. The money for arms and so-called aid which governments in countries of the South collect does not see the inside of a woman's handbag. The money that comes to any non-industrial country should not go into arms and should not go into corruption, which is what is often organized through so-called aid, but should go to carers, mostly but not only women. We ask the women of the world: How about it? And we hope we can come to you for that. Thank you.

Notes

1   In Norway, for the first two years of a child's life, mothers can choose between free childcare or cash payments from the State to care for the child themselves. While a majority took the childcare, they voted in support of mothers having the right to choose. We were told that many feminists opposed women having the money to be full-time mothers at home, and that immigrant women were more likely to claim the money. One consideration is that the jobs available to immigrant women are often hard and low-paid.

2   Selma James, "Strangers and Sisters: Women, Race, and Immigration (1985) (excerpts)," in Selma James, *Sex, Race, and Class: The Perspective of Winning—A Selection of Writings, 1952–2011* (Oakland: PM Press, 2012), 176.

3   "[B]ecause neither their husbands nor state officials were willing or able to satisfy their needs to produce food and secure cash income the women took drastic action. In Maragua and elsewhere in Kenya, women uprooted coffee trees and used them for firewood. In 1990 women responded defiantly to the longstanding deterrent. . . . Soon uprooting coffee was so widespread as to be unstoppable. The women in effect repudiated the law by direct action"; Terisa E. Turner, Wahu M. Kaara, and Leigh S. Brownhill, "Social Reconstruction in Rural Africa: A Gendered Class Analysis of Women's Resistance to Cash Crop Production in Kenya," 1997, accessed September 21, 2020, http://www.terisaturner.com/Counterplanning/c5.htm.

4   Alison Wolf, "Working Girls," Prospect, April 23, 2006, accessed September 20, 2020, https://www.prospectmagazine.co.uk/magazine/rise-of-professional-women-decline-female-altriusm; also see Alison Wolf, *The XX Factor: How the Rise of Working Women Has Created a Far Less Equal World* (New York: Crown Publishing Group, 2013).

France: Housework Must Be Waged— excerpts (2014)

I was invited to speak at a four-day forum, Penser l'émancipation, at the Nanterre University, in Paris. For the occasion, part of an interview by Joseph Confavreux with me was published in French in Mediapart.fr on February 19, 2014. The excerpts published here are from the original interview in English and were revised in 2020.

Do you think the Wages for Housework Campaign can achieve its goals?
We know a lot now about what not to do and we also know some principles of organizing. We know how, from time to time, to use the forces of the State on our behalf without joining it or giving anything away. That's what we have had to do because we are grassroots people who have little power. We never describe ourselves like that, but in fact we all [in WFH] feel that we are part of a great experiment, finding out who we are and how effective we can be as part of a collective. We are able to exercise individual talents and inclinations precisely because the collective is not a competition. It gives us the power to think our own thoughts and to invent solutions to all kinds of problems, organizational and political. It also enables us to respect our neighbours—our networks—even if they don't think as we do in any conscious or vocal way. It's been tremendous so far, and I am hoping to see it win.

The question of whether we will win, however, has to do with whether we can organize internationally. There is no other way to win now.

Second is whether we can be independent of the pimps of politics. Often it has been the left parties but not only them. It was also NGOs and most trade unions who kept us in check and prevented us from drawing out the connections among us and moving collectively. Obviously, this includes the political pimps of racism, of sexism, of the lesbian, gay, bi, trans, queer, because that is fundamentally how capital now governs, through the hierarchy among us headed by a sector of managers. They are so extraordinarily alike, whatever their race, their sexual orientation, their gender, as if they have been shaped by the same cookie cutter. They all think that what they must do is tell us what we should and especially what we should not do in order to win or even survive. And they've never won anything for us. They always mislead. Most of us work very hard to survive and hate having to put our little leisure time left over from work into politics, into the hard work of organizing to defeat them. We often let the political pimps stay in charge, and it is always—always—a mistake. You just have to make the commitment to get rid of them. Millions have to. But that's not always easy.

And as soon as many do, the work becomes so much easier, but at the beginning the inertia is great. So those of us who are trying to do it, we look like heroines of struggle. We are nothing of the sort. We are just like everybody else, except that we have decided that aside from survival, earning money or caring or both, that we are going to put every other moment we have into the business of changing the world. We are fighting for our lives. Even the media, and even in England, has had to acknowledge, for example, that there is such a thing as global warming. If we don't stop warming the globe, the globe will warm us.

Are unwaged labour and waged labour the same thing? In other words, is time the only measure of value?

The unwaged work we are talking about is unique; we produce labour power which is always indispensable to capital, and, thus, the labour of reproducing it is indispensable.

> It is the production and reproduction of the capitalist's most indispensable means of production: the worker. . . . The maintenance and reproduction of the working class remains a necessary condition for the reproduction of capital.[1]

The unwaged work of reproduction is not measured by time. Once it is not being paid for by the hour, they don't care how long it takes us. And unless workers cannot easily be replaced, they don't even care if we are reproduced.[2]

Marx attributes the production and reproduction of labour power not to caring work in the family but to the worker consuming the commodities bought with the wage received after s/he has done the work.

> [T]he individual consumption of the working class is the reconversion of the means of subsistence given by capital in return for labour-power

into fresh labour-power which capital is then able to exploit. . . . The individual consumption of the worker, whether it occurs inside or outside the workshop, inside or outside the labour process, remains an aspect of the production and reproduction of capital, just as the cleaning of machinery does, whether it is done during the labour process, or when intervals in that process permit. The fact that the worker performs acts of individual consumption in his own interest, and not to please the capitalist, is something entirely irrelevant to the matter.[3]

Why does Marx not refer to women's reproductive work? At that time in England's industrial centres, there was barely any reproduction beyond pregnancy and birth since the entire family was often in the factory. He says:

Compulsory work for the capitalist usurped the place, not only of the children's play, but also of the independent labour at home, within customary limits, for the family itself.[4]

Almost two centuries later, we've won some time to care and be cared for free of waged work—the working week is shorter in most countries, though people are still being worked to death in many places.[5]

We now look at *waged* and *unwaged* work differently but still inaccurately. Most of us accept that reproduction is work that mainly women do, some of which (from pregnancy to childbirth and breastfeeding) only women can do. We accept that society is dependent on that work. But this is not reflected in the way waged work is measured. A segment of the life not only of the waged worker but also of the unwaged worker is embodied in the products that capitalists sell for profit. We have struggled for this invisible, unmeasured and unvalued contribution to be counted—in time, skills, market value—and to be waged so that it is a power for the worker who contributes it.

Other workers have fought battles for unwaged work to be visible and waged, and sometimes we've won. In the 1930s, the miners' union in the US demanded the impossible: portal-to-portal pay. That is to say, when miners stepped on to mine owners' property, they often had to walk a long way to the pithead, change their clothes and get their tools: only after they had entered the pithead did their paid time begin. The time spent getting to the pithead, sometimes a mile away, and preparing for the shift was on their own time—unwaged. When John L. Lewis, president of the United Mine Workers (immigrant from Wales), demanded portal-to-portal pay, others agreed that it was unfair for workers to donate their time to the mine owners. After a long struggle the miners won.

This is a close parallel with unwaged caring work. It is invisible as work because it is unwaged. But as soon as the demand for payment is made, the time and effort become visible, and they are seen to be integral to re/production.

I referred to the portal-to-portal pay story in a speech in the US a couple of decades ago. In the discussion that followed, a man said, "We never thought we'd win portal-to-portal." He had been part of that struggle! Sometimes we demand what we are not sure we can win, but if our movement is strong enough, we surprise ourselves. And, in any case, we change the balance of power to be more favourable to ourselves.

Welfare is the wage that women in particular but also people with disabilities, the elderly and others have won by struggle for reproductive work, for caring, including for our own survival. We've had to fight to establish that while we don't work by the hour, in fact we work every hour—there is no end to caring and this caring makes human life and society (even profit-making) possible. Like the miners, once we demand payment for this work it becomes visible and recognized as work.

Marx usefully reminds us that once labour is embodied in a commodity, it is impossible to trace and identify which and how many human hands have produced it where. The reproductive work embodied in labour power—done (mostly) by a series of women, mothers, grandmothers, childcare workers, teachers . . . is invisible; they are all invisible. Demanding a wage for this work begins to end invisibility of who produces labour power.

Most invisible of all are the women who produced and reproduced the workers who become immigrants and refugees in other countries. Their struggles for the survival and education of their children have the first call on a wage for caring work from the country which is exploiting the labour power they produced and is, thus, exploiting them.

Aren't you afraid that such a demand as a wage for domestic labour could lead to a commodification of all kinds of human activities?
There is no escape under capitalism from money relations. We are not more commodified if we work for the market invisibly than if we work for the market and everybody sees that what we are doing is making human beings who will be workers for the market. Why should women who do reproductive work which is for the market be the *only* labour power which is not waged?

The idea that because we get no wages our labour power is not a commodity is a utopian fantasy.

Our work is invaluable. No amount of money can pay for it, but that does not mean that we should be enslaved by poverty and subservience for doing this work unwaged. Our work is not demeaned by money; it is more respected. We are acknowledged as workers, including by other workers. And this gives us, and other workers, more power against capital.

Who would pay the wage?
The State. Maybe employers too. Those with not only money but capital.

In a London tobacco warehouse I worked in, the women (not the men) got a paid day off before Christmas. It meant that the women who were doing the enormous work for Christmas, not only buying gifts but shopping for food in crowded supermarkets, which exhausts you while they're fleecing you, got paid time to do all that housework. The union had won a paid day off, not as holiday but as recognition that Christmas was work for women. That is wages for housework.

In Germany they also won some payment for the work you do for survival, for everybody's survival, at certain times of the year. Bits of wages for housework were won by women in a lot of places, but we've lost most of it now.

We have to remember, when workers first said I want a paid holiday, and I want unemployment pay, employers, and the public too, said: Are you mad? The companies will never give you something for nothing. We won that. And they tried to take it back. They have clawed some back, but we still have paid holidays, many of us at least, and we still have unemployment pay. That's one example of winning money for what looked like nothing.

I remember a silly feminist from the left who said, "You can't get wages for housework because it contradicts the laws of capitalism." Isn't that what we want to do? The laws of capitalism are not made by a God. They are not made by nature. They are man-made, and what man makes another man and maybe a woman can destroy. And that is what we are in the course of trying to do.

In the industrialized countries, a growing part of the domestic labour and the care is done by immigrants, mainly women.
Absolutely true, those of us who are domestic workers are poorly paid, but we're paid and have some recognition that we're workers! That work is sometimes the only way to escape war and occupation, extreme poverty, persecution,

domestic violence, but most commonly it is a way to feed and educate your family.

Does it change something about your demand for wages for housework?
Yes. It reinforces the demand, because the immigrant domestic worker is paid little, because neither she nor I is paid for our own housework. And the feminists who oppose wages for housework and fought against it with all their might may be the same women who underpay immigrant women who do their housework while they are earning good money and making a career for themselves.

When we demand wages for housework, the response of domestic workers in our network is: "Yes, this validates the work we do and the value that should be put on it." All of us are housewives, in fact. And demanding that domestic work be paid, be valued, be measured as a quantity of work that keeps the society going is in all our interests.

Under what conditions could sex, race, and class struggles converge?
There is no separate struggle of gender, of race, of nationality, of social and immigration status. They are autonomous parts of the same movement. They are often the same person. Women in the All African Women's Group which meets at our centre, some of them have fled from their countries because they are lesbian. Some of them have run from rape. Some of them have run because they are the "wrong" race or tribe. When they come to the UK trying to get asylum they have trouble, because they are the "wrong" race, they are the "wrong" sex, and they are mothers.

This business of sex, race, and class—you are not just one of these things, you are many things, every person is a member of many sectors. We each have to decide at what point we concentrate on what aspect of our struggle. This happens all the time.

I have to deal with ageism. That's a big struggle because capital does not believe that once you have retired from work you should stay alive. They think you have done their work for them, and it is time for you to move over, just get out. You become aware of the genocidal nature of capitalism, which, among other things, takes the form of ageism. On the other hand, my accent tells people that I am not UK-born. All of these are aspects of the divisions among us which we constantly confront in all kinds of ways. They don't always surface, but they are always in us as part of our struggle for survival and for liberation.

The terms of unity are that: from your own autonomous organization you find ways of addressing your problems, your crises, your struggle, and they are useful and important to other sectors who can join with you and with whom you can join. That's the terms of unity.

You have the power of your sector, which you find in autonomous collectivity. Autonomy does not mean separatism. Autonomy is your case against capital and your refusal to submit to other sectors that also have a case against capital but also have power over you and will use it. You refuse the power they have over you, and you let them know they'd do better if they'd join with you rather than try to push you around, rather than making you pay for what capitalism is doing to them. That's what women say to men, and they say that in all kinds of ways, not merely in all kinds of languages. They offer a route to power that strengthens women and weakens the common enemy.

That is what autonomy does. Separatism says my suffering is worse than yours, and therefore you must drop your own struggle and support mine. Autonomy says my power is the power of my sector, my collectivity, focused on ending the exploitation of my sector as part of ending my exploitation. I'm happy to share that power with you and your collective struggle against *your* exploitation, if you also want to fight our common enemy and not demand that I give up any part of my struggle. That's all there is. It's not terribly complicated.

It is terribly difficult to do when the movement is low, but as soon as the movement comes up, even sporadically, you can see that people are ready to get together. They are attracted by the power other sectors have. It's so amazing.

So now when a Black man who was not armed is shot by the police, all kinds of white people are ready to agree with Black people that, "Yes, those police, that is how they are." They are not in immediate danger of being shot themselves, but they know their interest is to side with Black people. And increasingly some of them come from a mixed-race family. There is a lot of mixing in all kinds of places now, and the racism you used to expect is not necessarily there. If some white people are supporting people of colour against racism, you have to acknowledge that as a political fact of life.

That's another way of saying that you organize autonomously in your sector, but you support others who organize autonomously, not to persecute you, not to have power over you, but to undermine the power of those who have power over you both.

Don't you think that some struggles are more urgent than others?
No. I think every struggle is urgent to the people who are making it. I don't think that we should prioritize struggles. The question is: How can the power of one struggle reinforce the power of others? That's what we are addressing.

You know, confronting the police is desperately important if your son has just been shot by the police. On the other hand, if your daughter has been raped, you have to deal with the fact that you need the police, but the police don't want to catch the rapist. What do you say? Do you say forget about the rape? Or do you say forget about the shooting? No way. We have to deal with both, and we have to work to build a movement that deals with both. We have to draw out the connections between them. The same police who claim they don't have the forces to deal with rape have the forces to chase and shoot unarmed Black or immigrant men. I think that looking at it that way is more truthful, more realistic, and can lead to being more effective.

And by the way, they are the same police that persecute sex workers. They are the same ones that stop and search people on the street.

There has been an erosion of police accountability in the UK. They steal. They fabricate evidence. They lie on the stand. They have been responsible for the deaths of many people in Hillsborough[6]—now that has emerged after *twenty years* of campaigning. So why is that different from shooting Mark Duggan?[7] It is just kept separate in news broadcasts, so we never, never make the connection. We never see the spectrum of police illegality and brutality in our deepest hurts, and the crimes of the police against different sectors of us. Sometimes a particular case will rally the fury of different sectors to come together. They feel that this is their chance to make the case for all of us. Hillsborough was an example of that and so was the Orgreave police attack on the miners' strike.[8]

At different points, a struggle takes the lead spearheading everybody's need for change. Sometimes it's obvious, as with the miners' strike when we all knew—Thatcher and the whole working class—that if the miners lost, we all lost. The Black Lives Matter movement now is everybody's struggle, and people are increasingly aware of that. If Black lives don't matter, then nobody's lives matter. It is indicating that others can join for Black lives and for their own lives internationally. That is very new.

A final word on the environment. I finally figured out the obvious. The reason the State seems stupid and paralyzed in the face of the horrendous floods which are predicted to worsen is because the only way to fix it is to change. They can't change. They can't conceive of shaking up the power structure. This would shake our subservience, and this terrifies them. Capitalism is suicidally greedy, and they can't stop. We have to stop them, or we are doomed.

Notes

1   Karl Marx, *Capital*, vol. 1 (London: Penguin Classics, 1990 [1867]), 717–18.
2   Until the abolition of the slave trade in countries like Haiti before its revolution, field slaves were worked to death, living only a few years after landing from Africa; they were then replaced with new Africans. In England, during the industrial revolution, life expectancy among working-class people in Liverpool, for example, was 15 years as a result of slum housing, inefficient sewerage, and impure water supplies (Edwin Chadwick, *The Sanitary Condition of the Labouring Population of Great Britain*, 1842).
3   Marx, *Capital*, vol. 1, 718.
4   Marx, Ibid., 517.
5   In 2016, *China Daily* reported that six hundred thousand people die yearly from overwork in China. The Japanese have a word for it: *Karoshi*, literally *"overwork death."* Just because there is no word for it in English doesn't mean it isn't happening in the West.
6   On April 15, 1989, in Hillsborough Stadium in Sheffield, England, 96 Liverpool football fans were crushed to death and 766 others injured after police opened a gate leading to already packed pens. It was the worst sports disaster in UK history. The police blamed the fans as drunken hooligans. After decades of families campaigning, an inquest found the police guilty of gross negligence, but the prosecution that followed did not convict them. This was the same South Yorkshire Police that attacked the miners at Orgreave (see note 8 below) and allowed an estimated 1,400 underage girls, many of them in the care of the State, to be raped and sexually abused for years.
7   Mark Duggan, a twenty-nine-year-old Black man, was shot dead by police in Tottenham, North London, on August 4, 2011. The killing sparked massive uprisings in several cities.
8   The Battle of Orgreave was a turning point in the historic year-long miners' strike and in police violence in the UK. On June 18, 1984, police with truncheons charged on horseback against the ten thousand picketers, injuring and arresting many. The prosecutions soon collapsed, and no police were ever charged.

What's a Nice Girl Like You Doing in a Job Like This? A Comparison between Sex Work and Other Jobs Commonly Done by Women (2019)

In February 2019, the English Collective of Prostitutes (ECP) launched a survey in Parliament comparing sex work with other jobs identified with women. As the first public spokeswoman for the ECP, I was asked to open the event. This is my speech with a few necessary edits.

First of all, this survey reminds me that when the women's movement began and for some time after—I think it continues up to today—we were told that our liberation was dependent on taking a job outside the home. Now we know from our own experience what these jobs are. Sex work was not included as one of the options. The other omission was how low the pay is. In fact, sex work is very often part of the work, even if you are not a sex worker. I know as a waitress, there was nothing like a smile to get the tip you deserved, that should have been ours in the first place.

I remember that when the liberation through work argument was made, one woman said, "You can't tell my mother that, she's been out there for twenty years and she's exhausted." Her mother had raised children while doing this "liberating" work. This reminds us that many working-class women have always had to work outside the home because the man's pay (if there is a man) barely covered the family's expenses.

This survey gives us not merely a comparison between different areas of work, but it also tells us what work women are spending their lives doing and how little we earn for it. I think that's vital information which we have to thank the English Collective of Prostitutes (ECP) for gathering.

Secondly, we have to remember that a lot of the work women do, as many people have commented, is an extension of work we do at home without wages. People have noticed that, but they haven't noticed that sex work is much the same.

We are sex workers, we women, a little bit, or maybe sometimes, in how we relate to men. We have always used our sex because there is no equality, we are the financially weaker sex. Because there is a power relation between ourselves and men, let alone the class relations, that we confront; and, therefore, we use what is available to us when we have little or nothing else. We have our sexuality, and we bargain with it when we have to. Some politicians and media are now calling sex work "survival sex." Are they really telling us that they didn't know that sex work was always for survival?

I want to briefly describe what happened when women who formed the ECP came out in the Wages for Housework Campaign and said, "Well, actually, you know, we work as prostitutes." And we said, "We are interested." We were interested first of all in how much money they made, and it was a lot more than most of us were making and certainly much more than we got on benefits as single mothers. And it was terribly important to us that the sex workers had money. We didn't benefit financially from it. They didn't fund us. But it was really important that we had women among us who had money and, even so, wanted Wages for Housework to acknowledge their work.

We used to ask: Does good money make women bad? And, in fact, it does. People know that, and some of them don't like the idea of working-class women having too many choices and more time than an 8–5 job gives us. And I think part of the reaction to prostitution, part of the reaction to women increasingly using this as a way of getting money, is that it upsets such people, because they feel we are out of their control. That's a very serious question for women and for men, and it always has been considered fundamental to the women in the Wages for Housework Campaign. And when the government said that they didn't have money for this or money for that, there were some well-paid hookers who were members of the ECP, and they would get up and say, "We have seen the money they say doesn't exist." It was a pleasure and a strength. It was terribly important for us and for our determination not to be poor and dependent.

When the ECP asked me to be their spokeswoman because they couldn't be public, I didn't hesitate. It seemed to be the most natural thing in the world for me, a respectable married woman, to speak for sex workers. I had one condition, that they educate me so that I could represent them.

In the Campaign there was one woman, a personal friend of mine, an academic; she was very upset by her sisters doing that work and sat down with them trying to convince them to give it up. She didn't succeed. The rest of the women had no problem at all and did absolutely understand. Sex workers in our organization, who were part of us in every way, really contributed to our clarity about our own sexuality and made us more aware of what we were doing with our lives and why we had so little and how wrong it was that we didn't have much. They gave us a standard: women could have money. They could be working-class, only they had money. It was of great benefit to know that.

I think that now we have to look again at what the Swedish model (to criminalize the clients of sex workers) is about. We have to know that it is proposing that all of us have no choice but to do the work that's expected of us and under the conditions that were described tonight. We have to remember, those of us who are sex workers, that if we give up sex work, this is what awaits us. I remember the Thai women saying that in Thailand, Empower, their organization, very powerful and very brilliant, said, "Well, we have two other choices if we're not on the game;[1] we can be in sweatshops—what a thrill!—or we can live hand to mouth doing farmwork in the countryside." So, to the people who criticize the way we work, those of us who are sex workers, the way we earn our living, we ask that they acknowledge how limited our choices are. And we wonder why they never noticed! That is terribly important.

Finally, thinking about the fact that 86 per cent of the austerity cuts have fallen on women (and that means children also suffer) at the same time that the Swedish model is being put forward with more urgency, we have to wonder how they are connected. We have to wonder why, at this moment in time, when women are in the worst position we have been in for many a day, somebody would come and try to interfere with a few of us at least, and many of us probably, using another way of feeding ourselves and feeding our families. Prostitution, sex for money, has been the way that women traditionally, when we had nothing else, have used. It's got us out of a lot of scrapes. It doesn't mean that we've won; it means we haven't lost.

What the women here tonight are making clear is that the jobs they have had to do, whatever those jobs are and however we feel about them, they are also about survival, about not losing. And this is what unites us. There is power for all of us in accepting each other and anything we have had to do to survive.

Notes

1   "On the game" is an informal British expression for sex work.

An Income to Care for People and Planet

(2020)

with Nina López

A Dazzling Array of Skills in an Endless Variety of Circumstances

Women reproduce the whole human race; in the course of which we reproduce the working class—that is labour power, the basic capitalist commodity. We get no wages for this work. Since 1972, the International Wages for Housework Campaign has worked to establish the importance of these obvious facts of life.

Once the Covid-19 pandemic threatened the whole society, it was impossible to continue to hide or dismiss the daily caring work on which, pandemic or not, society depends for survival and the workers who do it within the family for no wages and outside for poverty wages. These workers are overwhelmingly women.

Women's capacity to populate the world and to breastfeed the newborn, fundamental to any society, should have been a source of power for us. Instead we were robbed of the financial recognition and support that this unique contribution should entitle us to. Instead, we have had to be dependent on the wages of other workers, that is men. When we earned our own wages, they were lower than men's, and we were financially punished every time we went on maternity leave or had to meet other caring obligations.

Our unwaged caring work went well beyond the boundaries of raising children and servicing the wage earner, embracing extended families and social networks. It was expected of us; it was assumed to be our biological nature. Traditionally the woman who didn't marry cared for the elderly relatives and could be called on by any family member.

All the injustices that the women's movement has targeted, which shape our lives and relationships—rape and domestic violence, pay inequality, exclusion from land ownership, sexual repression, lack of power in the family and in society generally—can be traced to women's lack of financial power.

Some injustices have been removed or at least reduced, in some countries more than in others, by years of struggles, such as gaining the vote, the right to be educated and to go out to work so we could earn money of our own, inheritance rights and winning benefits, including for single mothers and children. But the weight of care within the family has barely shifted from women's shoulders anywhere, and we remain the poorer sex, especially once we become mothers.

In 1980, the ILO estimated that women did two-thirds of the world's work for 5 per cent of its income. Forty years later, women and girls do more than three-quarters of all unpaid care work a total of 12.5 billion hours a day, the greater part in the Global South, without washing machines and often without piped or even clean water.[1] The pay gap for mothers in the UK is 33 per cent by the time their first child is twelve years old, and even greater for working-class women.[2]

Yet demanding payment for the caring work on which society and the economy depend has been "controversial." Feminists generally have been anxious to distance themselves from housework and the slave aspects of being "just a housewife"—unpaid, financially dependent on a man, at everyone's beck and call, and often cut off from participation in the world outside the family. They could not see that housework was also integral to caring, even when the caring was for them.

Housewives saw this work not as a choice but as necessary to creating a framework for the life of a family and for raising children as part of a community. We knew what our work achieved and how dependent people were on it. In 1985, we wrote:

> Caring for others is accomplished by a dazzling array of skills in an endless variety of circumstances. As well as cooking, shopping, cleaning and laundering, planting, tending and harvesting for others, women comfort and guide, nurse and teach, arrange and advise, discipline and encourage, fight for and pacify. This skilled work, which requires judgement and, above all, selfdiscipline and selflessness, is most often performed within the family. Taxing and exhausting under any circumstances, this service work, this emotional housework . . . is done both outside and inside the home.[3]

The mother, the granny, the auntie, the sister were the first line of protection: while you were yourself under attack, you were there defending your children and siblings in the schools and on the street in a class society which is steeped in racism and every kind of prejudice.

When children were disabled, the mother was likely to be the first defender against pressure from doctors and social workers, including to give them up to institutions. Facing down social stigma, many mothers were impelled to fight to keep and care for their children, appreciating their zest for life, abilities, and relationships and encouraging them to expect support. Mothers demanded resources to enable survival and independent living, and compensation when industrial polluters and pharmaceutical companies were to blame. They fought to be heard by a healthcare system which dismissed mothers' observations as "anecdotal" and backed Big Pharma.[4]

Community struggles have always been dependent on housewives organizing against evictions, rises in the cost of living, cash crops replacing subsistence farming, mining, fracking, and other corporate assaults.

Caring for human life which will become labour power for capital is hard work. On the one hand, you want your children to "do well," but that means accepting authority and competing with others. On the other hand, you want them to be happy and true to themselves, which often results in standing with others against authority. It is never easy to balance these contradictions.

Even when not identified as "housewives," we found ourselves doing emotional housework, including for each other, which men did not usually do but somehow expected from women, even if we were lesbian, even if we were strangers. We knew that putting down housewives was accepting the male standards we had rejected.[5]

Women wanted recognition and support for all this work, as well as more time away from it, and were resentful at how little our needs were considered or even noticed. While we agreed with most of the feminist demands, we were furious that many who claimed to speak for women's liberation had a similarly low estimate of us as men did. They were fixed on the notion that a wage for housework would institutionalize women in the home rather than give us the power to reshape the relationships in the home and outside. Demands for money for women's work in the family, which in the UK had roots in the work of Eleanor Rathbone,[6] the suffragette who campaigned and won Family Allowance, and in the call from Virginia Woolf for a living wage for mothers,[7] were dismissed or ignored. In the US, Johnnie Tillmon, from the 1960s and 1970s massive National Welfare Rights Organization led by Black single mothers,[8] was also ignored when she called for "paying women a living wage for doing the work we are already doing—child-raising and housekeeping."[9]

Feminists' rejection of such a wage made it harder for anyone who wanted to pursue this financial demand.

Even when we won some recognition—as we did during and after the UN Decade for Women (1975–1985), when we successfully lobbied for governments to measure the quantity of unwaged work and agree that its economic value should be included in national accounts[10]—demands for money were opposed. The feminist mantra that we should get men to share the caring and go out to work prevailed, bypassing single mothers and discouraging those who might have preferred more time with their children or whoever they were caring for with less financial pressure. As a result, the newly gained visibility of women's unwaged work did not bring the financial recognition that it deserved and that we had hoped for.

Even counting the work was sometimes contentious because it pointed to payment. But then grants were offered for devising ways of counting, and a number of feminists applied. One academic was profoundly interested in all we had to say about the advantages and pitfalls of different ways of counting—she got a million-dollar grant for repeating it to the US Bureau of Labor Statistics. Another wrote a book mentioning some of the groups in our network, which she had never met, as if they were her network—very wearing.

Twenty-five years on, especially since the Covid-19 virus hit, it is undeniable that waged and unwaged carers are the front line, and that we depend on them for survival. All of a sudden it is becoming clearer to the chattering classes that we have *always* depended on carers for survival—as infants, as elderly, and as everyone in between. The volume of thanks carries with it the question of payment—a living wage if you were low-waged and a living wage if you were unwaged. When caring was not acknowledged, it was important to demand that it be measured and valued as most work is. To make that same demand today, when it is acknowledged as crucial work and measured and valued many times over is to avoid the payment, denying the worker the money she has earned.

Some people are writing about caring now as if they have just discovered it, having spent years avoiding or denying what others were crying out for. Their "discovery" is turning a century-old struggle for wages for housework into a niche industry where some will be paid (well) to research, write, speak about, and plan for the "betterment" of mothers and other carers—always withholding the wages from the worker. Thus, leaving untouched the power relations of caregivers—especially mothers who are unwaged—to the society.

This veneration of caring is perfectly acceptable, in fact helpful, to the State—it enhances their credibility, while hiding our exploitation. It is much like the charity of NGOs that fundraise billions to help "the poor" only to drive around quake/cholera-torn Haiti in their 4x4s, housed in luxury hotels, while "the poor" remain in camp cities, with no food or piped water.[11]

It is hard to fathom why, over the past fifty years, so many feminists who are professionals have been so consistently, even emotionally, hostile to women getting paid for caring they are doing in the family. Certainly, it has to do with feminist rejection of any identification with this work, which, though life enhancing, is demeaned for lack of a wage, which in turn demeans the women who do it and, by implication, all women.

But even academia is today full of precarious, poorly paid or unpaid, mainly younger, scholars. Some of them are politically engaged with the movement for financial recognition, including for the caring work they are themselves doing as mothers and/or daughters. (See comment from Ireland's GWS following this piece.) Universities don't always take kindly to lecturers who organize with cleaners and secretaries, but such connections are beginning to win battles.

And they are helping to expose those women who have risen into management and professions, while the majority of us go out to a job, not a career, and struggle with not enough money and with overwork. This is compounded for those of us who are women of colour or immigrants or both and/or have a disability and are usually lower down in the wage hierarchy. Claims of "sisterhood" ring hollow given the widening gap between most women and an increasingly integrated political and managerial class.

We didn't give up. Following the UN decision, Trinidad and Tobago, where Clotil Walcott, a working-class organizer who headed the Wages for Housework Campaign there and founded the National Union of Domestic Employees, bringing unwaged and low-waged workers together, passed legislation to count unwaged work—the first in the world![12]

When Venezuela agreed a revolutionary constitution with Article 88,[13] which recognized "work at home as an economic activity that creates added value and produces social welfare and wealth" and entitled housewives to social security, we made sure the world knew about it.[14]

And we mobilized against attempts to wipe out past gains, such as Article 41.2 of the Irish constitution, which, despite its outdated and sexist language, recognizes that women in the home contribute to "the common good," and that the State has a responsibility to ensure they are not forced out to work by financial need.[15]

In recent decades, work outside the home has increased many women's financial independence, and given scope to interests, talents, and aspirations which had been neglected by having to meet caring obligations. At the same time, many were driven out as one wage could no longer support a family, and benefits and services on which single mothers in particular had relied evaporated.[16] Once we were out to work full-time, it became obvious that much of the invisible work on which the whole society rested was being left undone. It caused a "crisis of care"—from the rise in the mental and physical ill health of children to the neglect of disabled and elderly relatives.[17] This is especially true in Western countries, where the extended family is much less available to share the responsibility for other family members, and only women on higher incomes can pay for a domestic worker, a nanny, or a carer—usually a low-paid immigrant woman.[18]

This connection between women going out to work and the neglect of unmet physical and emotional needs is still to be addressed.[19] With the Covid-19 crisis, women were told to leave their jobs and were then locked down with children and sometimes with violent men. Elderly parents had to fend for themselves and got ill and even died, including from the State-imposed isolation. Later the children were sent back to school, whether their parents felt it was safe or not, because the "economy" needed the mothers.

It is a dynamite subject, since women are now integral to the waged economy and are expected to keep their nose to the grindstone, even to the detriment of their families.

The celebrated rise of the career woman has not helped the grassroots mother whose benefits have been cut and who has had to take a low-paid job or several, subsidized by food banks or "survival sex."[20] Nor has it helped the mother of a disabled child whose full-time caring is rewarded with a paltry Carer's Allowance. (In the UK and US, these are the mothers whose poverty makes them most vulnerable to having their children taken from them by the State, especially if they are women of colour and/or immigrant, and/or victims of domestic violence.)[21] And it certainly hasn't helped the mother who has had to leave her children in the village miles away to be raised by their grandmother, while she goes to the city to send back money earned by domestic, factory, or sex work.[22] The trauma caused to children by this separation is the price they are forced to pay for survival.

Even the career woman pays a price. In order to compete in the job market and safeguard promotion, motherhood may be postponed beyond the biological clock. This makes pregnancy less likely, riskier, and often dependent on fertility treatments, the complications from which are rarely mentioned.[23]

The fact that women have had to struggle to win a few weeks off to recover from childbirth and to feed newborns with breastmilk, the food tailored to the child's individual needs, tells us that the emergence of new life is to employers merely a temporary halt in what really matters—the flow of production.

Women are exhausted from trying to fit two or three days of work into one. The situation is so desperate that waged workers have demanded and sometimes won (paid) time off to attend to a health or other emergency in the family.[24] And while the crisis of care is widely discussed by governments, the media, and academia, any mention of money for the mother or other unwaged primary carer is avoided.

Instead, we hear of extending childcare and care homes so the economy is not deprived of "women's full potential as human capital,"[25] of closing the "employment gap" so as many women as men are out to work by extending the care sector which employs mainly women who should get more "training and professionalization,"[26] and even of government plans to replace carers with robots, already the case in Japan and elsewhere.[27]

While women and other primary carers want and should have access to well-resourced childcare where their children are safe and happy, most mothers of young children don't want to be in full-time employment, but they are forced to by financial necessity. Child psychologist and bestselling author Oliver James advocates that "parents should be given the option of one of them being paid the national average wage while they give up work to care for any children under the age of three."[28]

We don't see such proposals on any government agenda. They are still social distancing themselves from paying any carer a decent wage to show how much she (and it's almost always a she) and the people she cares for are valued. But a few legislators, with whom we have worked over the years, are finally demanding that "work" be redefined to include caregiving in families[29]—definitely a step in women's and children's direction.

Risking Life and Limb for Climate Justice

In the last few years, the movement to stop climate change and the extinction of life on earth exploded onto the streets in many countries, forcing governments and the media finally to acknowledge the urgent deadline to end and reverse the destruction of the natural world and human society with it.

Environmental struggles are far from new, and women have been prominent in them: protecting or reclaiming ancestral land from mining, dams, military bases, pipelines, cash crops, factory farms, and a variety of multinational takeovers that have led to poisoned land and water, disease, disability, death, displacement and destruction of communities, and mass migration to the city or to other countries.

But opposing "progress" and "development" in order to preserve your way of life and your connection with the natural world was assumed to be irrelevant, backward, and a losing battle. Yet Indigenous communities, who are less than 5 per cent of the human population, support around 80 per cent of the planet's biodiversity.[30]

The climate justice movement in the Global North is only now beginning to recognize the herculean efforts of thousands of Indigenous and other communities, in both the Global South and North, who risk life and limb to save the land from multinationals backed by dictatorships, imperialist governments, and their militaries. These struggles—from Brazil, Haiti, and Thailand to India, Nigeria, and Palestine—are rarely acknowledged as part of the *front line of the climate justice movement*.[31] And we still face the force of organizations, including trade unions, North and South, which support "development," because it provides jobs, even though such development ruins the health of workers and their communities, as well as destroying the natural world.

In 2019, we were introduced to the Green New Deal for Europe (GNDE) as it was being drafted. It addresses itself to what needs to be done in Europe, but also to what Europe must pay for its imperialist past and to "take action to redress extraction, exploitation, and inequality in Europe and around the world."[32]

GNDE proposals included "implement[ing] a Care Income to compensate activities like care for people, the urban [and rural] environment, and the natural world."[33]

This built directly on what we had been doing, and we helped develop it further. We spelt out that it was women, starting with mothers, who had been doing most of the caring work all over the planet to accomplish the reproduction of the human race—in both the urban and the rural environments. Our proposals were welcomed, and most were incorporated into the GNDE.

In publicizing the Care Income and what it can practically achieve, we assumed it had to be global.[34] The Care Income was embraced by our international network, because it can bring together the movement for the survival of all life on earth and our liberation. Both those based in rural areas (in India and Southeast Asia, for example) and those in cities (in Peru, Ireland, US, UK. . .) are involved in a variety of struggles and in mobilizing support for them.

In the 1980s, we had made women's case against nuclear power and had spoken out against the *environmental racism* of using communities of colour, South and North, as dumping grounds for industrial contaminants and pollution.[35]

In preparation for the new millennium, we had called for a global women's strike for March 8, 2000—women in over sixty countries responded. The Wages for Housework Campaign has been known as the Global Women's Strike (GWS) ever since. We demanded: payment for all caring work in cash, land, or other resources; pay equity globally; food security; paid maternity leave and breastfeeding breaks; cancelling "Third World" debt; accessible clean water, healthcare, housing, transport, and literacy; non-polluting energy and technology; protection and asylum from all violence; freedom of movement.[36] The money was to come first of all from military budgets, starting with the biggest, the US, which is also the biggest polluter.[37] We summed up our perspective as: "Invest in caring, not killing."

In 2013, we issued an international petition demanding a "Living Wage for Mothers and other Carers."

The Soil and the Worker

While Karl Marx concentrated on the exploitation of workers, he has given us a much more holistic view—as usual!

> [A]ll progress in capitalist agriculture is a progress in the art, not only of robbing the worker, but of robbing the soil; all progress in increasing the fertility of the soil for a given time is a progress towards ruining the more long-lasting sources of that fertility. . . . Capitalist production, therefore, only develops the techniques and the degree of combination of the social process of production by simultaneously undermining the original sources of all wealth—the soil and the worker.[38]

Today, a century and a half later, we can take the soil to stand for the natural world and the worker to stand for the human race. Both plundered by capitalist production and accumulation enforced by imperialism, war, and military dictatorships. Thus, caring for people and caring for the planet are integral one with the other.

Indigenous people everywhere have shaped their societies on that premise. In rural areas of the globe where people are directly dependent on the natural world for their livelihoods, the struggle for human survival and for the survival of the planet are one indivisible whole. In the city, the natural world appears more distant, and we are trained away from paying attention to it—it must become integral once again. We must reject the theory, the training, the habit of human supremacy over nature: behaving as the führers of the planet, and allowing capital's suicidal greed to use science and us to dominate, exploit, and exterminate the natural world.

Women's reproduction of the human race is a combination of biological and social labour. What is physiological, what is social and what is individual—together form one indivisible whole. If we were not in a capitalist society, we would assume this. Under capitalism, we are urged to separate our physical nature as mammals from our social relationships. What we have in common with other life is downgraded as lacking in consciousness and dismissed. It is not treated as a social contribution which society must respect, resource, and protect. Like the rest of the natural world, it is free for capital to plunder without mercy.

We are educated to value what is manufactured over what is naturally and freely produced. This is the story of breastfeeding, the food that every mammal produces and offers to its young; only the human mammal is urged to offer instead the "junk food" manufactured for profit.[39]

As we reclaim our right to concentrate on protecting and regenerating the natural world, women can again reclaim the uniqueness of our contribution to human society, of biologically and socially reproducing the human population.

Healthcare too must be re-evaluated. Under capitalism, it is based on a technology which represses symptoms to impose a "cure" rather than on respecting and strengthening the body's own efforts to restore health. Western drugs that prioritize profit rather than health and cause serious, often lethal, side effects have replaced nutrition and a variety of therapies developed over centuries by many societies.[40] There is a conflict of interest between our health and Big Pharma, whose profits depend on our dependence on their products. We stay alive but increasingly in a state of chronic ill-health, which invites additional prescriptions.

Everyone knows that the technology of advanced capitalism, starting with weapons of war, bears full responsibility for the climate emergency. (And though we're told that's what we should want, we would have chosen differently if we'd been asked.) Technology is about what is profitable, how to efficiently exploit us, what will sell, and what wars to have. What happens to people and planet as a result is not a factor in the calculations—unless it provokes a movement that challenges the power of the elites.

The vast majority of people in the Global South, where so many raw materials are extracted and so many (proxy) wars are fought for their control, are deprived of the benefits of the technology we have all been exploited to produce. Only recently, in response to the movement against climate change, have less polluting technologies been on offer, and even these are often problematic. This reality, which has been imposed from above, seems fixed, inevitable, even natural. But it is most unnatural.

A Care Income—a Global Perspective

Demanding a Care Income can transform the end and aim of the economy from pursuing economic growth, capital accumulation, and jobs that are destructive of both workers and the environment to pursuing health and well-being of people and planet. These must be the measure of progress.

A Care Income sheds light on society's necessity to prioritize, respect, and support its own reproduction. It can pay a living wage to mothers and other primary carers of people, thus beginning to end poverty, starting with that of mothers and children, the poorest everywhere. Domestic workers in Peru, part of our network, are now demanding "a living wage for caring work in your own home and in the home of others."

A Care Income speaks to the increased awareness provoked by the Covid-19 pandemic that caring work is central to society, and that no worker should be without rights. Yet unwaged family caregivers, beginning with mothers, have no income and, therefore, few rights.[41] Women in the US have pushed for rescue packages to include family caregivers. It raises the status of caring and, therefore, of everyone doing this work, waged or unwaged, starting with the many care workers who are women of colour and/or immigrants and are grossly underpaid and threatened with deportation.

A Care Income speaks to the movement to end government subsidized factories in the field, which torture animals, poison the soil, and undermine local food production. It can increase the power of Indigenous communities and small farmers, the carers for the soil, providing land, water, and seeds that ensure food and economic independence, and methods of organic agriculture which can regenerate the health of people, wildlife, and the soil. As women in the Southern Peasant Federation of Thailand who are supporting a Care Income have said: "We care for the land in the same way we care for our families, trying always to do what is best for life and wellbeing of all."

This can save mothers and whole communities from having to migrate for financial reasons, leaving children with grandmothers who must raise two generations without recognition or support from the State.

Even considering a Care Income opens the way for all genders to rethink how we relate to each other and to the natural world, what we produce, and what we may want to refuse to produce. Once we are collectively respectful of all life—including our own—our standards are transformed.

A Care Income can undermine the division of labour between women and men, as caring activities which have been demeaned for so long can be re-evaluated. Caring that is respected and financially supported can be much more attractive to all genders—to fathers, and mothers too, who have never had time to know their children as they wanted to.

A Care Income can establish our right to care and to be cared for, that is, to build relationships of mutual care—across generations, dis/abilities, cultures—which we want to have the power to define and redefine according to what we need, know, and can contribute. This focus on life and relationships strengthens disabled people's demands for independent living. It is the opposite of caring work as capital conceives and imposes it: impoverishing, restricted, devalued, and squeezed in before and after waged exploitation.

A Care Income can provide security and support to all those who are working for protection and justice for the community and the environment, including by campaigning to stop destructive "development" and to return habitats to the wildlife and/or the subsistence farming from which they were stolen.

It can enable us to reclaim our sociobiological contributions and experiences. If we respect and defend biodiversity in the natural world, we must respect and defend our own biology. New life must have the time and attention it needs to develop its relationship to the world it has entered. Mothers must have every support for breastfeeding and not be under pressure to "make a living." These are the considerations for paid leave for mothers and other caregivers of newborns.

A Care Income can help dissolve the prejudices against women and communities from different cultures and technologies. We will begin to see what each of us has been up against and the brilliant solutions people find for survival, for ourselves and others. This can inspire new technologies and practices that do not pollute, do not exploit, do not destroy communities and ways of life but enhance them.

It can strengthen the movement against war and its mass murder of humans and other life, ecological devastation, and destruction of the historic remains of former societies (for example in Afghanistan, Iran, Iraq, and Palestine).

A Care Income is different in its aims and impact to a basic income. Proposals for this vary widely: some intend for it to end poverty;[42] others would use it to cut benefits, cut jobs through automation, and give us just enough to prevent "unrest."[43] None we know prioritizes caring work for either people or planet or pays a living wage to the (mainly) women who have earned it by doing this work 24/7. To address this, some like the National Welfare Rights Union in the US are sensibly suggesting that a Care Income should be paid on top of a basic income, and the Poor People's Campaign has included it in their 2020 Jubilee Platform.[44]

There is enough money. The unprecedented wealth held by the over two thousand billionaires in the world is an indication of this. The top eight billionaires own as much combined wealth as "the poorest half of the human race."[45] This is obscene. It is also terrifying. How can most of the people in the world have any decision-making power about their own lives and the planet we share when two thousand people, their empires, and the governments and media they control have so much influence over all economic, political, and military decisions? Collectively we have a claim on that accumulated wealth since it is our work that produced it and our world that it has polluted in the course of producing it.

A Care Income calls forth a revolution in decision-making and in production, so that what is produced anywhere no longer threatens life on the planet but serves it. Only a massive global movement can achieve that change in collective power and in direction—a movement which is by nature anti-sexist, anti-racist, and anti-capitalist, so that it can prevent fossil fuels from being replaced by "green" technologies that bring to the Global South and elsewhere a new level of plunder, pollution, and extinction.[46]

A Care Income can strengthen the struggles many people are already involved in and help build the movement for people and planet globally.[47]

A Care Income faces opposition, not because it is impractical, but because it threatens the established order of priorities, because it defends the natural world, because it attacks poverty, and because it begins with women but embraces everyone—it invites all genders to look again at the work we do and the lives we live.

The time is now.

Notes

1   Oxfam values this work at $10.8 trillion a year, based on legal minimum wages in different countries, which they consider a great underestimate; see Max Lawson, Anam Parvez Butt, Rowan Harvey, Diana Sarosi, Clare Coffey, Kim Piaget, and Julie Thekkuda,"Time to Care," Oxfam International, January 20, 2020, accessed September 21, 2020, https://www.oxfam.org/en/research/time-care.

2   "Understanding the Pay Gap in the UK," Office of National Statistics, January 17, 2018. On average, UK women earn 43 per cent less than men from paid work; see "Spirals of Inequality," Women's Budget Group, 2020, accessed September 21, 2020, https://wbg.org.uk/wp-content/uploads/2020/04/Spirals-of-Inequality-final-1.pdf. Professor Alison Wolf's breakdown of the income gap by class in the UK found that a "female graduate born in 1970 who has two children can expect lifetime earnings that are 88 per cent of her husband's, whereas for those with middle-level qualifications the figure falls to 57 per cent, and for those with no formal qualifications at all to only 34 per cent"; see Alison Wolf, "Working Girls," Prospect, April 23, 2006, accessed September 20, 2020, https://www.prospectmagazine.co.uk/magazine/rise-of-professional-women-decline-female-altriusm.

3   Selma James, "The Global Kitchen" (1985), in Selma James, *Sex, Race, and Class: The Perspective of Winning—A Selection of Writings 1952–2011* (Oakland: PM Press, 2012), 167.

4   The UK National Health Service, that extraordinary achievement of the post–World War II working-class movement led by Health Minister Aneurin Bevan, is increasingly being privatized and in the grip of Big Pharma. Mothers are the first to question vaccines and other established procedures when their children have adverse reactions to them, and to practice alternative medicine such as homeopathy if they find it effective. Homeopathy used to be freely available on the NHS, and there were a number of homeopathic hospitals, but they were attacked by the medical and pharmaceutical industries. Only the Glasgow Centre for Integrative Care remains.

5   In 1970, Kate Millett, in her best-selling *Sexual Politics* writes, "Virginia Woolf glorified two housewives, Mrs. Dalloway and Mrs. Ramsay," a criticism of Woolf. Far from glorifying these two housewives, in *To the Lighthouse*, Woolf breaks new ground by describing Mrs. Ramsay's exhausting emotional housework and her husband's insatiable demand for it as rape ("the beak of brass, the arid scimitar of the male, which smote mercilessly, again and again, demanding sympathy.") Nor is there glory in Woolf's description of Mrs. Dalloway's work (*Mrs. Dalloway*): she organizes a (political) party for the heads of professions and government, among whom is the psychiatrist who has driven a traumatized war veteran to suicide. Woolf had plenty of experience with psychiatrists, and she implies that the other guests are of a similar ilk. This great novelist conveyed the tragedy of the work women of her class spent their lives doing as part of a monstrous social order; Kate Millett, *Sexual Politics* (New York: Doubleday and Company, 1970), 139.

6   It is shocking that the woman who fought for mothers to be financially rewarded for their work, in the knowledge that this was also the best way to eliminate child poverty, has been barely recognized by feminists; see "Child Benefit Has Been Changing Lives for 70 Years. Let's Not Forget the Woman Behind It," 27–29, this volume. To begin to right that wrong, "Remembering Eleanor Rathbone: Mother of Child Benefit," Crossroads Women, accessed September 21, 2020, http://crossroadswomen.net/live-projects-and-campaigns, interviews mothers about what Family Allowance meant to them.

7   In 1938, Woolf said: "[Woman] must make it her business to press for a living wage . . . a wage to be paid by the State legally to the mother . . . for the work of bearing and bringing up children, a real wage, a money wage, so that it became an attractive profession instead of being as it is now an unpaid profession, an unpensioned profession, and therefore a precarious and dishonoured profession"; Virginia Woolf, *Three Guineas* (New York: Penguin, 1983 [1938]).

8   They were part of Martin Luther King Jr.'s Poor People's Campaign in 1968, and today's National Welfare Rights Union is part of the new Poor People's Campaign: A National Call for Moral Revival.

9   Johnnie Tillmon, "Welfare Is a Women's Issue," *Ms.*, 1972; republished in Gwendolyn Mink and Rickie Solinger, eds., *Welfare: Documentary History of US Policy and Politics*, (New York: New York University Press, 2003), 373–79; also available at Vancouver Rape Relief and Women's Shelter, accessed September 21, 2020, https://www.rapereliefshelter.bc.ca/learn/resources/welfare-womens-issue-johnnie-tillmon.

10 See Nairobi Forward-Looking Strategies for the Advancement of Women, United Nations, July 26, 1985, paragraph 120, accessed September 20, 2020, http://www.un-documents.net/nflsaw.htm; Beijing Declaration and Platform for Action, UN Women, September 1995, paragraph 206, accessed September 21, 2020, https://www.un.org/womenwatch/daw/beijing/platform.

11 See "Haiti: NGO Crimes Go Far Beyond Oxfam," 100–2, this volume.

12 The Counting Unremunerated Work (No. 2) Bill, 1995, Parliament Republic of Trinidad and Tobago, December 12, 1995, accessed September 21, 2020, http://www.ttparliament.org/publications.php?mid=28&id=398, was put forward by Independent senator Diana Mahabir-Wyatt.

13 The Bolivarian Republic of Venezuela's constitution of 1999, with Amendments through 2009; Constitute, Article 88, accessed September 21, 2020, https://www.constituteproject.org/constitution/Venezuela_2009.pdf?lang=en; Article 88 reads: "The State guarantees equality and equity between men and women in the exercise of their right to work. The State recognizes work at home as an economic activity that creates added value and produces social welfare and wealth. Housewives are entitled to Social Security in accordance with the law."

14 We organized speaking tours of Spain, the UK, and the US for Venezuelan women and published Nina López, ed., *Creating a Caring Economy: Nora Castañeda and the Women's Development Bank of Venezuela* (London: Crossroads Books, 2006), also in Spanish as *Creando una economía solidaria: Nora Castañeda y el Banco de Desarrollo de la Mujer de Venezuela*.

15 Maggie Ronayne, "Invisibility Would Undermine Carers' Struggle for Equity," *Irish Times*, July 13, 2018, accessed September 21, 2020, https://www.irishtimes.com/opinion/invisibility-would-undermine-carers-struggle-for-equity-1.3563054.

16 About a quarter of children in both the UK and the US live with one parent, overwhelmingly the mother, and no other adult, compared to about 7 per cent around the world; Pew Research Center, December 12, 2019, accessed December 20, 2020, https://www.pewresearch.org/fact-tank/2019/12/12/u-s-children-more-likely-than-children-in-other-countries-to-live-with-just-one-parent. Department of Work and Pensions records show 134,044 households had support capped, with single mothers accounting for 114,337. "Benefit cap: single mothers make up 85% of those affected, data shows," Rajeev Syal, *Guardian*, January 4, 2019, accessed December 15, 2020, https://www.theguardian.com/society/2019/jan/04/benefit-cap-single-mothers-make-up-85percent-of-those-affected-data-shows

17 During Covid-19, the treatment of the elderly by some governments has bordered on genocide. In Sweden, which is promoted as a model of women's equality, several regions had issued guidelines ordering that no care home residents should receive hospital treatment for any illness or injury at all. Some doctors had recommended palliative care without even looking at patient records"; Richard Orange, "As the

Death Toll Soars Ever Higher, Sweden Wonders Who Is to Blame," *Guardian*, December 20, 2020, accessed December 21, 2020, https://www.theguardian.com/world/2020/dec/20/as-covid-death-toll-soars-ever-higher-sweden-wonders-who-to-blame.

18 Eighty-six per cent of government cuts have targeted women; see Women's Budget Group, *The Impact on Women of the 2016 Budget* (London: UK Women's Budget Group, 2016), accessed September 20, 2020, http://wbg.org.uk/wp-content/uploads/2016/11/WBG_2016Budget_FINAL_Apr16-1.pdf.

19 "With so much of our long-term health tied up in our crucial first foods and what we eat as children, we must acknowledge the political and health functions of the home and motherhood. Yet the public health aspect of the home has been completely left out of the conversation about food, health, and politics—and the only way to change this is to assign real value to the work done in the home. When it comes to public health measures, breastfeeding, in addition to cooking and preparing healthy whole foods, is one of the most significant activities"; Kristin Lawless, *Formerly Known as Food: How the Industrial Food System Is Changing Our Minds, Bodies and Culture* (New York: St Martin's Press, 2018), 217.

20 English Collective of Prostitutes, "ECP Submission to Work and Pensions Committee Inquiry into Universal Credit and 'Survival Sex,'" May 2, 2019, accessed September 21, 2020, https://prostitutescollective.net/submission-to-work-and-pensions-committee.

21 See Anne Neale and Nina López, for Legal Action for Women, *Suffer the Little Children and their Mothers: A Dossier on the Unjust Separation of Children from Their Mothers* (London: Crossroads Books, 2017); Legal Action for Women coordinates the campaigning coalition Support Not Separation in the UK. Also see the award-winning documentary Every Mother Is a Working Mother Network, *DHS, Give Us Back Our Children* (excerpts) (Philadelphia: Scribe Video Center, 2019), accessed September 21, 2020, https://www.youtube.com/watch?v=OHLNsIlxFsQ.

22 See Empower Foundation, *Sex Workers and the Thai Entertainment Industry*, July 2017, accessed September 21, 2020, https://tbinternet.ohchr.org/Treaties/CEDAW/Shared%20Documents/THA/INT_CEDAW_NGO_THA_27511_E.pdf; the Empower Foundation submission to the Committee on the Elimination of Discrimination against Women highlighted the fact that over 21 per cent of children in Thailand are in the care of extended family, most often the grandmother, as mothers are forced to migrate to find waged work in the city.

23 Adoption by professional women and gay men, using lower-income surrogate mothers to carry the child or being offered one of the children taken into "care" by social services without the consent of the birth mother, has become more common—another expression of the class divide among women.

24 See "What Women Want 2.0," 30–32, this volume.

25 Vicky Pryce, *Women vs. Capitalism: Why We Can't Have It All in a Free Market Economy* (London: C Hurst & Co, 2019), 82–83.

26 Women's Budget Group, "Investing in the Care Economy to Boost Employment and Gender Equality," 2016, accessed September 21, 2020, https://tinyurl.com/y2np4sou.

27 The UK government is researching the development of robots that could fulfil tasks such as "helping an elderly person up after a fall . . . delivering food to an older person at mealtimes, and even ensuring they take crucial medication at the correct time"; Department for Business, Energy and Industrial Strategy, UK Research and Innovation, and the Rt. Hon. Chris Skidmore MP, "Care Robots Could Revolutionize

UK Care System and Provide Staff Extra Support" (press release), October 26, 2019, accessed September 21, 2020, https://www.gov.uk/government/news/care-robots-could-revolutionise-uk-care-system-and-provide-staff-extra-support. Some countries are already using robots to avoid having to raise the wages of carers or having to employ immigrant workers; Daniel Moss, "Graying Japan Wants Automation, Not Immigration," *Japan Times*, August 28, 2017, accessed September 21, 2020, https://tinyurl.com/y4d89skm.

28 In 2007, James put the sum at about £20,000 (approximately $40,000) a year. He excludes families who are rich, the 1% of people who earn more than £100,000 (approximately $200,000) a year or who have large capital assets. He also proposes that the richest must be divested of a significant portion of their wealth: Oliver James, *Affluenza*, (London: Vermillion, Penguin, 2007), 493–94.

29 The Worker Relief and Credit Act (WRCR HR5271) introduced by Rep. Gwen Moore (WI) and Rep. Marcia Fudge (OH) would redefine workers to include unpaid family caregivers and students. It would get cash directly into the hands of mothers, other caregivers, and students. It is estimated that it would help alleviate poverty by 30 per cent, particularly among Black, Indigenous, and Latina caregivers.

30 Patrick Greenfield, "Trust Our Expertise or Face Catastrophe, Amazon Peoples Warn on Environment," *Guardian,* January 28, 2020, accessed September 28, 2020, https://tinyurl.com/sofrz9l; Elaine Jung, "Earth Day: Meet the Original Eco Warriors Protecting the Planet," BBC News, April 22, 2020, accessed September 28, 2020, https://www.bbc.com/news/science-environment-51806291.

31 Protection International works with women human rights defenders in Thailand and other countries. The Palestinian struggle against environmental destruction is one with the struggle against Israeli occupation. As a result of Israel's siege of Gaza, and its repeated bombing of water, sewage, and power infrastructure, less than 5 per cent of water from Gaza's single fresh water aquifer is fit for human consumption—a leading cause of child deaths.

32 "The goal is to move beyond symbolic commitments to 'anti-colonial action' to consider meaningful contributions to repairing the past in the form of infrastructure funding, technology transfers and resources for displaced communities"; *Blueprint for Europe's Just Transition*, edition two, Green New Deal for Europe, December 2019, accessed September 28, 2020, https://tinyurl.com/y7ceugoy.

33 Ibid., 37.

34 See "A Care Income Now!," 82–83, this volume.

35 Wages for Housework Campaign, *Refusing Nuclear Housework: Women's Case against the Building of Hinkley "C" Nuclear Power Station* (London: Wages for Housework Campaign, 1989). In 1995, International Black Women for Wages for Housework hosted the workshop "Opposing Environmental Racism & Sexism" at the NGO Forum of the UN Conference on Women in Huairou, China.

36 These were the demands of the Global Women's Strike we called for March 8, 2000; for the full demands, see "Global Women's Strike International Demands," in Selma James, *Sex, Race, and Class*, 238.

37 The US military has also caused the desertification of 90 per cent of Iraq; Whitney Webb, "US Military Is World's Biggest Polluter," MintPress News, May 15, 2017, accessed September 21, 2020, https://www.ecowatch.com/military-largest-polluter-2408760609.html.

38 Karl Marx, *Capital*, vol. 1 (London: Penguin Books, 1976), 638.

39 See Solveig Francis, Selma James, Phoebe Jones, and Nina López, *The Milk of Human Kindness—Defending Breastfeeding from the Global Market & the AIDS Industry* (London: Crossroads Books, 2002), 84; also see, "The Milk of Human Kindness," in Selma James, *Sex, Race, and Class*, 224–29.

40 Even the massive traditional herbal systems of China and many other countries are largely hidden or ignored in the West.

41 A UK poll found that "eight out of ten people want to prioritize health and well-being over economic growth, and six out of ten still want to after the pandemic ends"; "8 Out of 10 Agree: Public Health before Economic Growth," Positive Money, May 18, 2020, accessed September 21, 2020, https://www.youtube.com/watch?v=0YzRKIqng2U. The pope, speaking of those who "live from day to day, without any type of legal guarantee to protect you," including "the different kinds of caregivers," called for "a universal basic wage which would acknowledge and dignify the noble, essential tasks you carry out. It would ensure and concretely achieve the ideal . . . of no worker without rights"; see Pope Francis, "Letter of His Holiness Pope Francis to the Popular Movements," Libreria Editrice Vaticana, April 12, 2020, accessed September 21, 2020, https://tinyurl.com/y4chcqzf.

42 For example, the Ingreso Mínimo Vital (Minimum Living Income) introduced by the Spanish State in 2020.

43 John Clarke, an organizer with the Ontario Coalition Against Poverty for nearly thirty years, offered a scathing critique of the Canadian provincial government's trial use of a basic income and its impact on disabled people.

44 The Poor People's Campaign Jubilee programme issued on June 20, 2020, includes: "Establish a universal and guaranteed adequate income. Include a care income to recognize the economic contribution of routine housework, childcare, tending to the elderly and other household or non-household members and other unpaid activities related to household maintenance. Redefine welfare as a right that strengthens our society."

45 Deborah Hardoon, "An Economy for the 99%," Oxfam International, January 16, 2017, accessed September 21, 2020, https://www.oxfam.org/en/research/economy-99.

46 One example is the extraction of lithium for electric car batteries, which is destroying ecosystems and poisoning water and soil in South America and increasingly in Africa, Australia, and China. Another is the expansion of large-scale monoculture tree plantations which threaten to replace ancient forests in many countries of Africa.

47 Since the Green New Deal for Europe, we have been working with Stefania Barca and Giacomo D'Alisa, both active in the Feminisms and Degrowth Alliance, and have together published *Renta de los Cuidados ¡Ya!* (Barcelona: Icaria Editorial, 2020), accessed February 24, 2021, https://icariaeditorial.com/libros-libres/4684-renta-de-los-cuidados-ya.html.

How Some of Our Network See the Care Income We Are All Campaigning For
(2020)

Thailand
These two communities are part of the Women Human Rights Defenders' Collective which includes women who are Indigenous, disabled, lesbian, Muslim (from the Deep South), sex workers, fighting for natural resources and the environment (e.g., resisting coal power plants, potash and gold mining, and mega-dam projects), reclaiming and farming land, fighting for rights to the sea, for land reform (in the Northeast), for democracy, refugees, migrants, former prisoners, lawyers who represent various communities under threat (and who are under threat themselves), rural, the Assembly of the Poor, from the slum communities, garment workers (Tri-Arm), and street vendors.

North East Anti-Mining Community
I wake up at 2:00 a.m. to go and tap rubber from the trees for the plantation owner. By 6:00 a.m., I head home in time to get breakfast for my daughter and husband. The daily chores of keeping the house and working in the vegetable garden take up the afternoon.

On most days, there will be some work that needs attending to for our campaign against the mining company, which is intent on poisoning our soil and water. The company has filed several lawsuits against me and the other village women. Sometimes soldiers or authorities come to check on me, which is intimidating.

My evening is spent making dinner, listening, encouraging, and cleaning up ready for the next day. I go to bed about 9:00 p.m. This is the hour I do most of my worrying and planning. I worry about the future of my daughter. I worry about the poisons from the mines. I worry about our debts and whether there will be enough money for school fees, food, clothes. I worry about going to prison.

I am awake nineteen hours each day. Of this, twelve hours are spent doing the unwaged work of caring for others, i.e., my family, community, and the environment. The four hours I spend tapping rubber is the only work that is waged. If it's raining it cannot be done. . . . Sometimes I hope for rain so I can rest. Sometimes I hope for clear skies so I can earn money.

What would a Care Income mean to me? Some people say time is money, and this money would give me time. Time to grow more food; time with my husband and daughter; time to strengthen the resistance to mining and other injustices. My family and our community would be secure, and security brings dignity and freedom. No more having to choose between sleep or money!

Four Region Slum Network

I live in the famous and oldest slum of Bangkok, Klong Toey. I'm a single mother with a young daughter and a brother who both have disabilities and chronic health problems. My elderly mum also lives with us and is dependent on me.

I get up at 1:00 a.m. and cook the rice and pork to sell later before going to my taxi job. I am a motorcycle taxi driver from 3:00 a.m. to 7:00 a.m. every day. Later I take my daughter to school, which is far from our home. I sell sticky rice and pork outside the gates there for an hour or so before going home to get my mum's lunch and do the household chores. There are visits to the clinic and sometimes the hospital.

I am also the elected and unpaid chairperson of the Four Region Slum Network, which represents the millions of people who live in the slums. Every day there is work to do in our community fight against the threat of eviction and other issues of poverty and State discrimination.

I pick my daughter up from school, and we go back home to prepare dinner and get school clothes ready, etc.

We have a very low income, so must live day to day. Any emergencies, even a small one like a flat tire on my motorcycle, can mean we are in big trouble.

A Care Income would be a secure foundation for me. It would mean I could do more work of caring for my daughter and the community. This would be good for our family and good for society. The government could provide community housing to mothers and carers as part of the income. Paying us a wage, in cash or in housing, would mean we could solve many of the problems of slums and poverty ourselves. We don't lack capacity; we lack money!

India: Nawa Chhattisgarh Mahila Samiti

So many people are protesting about climate change. It's getting hotter—48°C in Chhattisgarh. People are fighting against mining companies, including British: iron, coal, uranium polluting land and water. They steal water from the village areas and cut down trees. Due to the cutting of the forest, all the villagers' resources are being depleted. The water level is also getting very low and due to that people are facing a lot of problems with drinking water. The company is buying the people's land, so their land is being snatched from them. Adivasi and Dalit women are campaigning strongly against the companies in forest areas where they live, to get them to leave. We need a Care Income.

Naya jamana aayega! A new age is coming!

Peru: GWS and Federación Nacional de Trabajadoras y Trabajadores del Hogar

We work in our home and in the home of others. As a domestic workers' trade union, we campaign for legislation based on ILO Convention 189, won by international organizing over decades: an eight-hour workday, paid maternity leave, paid holidays, a written contract, the right to unionize, etc. As the GWS, we also campaign for a Care Income—a living wage for the work we do in our families and communities, for the environment, and for human rights.

Caring work does not distinguish culture, ethnicity, origin. But in Peru, most of us who do caring work for others are Indigenous women and girls who migrate from the countryside to the city or to another country. We create time for others to pursue their careers and improve the standard of living of their families. But what about our families? Many of us work several jobs and are forced to leave our children at home on their own for long hours—with a Care Income we could stop doing the triple day.

The pandemic has shown that caring work is the most humanitarian work in the world. It demands effort, time, dedication, preparation, skills, and abilities. It is highly responsible work, because we care for lives. There must be a budget for it; reducing people to extreme poverty before they can access social programmes leads to exploitation and corruption. The elimination of poverty must be a priority for all who claim to defend the rights of women. Without financial recognition for caring work, such elimination is impossible.

Ireland: Global Women's Strike

Article 41.2 of the 1937 Irish constitution says: "[T]he State recognizes that by her life within the home, woman gives to the State a support without which the common good cannot be achieved. The State shall therefore endeavour to ensure that mothers shall not be obliged by economic necessity to engage in labour to the neglect of their duties in the home."

Because the language is outdated and sexist, some feminists have wanted this article removed. They seemed unconcerned that women who do this work would be angered by losing this pathbreaking recognition of the State's responsibility to family carers.

Unwaged caring in the home has been used to lower women's wages and status on the job market. In 2014, an equality tribunal ruling noted that academic women applicants for promotion at the National University of Ireland Galway seemed to be disadvantaged when they declared their caring responsibilities. The ruling triggered a movement I have been involved in for pay equity and gender equality in higher education, which has been extended to all grades—from cleaners and administrative staff to lecturers and professors.

Acknowledging that in most families, everywhere, mothers are the primary carers does not chain women to this work. It simply points to this important contribution on which society—"the common good"—depends.

The Care Income has given us new impetus to demand that the constitution be updated so everyone doing this work, of whatever gender, is afforded the dignity and financial support they deserve.

A Care Income Now! (2020)

On March 27, 2020, partly in response to governments' handling of the Covid-19 pandemic, GWS and Women of Colour GWS, together with the Green New Deal for Europe, issued this Open Letter to Governments.

Every day and in every emergency, unwaged or low-waged caregivers, urban and rural, mostly women, often immigrant women, struggle to protect and care for people of every age and condition. But this work is kept invisible and, therefore, **there is never a relief package from governments for caregivers, only more work**, especially with the advent of Covid-19.

In 1980, the ILO estimated that women did two-thirds of the world's work for 5 per cent of its income. Today **women and girls do more than three-quarters of all unpaid care work**—a total of 12.5 billion hours a day.

The coronavirus pandemic came on top of the climate pandemic, the poverty pandemic, the war pandemic, and the rape and domestic violence pandemics, which have hit single mother families, ill, disabled and older people hardest. It is exposing weaknesses in our ability to resist and survive physically and financially—from immune systems already compromised by poverty, discrimination, pollution, war, occupation, displacement, and other violence to inadequate health care and inadequate incomes, especially in the Global South, in communities of colour in the North, and among refugees everywhere.

In response to the virus, country after country has been shut down—from workplaces to schools and transport—and proposals to replace lost wages are being debated. These drastic measures show that **governments can take swift action and find money to deal with "emergencies"—if they want to**. At this critical moment, we must insist collectively on what we need. We fear that governments may use increased emergency powers to transfer wealth from taxpayers to corporations, and even to impose further controls, surveillance, and restrictions on our movements and our lives well after this pandemic is over.

The market values unwaged work at $10.8 trillion but never suggests that women should get any of it. Instead we are advised to get an education and a better paid job. We, of course, have a right to that. But it does not deal with **the indispensable work of life and survival**—from breastfeeding to elder care. Only increasing the status, power, and income of caregivers can do that.

In the 1980s, the **Women Count—Count Women's Work** petition issued by the International Wages for Housework Campaign gave voice of a hidden mass movement for recognition of this work. It was signed by 1,200 organizations representing millions of women worldwide, resulting in the 1995 UN decision that governments measure and value unwaged work in national accounts.

The **Green New Deal for Europe** takes this forward. It looks at what work is needed for social and environmental well-being and what work is not and proposes a Care Income as a key part of its programme for climate justice. At last protecting people and protecting the Earth can be equated and prioritized over the uncaring market—a major step in transforming the world and saving it. We need this everywhere.

We demand a CARE INCOME across the planet for all those of every gender who care for people, the urban and rural environment, and the natural world.

This open letter has thus far been translated into Arabic, Bahasa, Burmese, Dutch, French, German, Greek, Hindi, Italian, Mandarin, Romanian, Spanish, Swahili, Thai, Turkish, and Urdu.

You can endorse it at: https://globalwomenstrike.net
and contact us at: careincomenow@globalwomenstrike.net
http://www.gndforeurope.com

With CLR James at his sixtieth birthday celebration in Trinidad, 1961. (© Selma James)

Margaret Prescod shaking hands with Frankie Mae Jeter, Beulah Sanders, and Johnnie Tillmon after winning the resolution that welfare should be called a wage, National Women's Conference, Houston, 1977 (Photo from *The Spirit of Houston: An Official Report to the President, the Congress and the People of the United States*, March 1978).

Time Off for Women at Greenham Common Women's Peace Camp, October 1986: Sarah Hipperson of Yellow Gate, which hosted the event, is speaking. She was a Scottish former midwife and magistrate who lived at the camp for many years to protest against the US nuclear cruise missiles based there. The Peace Camp scored a victory, with the military base closed and the land restored to common use.

With Ralph Ibbott, c. 2010, preparing his book *Ujamaa: The Hidden Story of Tanzania's Socialist Villages* for publication.

Andaiye (Guyana) in Los Angeles in 2007 on a US speaking tour with me, which Phoebe Jones (GWS Philadelphia) coordinated.

Lori Nairne (1951–2017), a member of Queer Strike, which spearheaded the "Grand Marshall, Not Court Martial" campaign, which named whistleblower Chelsea Manning Grand Marshall of the 2014 San Francisco Pride March, banned military recruiters, and removed pro-corporate Pride board members. Lori was a nurse and a homeopath. Our international network greatly misses her and the holistic knowledge and skills she was always happy to make available.

With (from right to left) President Jean-Bertrand Aristide, Margaret Prescod, Aristide's wife and colleague Mildred Trouillot, their daughters Michaelle and Christine, March 18, 2011, the day the Aristides returned to Haiti after seven years of forced exile.

Pierre Labossière of the Haiti Action Committee reporting back on the delegation to Haiti, which included Congresswoman Maxine Waters, Danny Glover, and Margaret Prescod, Los Angeles, June 15, 2019.

With (from left to right) Manju Gardia (Nawa Chhattisgarh Mahila Samiti, India), Fakhra Salimi (MiRA Pakistan/ Norway), and Rea Dol (SOPUDEP, Haiti), GWS international conference, London, 2015.

Maggie Ronayne (GWS Ireland) speaking, with Liz Hilton (Empower, Thailand) and Cristel Amiss (WoC GWS, London) at the same conference

A number of us were outside the conference centre in London where Jeremy Corbyn's election as leader of the Labour Party was announced. Nina López, who co-authored some of the articles in this book, is on the left.

Speaking for the International Jewish Anti-Zionist Network outside Labour Party headquarters in 2018, during the protest against the IHRA definition of antisemitism being adopted. The section of the banner behind me reads BDS.

All African Women's Group, Women of Colour GWS, and supporters rally outside the Home Office in London to stop the deportation of a member, February 2017.

The US PROStitutes Collective welcomes Empower (Thailand) and the English Collective of Prostitutes, in Oakland, March 2018.

Mothers, family members, and supporters with DHS Give Us Back Our Children and Every Mother Is a Working Mother Network outside Philadelphia Department of Human Services, protesting the tragic and unjust removal of children by the child welfare system, June 15, 2012.

International Women's Day, 2018, London: a number of organizations came together for a speak-out across the street from Parliament, highlighting the State's brutal removal of children, especially from mothers who had suffered domestic violence.

Women of Colour GWS was invited to speak at the Migrant Justice Bloc of the Global Youth Strike, London, September 2019.

Taking part in the Extinction Rebellion Mothers' Nurse-in, London, October 2019.

Rev. William Barber II, co-chair (with Rev. Liz Theoharis) of the Poor People's Campaign, greets the GWS and Payday men's network delegations to the national PPC's Moral Action Congress, Washington, DC, June 2019.

Lima, Peru, March 8, 2019: GWS and the trade union FENTTRAHOP rallying for the domestic workers' rights law, which was finally passed in September 2020. Leddy Mozombite Linares, who led this struggle, is behind the banner, third from left. (© FENTTRAHOP)

Thailand: Women Human Rights Defenders' Collective (WHRD) celebrating the victory of the Dong Ma Fai community, which reclaimed its land after a twenty-six-year struggle against a limestone mining company, September 25, 2020. WHRD currently represents nineteen different sectors and struggles, some of which are part of the GWS network. (© WHRD)

Photos © Crossroads Audiovisual Collective, except where otherwise noted.

Chávez, Nyerere, Aristide versus Thatcher
(2013–2018)

Hugo Chávez Knew That His Revolution Depended on Women (2013)

with Nina López

And he wasn't the only one. Presidents of Tanzania and Haiti have both benefited from making women central to progress.

Guardian, March 8, 2013

The funeral of President Hugo Chávez of Venezuela took place on International Women's Day—a fitting day of departure for "the president of the poor," who was loved by millions, especially by women, the poorest.

When Chávez was elected in 1998, the grassroots movement took a leap in power, and women in particular were empowered. Women were the first into the streets against the 2002 US-backed coup; their mobilization saved the revolution. When asked why, woman after woman said: "Chávez is us, he is our son." He was an extension of who they were as strugglers for survival.

Chávez soon learnt that the revolution he led depended on women and said so: "Only women have the passion and the love to make the revolution." He acknowledged that the "missions"—the new social services which were at the heart of his popularity and which the State funded but did not run—were mainly created and run by grassroots neighbourhood women.

In 2006, when announcing the partial implementation of Article 88 of the new constitution recognizing caring work as productive—a breakthrough worldwide—Chávez said: "[Women] work so hard raising their children, ironing, washing, preparing food . . . giving [their children] an orientation. . . . This was never recognized as work yet it is such hard work! . . . Now the revolution puts you first, you too are workers, you housewives, workers in the home."

Chávez was not the first movement leader who went on to head the government to have understood women's centrality to creating the new society they were striving to build.

Half a century ago, Julius Nyerere, leader of Tanzania's independence struggle and its first president, aimed his programme for development at the elimination of two ills: women's inequality and poverty. He said: "Women who live in villages work harder than anyone in Tanzania, 'working' in the fields and in the homes."

"The truth is that in the villages the women work very hard. At times they work for 12 or 14 hours a day. They even work on Sundays and public holidays." Whereas the village men "are on leave half their lives."

Nyerere's *ujamaa* or "African socialism"—self-reliance and co-operation—was to keep Tanzania independent, by enabling it to refuse foreign loans. He insisted men must do their share. Equity was a question not only of justice but of economic necessity and political independence.

Encouraged by Nyerere, in one region, seventeen *ujamaa* villages created a communal society based on equity among women and men, children and adults—all contributed what they could, and all shared equally in the wealth produced. Their extraordinary society was destroyed by Nyerere's power-hungry colleagues against his will, but it showed us what is possible.

Closer to Venezuela, women gained recognition under Jean-Bertrand Aristide, Haiti's first democratically elected president (1990 and 2000). Determined to tackle extreme poverty and injustice, Aristide created a Ministry of Women's Affairs, appointed women to ministerial posts, supported girl domestic workers and survivors of military rape. As in Venezuela, women were the main organizers and beneficiaries of literacy and health programmes; the rise in the minimum wage benefited them especially—sweatshop workers are mainly women.

Young people's love for Aristide is legendary, but women's devotion has been as constant. Two months after the devastating 2010 earthquake, women collected twenty thousand signatures in three days demanding President Aristide's return from exile—they needed him for reconstruction. A year later, he was back, not as president but as educator, reopening the medical school he had founded for poor students, which the coup had closed.

In Bolivia, indigenous women were recognized as central to the mass mobilizations which propelled Evo Morales into the presidency. These included the "water wars" which drove the multinational Bechtel out of Bolivia (they privatized the water and criminalized people who collected rain water). In 2008, the women were prominent in surrounding Congress for several days while the new constitution was debated; the white parliamentary elite intended to absent themselves to prevent a vote. The blockade forced them to sleep in the building till the vote was taken. That constitution heralded a new level of power for women—from pay equity to recognition for the economic value of caring work.

As the president of the poor is laid to rest, the historic Operation Condor trial opens in Argentina, tackling the coordinated campaign of State terror of former Latin American dictatorships. We must recall a little-known aspect of Chávez's legacy. Venezuela's oil revenue supported Argentina's Presidents Nestor and Cristina Kirchner, enabling them to pass laws removing the military's immunity from prosecution. The Mothers and Grandmothers of Plaza de Mayo, who led the 1983 overthrow of the dictatorship, and who had long campaigned for justice for the thousands the dictatorship raped, murdered and disappeared, have long paid tribute to Chávez—a most unusual military man.

They, like women all over South America and beyond, will be watching anxiously to see that the gains of the Bolivarian Revolution are not undermined.

Thatcherism Hasn't Failed: It Has Infected All Our Politics (2013)

with Nina López

In Venezuela, Hugo Chávez's legacy on poverty is likely to get his chosen successor elected. We can't so easily vote out Margaret Thatcher's war on welfare.

Guardian, April 10, 2013

Another head of government died recently, who, like Thatcher,[1] was called divisive. But unlike Thatcher, President Hugo Chávez of Venezuela, the "president of the poor," fought for a caring economy and against the rule of the market. The "crime" he was accused of was to reclaim the oil revenue from local and foreign thieves, and use it to tackle poverty. Chávez is gone, but the voters are likely to re-elect Chavismo on April 14. Thatcher is gone, but Thatcherism has infected and discredited all mainstream parties, depriving us of a chance to turn it down.

The left misleads us and maybe itself when it says that Thatcher's policies, extended by New Labour, and then by the coalition, have failed. The drastic results of these policies were intentional. Their target was "the enemy within"—working-class power and the so-called culture of entitlement.

The Welfare State set out to ensure that no one, in the UK at least, would starve or freeze to death or suffer or die for lack of medical or other care. No elderly person would be deprived of the dignity of spectacles, dentures, or a hearing aid because they couldn't afford them. No homeless or disabled people need beg on the streets. No children excluded from school activities, because mothers couldn't pay. No single mother raising children was to be called "workless," skipping meals to feed them and forced to ditch them to submit to "workfare" or a starvation wage.

The Welfare State, with its unemployment and housing benefits and free healthcare, actually protected wages: employers could not force workers to accept low pay or unpaid overtime because of the job's healthcare provision, as they do in the US. Thatcher understood the connection between the social wage and workers' wages better than most unions.

She was the first prime minister to be more accountable to the international market than to the British economy. To enrich the global 1% she so brilliantly represented, our "entitlement" had to go, and she was just the one to do it.

She said "there is no such thing as society," and set out to prove it by promoting individual greed and competition for everything. Privatization was the single most massive attack on democracy we have seen. It destroyed the public's power to determine via parliament the services and prices of gas, electricity, telephone. The relative wealth of the UK 1% had been falling steadily for fifty years when Thatcher took power in 1979; since then it has climbed steeply and is almost back to 1918 levels. How dare her apologists and beneficiaries of her legacy refer to trade unions like the NUM [National Union of Mineworkers] as "corrupt" in the face of their bonuses and tax cuts!

The leading feminist Natasha Walter called Thatcher "the great unsung heroine of British feminism." While Labour was now "intensely relaxed about people getting filthy rich,"[2] ambitious feminism wanted to be let in to the boardroom and every corridor of power—that and little else is what they mean by changing the world. Thatcher came to personify those ready to push anyone aside to gain power in a man's world and strengthen that world with their ambition.

It is not true that Thatcher didn't care about the media. She worked to enhance its corporate power. Police charges against picketing union printers in Wapping enabled the Murdoch empire to flourish, ensuring their power and hers. Original, independent voices such as BBC director general Alasdair Milne were brutally silenced.

She was propped up by police who were encouraged to brutality against not only strikers but communities of colour, already hardest hit by unemployment: police powers were enhanced and their racism given free rein, especially with stop and search; CS gas was used on the mainland for the first time. In 1982, the English Collective of Prostitutes occupied a church for twelve days in protest against "police illegality and racism in King's Cross"—the area to which many sex workers, known as "Thatcher's girls," had travelled from high unemployment areas in the Midlands and the north. And in 1983, for the first time, children born in Britain to non-British parents were denied automatic citizenship, fostering further racism and discrimination in immigration policy.

In the north of Ireland, she had the army and the Diplock courts, which reached their peak in the mid-1980s. A friend of South African apartheid and mass murderers—from Kissinger and Pinochet to the Khmer Rouge after they had killed two million Cambodians—she was a zealous saleswoman for the arms industry. Without the Falklands/Malvinas War, which exploited nationalism (as Argentinian dictator Galtieri did), and which Labour would not oppose, she would never have been re-elected in 1983. Everyone knows that.

The passing of Chávez is mourned by the many millions who loved him in Latin America and everywhere. Thatcher's passing is marked by street parties in Brixton, Belfast, Bristol, Derry, Glasgow, and Liverpool, and seething bitterness among the mining families and communities she was allowed (including by scab union and Labour leaders) to destroy.

If they have no bread, let them eat from food banks—that's Thatcherism, the legacy we are still to bury before it buries us.

Notes

1   Margaret Thatcher was the Conservative British prime minister from 1979 to 1990.
2   Statement by Peter Mandelson in 1998, while secretary of state for trade and industry in Tony Blair's Labour government.

Haiti: NGO Crimes Go Far beyond Oxfam

(2018)

with Sara Callaway, Nina López, and seventeen others

Figures for earthquake relief range from $10 billion to $13.4 billion. Some of us who visited Haiti have seen little or no sign of that money, write activists.

Guardian, Letters, February 13, 2018

In 2008, some of us had written to Barbara Stocking, then Oxfam chief executive, objecting to a report that it sponsored, Rule of Rapists in Haiti, which labelled Haitians as rapists while hiding rapes by occupying UN forces. The year before, 114 soldiers had been sent home for raping women and girls, some as young as 11. No one was prosecuted. We wrote: "NGOs like Oxfam have known about rapes by UN forces, as well as by aid and charity workers, for decades. It's the pressure of victims, women and [children] in the most impoverished communities, who had the courage to speak out that finally won . . . public acknowledgement." There was no reply.

The latest revelations of sexual abuse by major charities (Report, 13 February) are but one facet of NGO corruption.[1] The people of Haiti were the first to free themselves from slavery, but the colonial "masters" they defeated—France, Britain, and the US—have continued to plunder and exploit, including through imported NGOs. Haiti has more NGOs per square mile than any other country, and it remains the poorest in the Western Hemisphere. Corruption begins and ends with neo-colonial powers.

While celebrated for "doing good," NGO professionals do well for themselves. They move between NGOs, academia, and political appointments, enjoying a culture of impunity while they exercise power over the poorest. [When she left Oxfam, Stocking went to academia, advising on "gender equality."][2] The Lancet described NGOs in Haiti as "polluted by unsavoury characteristics seen in many big corporations" and "obsessed with raising money."

Figures for earthquake relief range from $10 billion to $13.4 billion. Some of us who visited Haiti have seen little or no sign of that money. The public was outraged when they discovered the Red Cross intended to build a luxury hotel and conference centre in Haiti with some unspent donations. Big NGOs are far from non-governmental. For example, Oxfam receives millions from the UK government. USAID is another major funder. Unsurprisingly, NGO politics follow the cash.

In 2004, the US (backed by Canada and France) overthrew Haiti's democratically elected president Jean-Bertrand Aristide. He headed a popular movement to chart an independent course that would move Haitians "from destitution to poverty." His government supported small farmers, raised the minimum wage (the lowest in the Western hemisphere), built schools and hospitals. (UNIFA, his medical university, will be celebrating the graduation of its first class of doctors in March.)[3] The coup against him had NGO support. Charities thrive on the poor, not on ending poverty.

Signed by:
Cristel Amiss, Black Women's Rape Action Project
Andaiye, Red Thread, Guyana
Margaret Busby, publisher & author
Sara Callaway, Women of Colour Global Women's Strike
Luke Daniels, Caribbean Labour Solidarity
Jocelyn Dow, Red Thread, Guyana
Selma James, Global Women's Strike
Pierre Labossière, Haiti Action Committee
Emma Lewis, Caribbean Labour Solidarity
Dr. Altheia Jones-LeCointe, Trinidad and Tobago
Eddie LeCointe, Dominica
Nina López, Legal Action for Women
Ian Macdonald, Queen's Counsel
Rose Okello, All African Women's Group
Margaret Prescod, Women of Colour Global Women's Strike
Lawrence Renee, Payday Men's Network
Sidney Ross-Risden, Haiti Support Working Group
Becky Titah, All African Women's Group
Sam Karl Weinstein, Refusing to Kill Network
Nichola Marcus, Red Thread, Guyana

Notes

1   Robert Booth, "Oxfam Warned It Could Lose European Funding Over Scandal,"
    March 12, 2018, accessed September 22, 2020, https://www.theguardian.com/world/
    2018/feb/12/haiti-demands-oxfam-identify-workers-who-used-prostitutes.
2   This sentence was edited out on publication.
3   By 2020, UNIFA had graduated 230 doctors, 78 nurses, 88 physiotherapists, and 30
    lawyers. It has launched its most ambitious project to date, a Campaign for Dignity,
    to construct a new medical center and teaching hospital.

Ujamaa: The Hidden Story of Tanzania's Socialist Villages (2014)

Introduction

In 1961, following independence and a call by President Nyerere, farming families built the Ruvuma Development Association (RDA) in the south of Tanzania, developing their economy and transforming their rural society. The RDA grew to include seventeen villages and was destroyed after eight years by Nyerere's party. My introduction to Ralph Ibbott's book *Ujamaa: The Hidden Story of Tanzania's Socialist Villages* aimed to put his extraordinary account of what happened into a wider political context.[1]

People today have little awareness of the movement of many millions which chased the European imperialists out of countries they had colonized and subjugated for centuries. Yet this was a major turning point for most of the world, since most of the world had been colonized.

The first to gain national independence from Britain was India in 1947, after a struggle over generations. Clement Attlee, prime minister of the 1945 Labour government—itself a victory of those who were determined never to go back to pre-war depression and class degradation—proclaimed soon after the landslide election that tossed out archimperialist Winston Churchill that Britain was getting out of India.

But the catastrophic Hindu-Muslim split led to the partition of Pakistan from India. Mahatma Gandhi, India's internationally respected leader, opposed partition with all in his power, but he could not stop it. It cost millions of lives and dimmed the triumph of Britain's departure.[2] This should have warned us that political independence was not enough to ensure a compassionate future.

Nevertheless, when on March 6, 1957, the British flag was lowered on the colony of the Gold Coast and Ghana's Black Star flag replaced it, anti-imperialists everywhere were ecstatic with triumph and hope. Black Africa, maligned, demeaned, and brutalized in every way, was lifting itself up, able finally to show its own worth and determine its own future as much as any single country can—and maybe even to unite as a continent. The scourge of imperial occupation, a major source of the racism that justified the theft of great wealth in human labour and natural resources, was ending in Africa.

That the anti-colonial movement is largely unfamiliar now reflects the (mis)education we all receive, including from the media. The history made by unknown millions, when silenced people speak with action, is usually distorted when it is not censored. Such massive involvement of people on their own behalf is truly subversive, threatening a tide of change even in retrospect.

But the achievements of the anti-colonial movement could also be wiped from view by the dictatorships, proxy wars, and excruciating poverty that followed. How could such enormous tragedy be its outcome? The implication often lurking behind political and academic diagnoses is that more could not be expected, that people who have little can only accomplish little.

The RDA's history helps right this racist wrong.

The story begins with the extraordinary Julius Kambarage Nyerere, socialist and pan-Africanist who, in July 1954, formed the Tanganyika African National Union (TANU) to spearhead the struggle for independence from Britain.

Nyerere had lived in the village of Butiama until he went to school at age twelve. He was the son of a chief of the Wazanaki tribe, which had not been distorted into a steep hierarchy by the colonial administrators, as had some tribes. Shaped by traditional communal village life, he never ceased to see the world from the point of view of villagers. It was a crucial component of his leadership, an unalloyed and unique strength.

Nyerere was the first Tanzanian to go to university abroad (Edinburgh, 1949–1952, where he got a master's degree). It is known that in 1944 at Makerere University in Kampala, Uganda, he wrote a paper on "The Freedom of Women." He later commented: "My father had twenty-two wives and I knew how hard they had to work and what they went through as women."[3] Not too many men, African or not, acknowledged the hard work of women at that time. Or even today. This awareness ensured a more accurate view of who "villagers" were.

He returned from post-war socialist Britain to teach. This was when he gained the title of Mwalimu, or Teacher, as he was known from then on. A year later, earlier than he had planned, he threw himself into organizing for independence.

For Nyerere, political independence from any imperial power did not by itself ensure independence from Western economic, political, and military power. Describing independence as "the preliminary goal" made clear that it was crucial but not the movement's only aim.[4] This perspective was way ahead of the prevailing unrealistic view that all a colony had to do was win political independence for everything to change. How, when resources were so meagre? The wealth that had been stolen over centuries, including the wealth in people via the slave trade, was gone; the profits accumulated by those who had dominated were a power for them to continue to dominate. The forces ranged against "new countries" were formidable, especially dangerous when they were not acknowledged.

How to cleanse the society emerging from colonialism of the structures the imperialists left behind? What should and could replace them given the level of skills of the population who had been deprived even of literacy, let alone technical and scientific training?

We should remind ourselves that even people in the West who were committed to colonial liberation rarely considered that the form of government they lived under and often challenged should not be imposed on ex-colonies. The movement itself, blinded by euphoria at the moment of its greatest power, also seems to ignore the power of capitalism to recover and reconquer. As early as 1897, James Connolly, Irish socialist leader, told the nationalist movement:

> If you remove the English army tomorrow and hoist the green flag over Dublin Castle, unless you set about the organization of the Socialist Republic your efforts would be in vain.
>
> England would still rule you. She would rule you through her capitalists, through her landlords, through her financiers, through the whole array of commercial individualist institutions she has planted in this country and watered with the tears of our mothers and the blood of our martyrs.[5]

It is a lesson which has proven hard for anti-capitalist movements to learn.

The solution often proposed to all problems was Africanization—for local people to step into the posts the British were vacating. But it is those who fight for personal advancement who usually take charge, including of expatriate salaries that had always fleeced the population. They change little but the colour and accent (and nowadays also the gender, sexual preference, etc.) at the top.

A power-hungry elite was emerging in other newly independent countries. In 1961, agronomist René Dumont, committed to colonial liberation, reported on the response to this danger in formerly French colonies:

> In May 1961 a number of farmers north of Brazzaville said to me: "Independence isn't for us; it's for the city people." I heard the same criticism that year in Dahomey and Madagascar.[6]

He quotes the mayor of Ngongsamba, Cameroon:

> [T]he masses have the impression that national sovereignty has created a privileged class which has cut itself off from them. . . . [A] good number of our officials, scorning a real sense of public office and duty, are only interested in the advantages and privileges of their positions. . . . [A]t the rate we are going now, we are headed towards a worse colonialism, that of class.[7]

Dumont also considered independence as a preliminary goal and knew that what was essential was for the farmers to be enthusiastic enough to make "a massive effort." Ibbott reports that Nyerere read his book *False Start in Africa* and ordered copies to be distributed to his ministers.[8]

Also in 1961, Frantz Fanon, a psychiatrist from Martinique in the Caribbean, drew vital lessons from the Algerian Revolution against France, of which he was part. He was one of the earliest to identify even before independence the counter-revolution driven by the ambitious new elite. They were "a little greedy caste, avid and voracious," and the party heading the movement was "transformed into a trade union of individual interests . . . a means for personal advancement."[9]

TANU was the same. Already in February 1960, nearly two years before independence, Nyerere told a TANU conference:

> I have seen TANU officials getting drunk with power and scheming to undermine one another. . . . Too many big TANU officials seem to spend most of their time talking about their positions. To what sort of government would that lead when responsible government comes? You and I must reform because if we do not, we will be blamed by the 200 million in Africa. If we cannot reform, then we must destroy TANU because it will be of no use to this territory.[10]

(Note: for him, pan-Africanism was a political principle; they were accountable to all in Africa for what they did in Tanzania.)

Nyerere called it on the opportunistic use of race; it was "racialism." Merely replacing Europeans with Africans could not change the nature of the State that imperialism had carefully left behind, whose structure aimed not to liberate but to discipline and repress.

A profoundly radical alternative strategy was needed.

He spoke in Kiswahili, the language that almost everyone understood, irrespective of region or tribe. (Local languages were often spoken in the villages, especially by women.) Mwalimu, the teacher, spoke to the people via the transistor radio.[11] No electrification needed and relatively inexpensive, it was a way of organizing which brought town and country much closer. Change depended on the 96 per cent of the population scattered in the countryside. He informed his audience about the independence struggle and about the profound problems they would face once the colonizers had gone.

> [W]e are free already. What is freedom? It is the power we have to decide what is going to happen in Tanganyika and when it is going to happen and that power we have. All that remains is hard work. . . . We must spend our brains, we must spend our sleepless nights to see how we are going to give our people the water they need, to give them the schools they need, how are we going to give the people the health they require.[12]

Tanzania became independent in December 1961. Nyerere was its first elected prime minister. TANU's commitment to socialism was enshrined in its 1962 constitution: "To establish a democratic and socialist form of government."[13] What did this mean in practice?

Nyerere's strategy for economic and social development began not with academics or planners but with African farmers.

Brought up in "tribal socialism," as he called it, Nyerere had found, in fact, invented, the Kiswahili word which both named and explained his alternative strategy:

> "*Ujamaa*" . . . or "Familyhood," describes our socialism. It is opposed to capitalism, which seeks to build a happy society on the basis of the exploitation of man by man; and it is equally opposed to doctrinaire socialism which seeks to build its happy society on a philosophy of inevitable conflict between man and man.
>
> We, in Africa, have no more need of being "converted" to socialism than we have of being "taught" democracy.[14] Both are rooted in our own past—in the traditional society which produced us. Modern African

socialism can draw from its traditional heritage the recognition of "society" as an extension of the basic family unit.

. . .Our recognition of the family to which we all belong must be extended yet further—beyond the tribe, the community, the nation, or even the continent—to embrace the whole society of mankind. This is the only logical conclusion for true socialism.[15]

This was far from a narrow State plan; national, but also internationalist. People in industrial countries had fought class exploitation and privilege by voting socialists into power so the State would act for them. It was a triumph, despite drawbacks, when Welfare States were created with free national healthcare and education, affordable housing, and benefits. In Tanzania there were hardly any doctors, nurses, teachers, hospitals, schools, money—little to nationalize. But it did have a rich tradition of a communalist society which took responsibility for the care of its people.

With *ujamaa*, the population rather than the State would take charge of development on the basis of the communalism they already knew. While traditional society was generally presumed to be limited and limiting—what development overcame—Nyerere saw both its social value and its possibilities precisely for overcoming underdevelopment. Rural people using not an import but a native framework could develop their society without capitalism—in fact, while bypassing capitalism as an economic and social system. He was not applying any socialist theory, Marxist or otherwise,[16] but adapting the communal foundation of traditional society to modern needs, aspirations, and developing personalities. It was socialism without money, rooted in the soil that had shaped Tanzanians, most of whom had lived outside of the money economy. His strategy was bold; it was a strategy for a poor but sovereign country determined to pull itself out of poverty and remain sovereign.

In April 1962, a few months after independence, Nyerere resigned from the government to use the impetus and energy of the movement that had just won the "preliminary goal" to build the movement for *ujamaa* within the party and among the population. His resignation made clear that building the movement was his priority over governing; if the people had to do it, then the people had to be informed and inspired and mobilized. Already, he said, "there had been a general acceptance of the social attitudes and ideas of our colonial masters" and of the false promise of a quick route out of poverty via the money economy. The elite which had emerged in the party and the new State was ready to use this drift to the cash nexus to secure its position.

There was not much time; Nyerere had to act before the movement receded further and "tribal socialism" was swept away. African socialism—the people themselves building a communal agricultural economy—was in a race with the elite's gold rush for wealth and power.

> I have taken this action [of resigning] and won the support of my colleagues for it after a long debate that has gone on for days because of our firm belief that this is the best way to achieve our new objective, the creation of a country in which the people take a full and active part in the fight against poverty, ignorance and disease.[17]

He put running the government in the hands of Rashidi Kawawa, a government minister, and travelled throughout the country meeting with TANU members and with the public. He published three pamphlets. His *Ujamaa—the Basis of African Socialism* made the case against capitalism and for socialism, urging Tanzanians

> to re-educate ourselves; to regain our former attitude of mind. In our traditional African society we were individuals within a community. We took care of the community and the community took care of us. We neither needed nor wished to exploit our fellow men.
>
> . . .It is . . . up to the people of Tanganyika—the peasants, the wage earners, the students, the leaders, all of us—to make sure this socialist attitude of mind is not lost through the temptations to personal gain (or the abuse of positions of authority) which may come our way as individuals.[18]

Integral to the strategy of *ujamaa* was self-reliance. They had to do without loans and aid from abroad; both had strings attached. "For a community, self-reliance means that [Tanzanians] will use the resources and the skills they jointly possess for their own welfare and their own development." They would be neither wage slaves nor exploiters; rather, they would reshape their own society so that it ended poverty, ignorance, disease.

There are not many political leaders who can tell their voters who had just won independence that to stay that way they had only their own hard work to rely on. Nor was his view of traditional communalism in the least romantic. There had to be changes to overcome "two basic factors which prevented traditional society from full flowering."

The first was that women suffered from "ill-treatment and enforced subservience."

It is impossible to deny that women did, and still do, more than their fair share of the work in the fields and in the homes. By virtue of their sex they suffered from inequalities which had nothing to do with their contribution to the family welfare.[19]

The second was poverty.

Certainly there was an attractive degree of economic equality, but it was equality at a low level. The equality is good, but the level can be raised.[20]
...[T]here is an almost universal belief that life in the towns is more comfortable and more secure—that the rewards of work are better in the urban areas and that people in the rural parts of the country are condemned to poverty and insecurity for their whole lives.[21]

Increasing the scale of farming by families working together and using more modern methods of agriculture could increase yields. This was vital not only to attack poverty but to transform rural life so that it did not suffer the deprivation of the services and facilities available only in cities:

> The land is the only basis for Tanzania's development; we have no other. Therefore, if our rural life is not based on the principles of socialism our country will not be socialist, regardless of how we organize our industrial sector, and regardless of our commercial and political arrangements. Tanzanian socialism must be firmly based on the land and its workers. This means that we have to build up the countryside in such a way that our people have a better standard of living, while living together in terms of equality and fraternity. It also means that, in the course of time, the advantages of town life in the way of services and personal pleasures and opportunities must become available to those who work in the rural sector as much as those in urban areas.[22]

Rural society, from which economic change had to come, had to transform itself into satisfying and rewarding communities, no longer socially deprived backwaters.

The elimination of poverty that would make this possible required another change.

Women's subordination had wide economic implications.

> The truth is that in the villages the women work very hard. At times they work for twelve or fourteen hours a day. They even work on Sundays

and public holidays. Women who live in the villages work harder than anybody else in Tanzania. But the men in the villages . . . are on leave for half their life.

If men pulled their weight, this "could contribute more towards the development of the country than anything we could get from rich nations."[23] Men had to change as a socialist principle but also as an economic necessity. It is extraordinary how neglected are these prominent anti-sexist views.

There were no quick fixes, not from him. Government-managed schemes which were relatively well-funded had promised much but had failed, wasting scarce resources and discrediting ministers and their managerial methods. The lesson was that success depended not on investment but on the committed and collective self-management of the producers.

People's trust in the honesty of their leader enabled him to speak these truths. He seemed without personal ambition, the rarest and most vital quality of the head of government and the movement leader—he was both. He trusted in their ability to understand and consider what he was urging them to do. And he had the patience his strategy demanded to steer the whole society away from the imperialists' waiting jaws.

> We are now a poor nation; there is no short cut to prosperity; hard work and a deliberate decision by us to plan for a better future is the only way forward.[24]

> We must not try to rush this development; what matters is not the speed but the direction in which we move.[25]

On November 7, 1960, Ntimbanjayo Millinga, twenty-one years of age, a TANU Youth League member and secretary of his branch set off with fourteen other TANU YL members to build what later became known as an *ujamaa* village. All left family behind. Though young, Millinga had worked on a sisal estate and had training as a nurse; he had also been a trade union representative—all valuable experience.

Once they had built a shelter, the men cleared the bush and planted some acres of maize, a staple of the diet. But they had to return home for lack of food to sustain them till the first crop.

Some months later, in June 1961, Millinga tried again with three of the same men and some others. This time they stayed.

During this second attempt, Millinga attended a short course at the new Kivukoni adult education college in Dar es Salaam. Ralph Ibbott had been invited to speak there about his experience on a ten-thousand-acre multiracial cooperative farm at St Faith's, in apartheid Southern Rhodesia. He had worked for ten years with Guy Clutton-Brock, a dedicated, highly regarded anti-apartheid campaigner.

A new priest hostile to such anti-racism had pressed the church that owned the land into telling Ralph, his wife Noreen, and their three children (all born in Rhodesia) to leave. The Ibbotts were now living at Nyafaru, another multiracial cooperative farm on donated land.

Millinga invited Ralph to their new village of Litowa to advise them on improving agricultural methods. Ralph visited Litowa and met the other men. He saw what they were doing and with what commitment they were doing it. He was deeply impressed, especially with Millinga. This serious young man was clever, energetic, and a natural leader (others later described him as charismatic). Ralph wrote soliciting a donation, and a kind English woman sent £50 (approximately $140), which ensured the group could survive until the first harvest.

Millinga then spent some time with the Ibbotts at Nyafaru. They discussed Litowa and the Ibbotts' possible move there and drafted a constitution for the Litowans to consider.

This was Ralph's chance to do the collective development work which apartheid could never allow. He would work with people at the exciting moment when they had won their liberation from colonial rule. Most important, unlike in Rhodesia, the Tanzanian president himself was advocating what they were attempting: that they take charge of the economic and social development of their village. The Ibbotts would have an African point of reference, a talented, determined man, and could contribute to a project to which a whole village was dedicated.

The two men began a strong and productive friendship that lasted until Ntimbanjayo Millinga's death in 2008.

The Ibbotts returned to England, as they had planned. On the way, there was a quick visit to Litowa so that Noreen and the children could see where they would be returning to. Now Ralph was in search of funding. War on Want, the UK charity, agreed to give the Ibbotts the £50 (approximately $140) a month Ralph had asked for to stay and work in Tanzania. In April 1963, the family made the move to Litowa.

By this time their families had joined the men in Litowa. The women were nervous to leave all they depended on to join this village in the bush: Would it be able to feed the family? They slowly but steadily became full participants of the village. Not surprisingly, a decisive factor was that the children flourished.

Litowa was structured to encourage all to participate in decision-making. The key gathering was the *ujamaa* dinner of all the villagers two or three times a week, served by the girls and boys. This was where problems were confronted and decisions made, from how much of each crop to plant to when they could afford to invest labour and other resources in better housing.

Ntimbanjayo was the compassionate, respected leader, pulling people together, while gently but firmly raising criticisms of those who, for example, did not pull their weight. He in particular encouraged the women to speak up.

Talented organizers emerged, strengthening the collective. The man chosen to plan the fieldwork would present his plan, and then take up his hoe along with everyone else. Planners were still fieldworkers; so division of labour did not automatically divide the labourers.

All worked, and all work was respected. Most of the women came later to the field, so they could care for the children and do other household work.[26] Elderly and disabled people who could not do heavy fieldwork often had the job of frightening away the baboons who wanted to share in the lovely food the people had planted. (Later, they might help with childcare.)

And when any of the crop was sold (planting some tobacco as a cash crop was a government requirement), the cash remaining after social needs were met was divided equally among all, women and men, fieldworkers and baboon scarers. The RDA's pay equity was probably among the first anywhere. Not much money was at stake but its equal distribution was in keeping with socialist values. (Equity was growing in other directions. Domestic violence was not approved of by the villagers, which proved an effective deterrent.)

There seem to have been constant consultations, as there were always expanding or diversifying projects, or villagers were receiving visitors or travelling to other areas to explain what they were doing and how.

Though Ralph could be called on at any time for his opinion or advice, and Noreen was always contributing to village life, the Ibbotts never attended communal decision-making meetings. This was a principle which they, at least as much as others, were determined to uphold. It had to be the villagers who made and saw themselves making all decisions.

Ralph, trained as a quantity surveyor, had many practical skills. After the years at St Faith's and Nyafaru, he knew something about agriculture in Africa and about working collectively. One stunning contribution was installing a hydraulic ram by a waterfall on the Luhira River to enable water to be piped to Litowa. It was a boon, especially for the women and children who traditionally transport water. It lifted the whole village.[27] Similar was planned in other villages.

Noreen was one of those creative housewives who, eminently flexible, can make herself useful anywhere and find or invent practical solutions to most problems. Like Ralph, what she didn't know how to do and thought would be useful to the village, she sent to England to learn about. When Litowa decided to rear sheep, she imported a spinning wheel, taught herself to make yarn, and then trained others. She took her children into the forest to find natural dyes. And she taught people to knit: men as well as women could be seen walking in the village knitting wool garments for the high-altitude winter.

It was Noreen who suggested to Ntimbanjayo that the village organize childcare. She saw hungry and cranky children whose mothers hadn't arrived back from the fields. The village could take on feeding and caring for them until their mothers' return. The village agreed. It was set up and was a great success.

Nyerere was opposed to Africanization, among other reasons, because he was determined that people should have access to the skills and expertise of non-Africans like the Ibbotts who had come to help rather than to dominate or profit. He thought in particular socialists who had little scope in their capitalist countries could put their commitment and skills to work in Tanzania. Others besides the Ibbotts had come and were welcomed by the villagers. One of the teenage Harvard undergraduates, who stayed for shifts of one year, wrote a lively book about her year of hard work, learning from Litowans, including about her native US.[28] Because villagers were committed to and in charge of what they were doing, they got the best from working visitors; and the visitors were amply rewarded by the harmonious and expanding life the village offered.

The size of the village helped determine participation. Litowa's population was not to exceed about eighty families, maybe four hundred people—a number often discussed. More than that could prevent every individual's participation. Farmers who heard about the success of Litowa (and later other villages) would come to join. But *ujamaa* could only be built by the willing. Interested people were invited to stay and work in the village for a few weeks to ensure that this was the life they wanted. If it was, they would be encouraged to join a smaller village or helped to start their own village (a number of villages were formed this way).

Limiting the numbers but graciously incorporating new people is a widely applicable principle where the aim is involving everyone. It can work even in large factories, offices, hospitals, neighbourhoods. The units can then coordinate, as ultimately the villages coordinated.

When there were three or four villages, the Ruvuma Development Association came together. It was mutually helpful, sharing skills, practices, and resources. A carefully chosen group was formed to help with this and help newcomers to get started and to integrate. It called itself the Social and Economic Revolutionary Army, or SERA.

It's hard not to be impressed by the generous caring welcome, despite slender resources, extended by SERA to strangers who wanted to join in building *ujamaa*. It could only spring from the kind of caring society most of us want for ourselves. The thoughtfulness with which people were incorporated helps explain why almost all the villages that started thrived. (One village failed, and Ralph explains why.)

There was as much consultation and joint decision-making among the villages as distance and difficult transport permitted. Their major joint enterprise besides SERA was the school at Litowa, which educated the children from all the villages. Litowa boarded them during term time. It was perhaps the single greatest achievement of the RDA.

Led by a head teacher, the school had student self-government. More important, it had rejected the competitive principle of most formal education as we know it, which prepares the young to compete with each other to move up in the social hierarchy: to rise out of poverty, not to eliminate poverty. This usually results in the child rejecting his own community, especially if it is rural (read: "backward"). The purpose of the Litowa school was to educate children to be part of the development of their rural society. It deserves a book in itself. Certainly, those interested in education might want to study the documents, especially one by Suleiman Toroka, the head teacher of this great and innovative school, who became a member of Litowa village.[29]

No wonder then that when President Nyerere was asked by anyone at home or from abroad what he meant by *ujamaa*, he sent them to the RDA. The RDA, he said, that is *ujamaa*.

He always supported the villagers. He had been confident that what he had proposed would work. But now he had brilliant proof. His key writings, published as *Ujamaa* in both Kiswahili and English, a small popular book "for leaders and educators of the new Tanzania," mention the RDA twice.

Any model which is drawn up should just be a guide which draws the attention of the people to the decisions which have to be made by them; each village community must be able to make its own decisions. Nonetheless, the experience of existing *ujamaa* villages, such as those now operating within the Ruvuma Development Association, could be helpful, and the ministry of local government and rural development should try to make this experience available to people from different parts.[30]

[N]othing succeeds like success! If we can get a few of these village communities working in every area, their success will lead to others also being started. . . . [The] *ujamaa* villages in the Ruvuma Development Association have grown out of a beginning made by ten individuals.[31]

Almost from the beginning there was opposition, first to Litowa, then to the RDA as a whole. Ralph Ibbott's epilogue reports:

[T]he antipathy to the RDA . . . came from the top: from the central committee, government ministers and, with rare exceptions, top civil servants—what amounted to the whole political establishment. The RDA would not have been allowed to exist as long as it did had it not been for Nyerere's commitment to it.

The villagers sidestepped disapproval, disdain, and even sabotage from above as much as possible, often with the president's help. And since he was unambiguously and publicly on their side, it never threw them off course. They were TANU. They were *ujamaa.* And they were growing and gaining in confidence and reputation.

By the mid-sixties, Millinga had become a member of parliament—the RDA had decided he would represent them nationally, and Nyerere asked for Millinga to work closely with him. The president tried to use him and other RDA members to educate party leaders about *ujamaa.* But the problem was not lack of education; it was hunger for power. They had no wish to learn from "ignorant peasants" who were autonomous of them. It was a waste of the RDA's time. That Nyerere continued to try to persuade them of the value of what they hated—the power of the people—could only mean he didn't know what else to do.

In February 1967, Nyerere had made a great effort to renew TANU's commitment to socialism and to curb ambition in party and government. He issued the acclaimed "Arusha Declaration" calling for the nationalization of some industries,[32] for which there was general support. Part Five (the Arusha resolution known as the "Leadership Code") limited the wealth politicians could accumulate—this caused uproar.

Later that year, he published "Socialism and Rural Development," which he said was part of the "Arusha Declaration." The clarity of this renewed case for socialism is breathtaking: more confident and concrete—as though the people themselves had written it. In a sense, they had, since it was informed by what the RDA was actually mastering as he wrote. We must give the RDA the credit they deserve for their contribution to this historic document.

With this declaration in hand, Nyerere resigned the presidency a second time, again prioritizing the strengthening of the movement over governing. He concentrated on the grassroots of the party, the natural transmission belt to and from the people. He led marches and meetings, celebrating the power of the grassroots as expressed in this great declaration. It was enthusiastically received by the public and adopted by the party and the government. But changes were introduced to the "Leadership Code," blunting its impact on the party and government elite. They were shaken, but not enough.

Nyerere had worked to avoid Tanzania becoming a society torn by the disparity of class power. But the seeds of class conflict were sown from the moment the movement formed to win State power. What had got the British out was a movement of the entire country, with all its sectors and tendencies. Once they left, however, the new elite defended the colonial hierarchy and salary scales they were in the movement to collect. As is usually the case, they considered it unjust for them to be denied what the former rulers had but were oblivious to the injustice they perpetuated against others condemned to work hard to pay for their greed. Few at the top escape becoming psychopaths, insensitive to the pain they inflict on the less powerful, man or beast.

Nyerere had been particularly outraged when, in 1966, the university students who had gotten free education refused to spend time in national service to the community and fought to move straight into the high-salary jobs. How could *ujamaa* flourish under or even alongside such avarice?[33]

Finally, in September 1969, there was a decisive confrontation on the RDA at a stormy meeting of TANU's central committee. Although no vote was taken, twenty-one out of twenty-four members pressed for the RDA to be banned and TANU to be in charge of all *ujamaa* developments. The president was defeated. He was about to leave the country on government business the following morning. As soon as he was gone, the minister for rural development and others travelled to Litowa and enforced the order, destroying years of precious work and equipment. Ralph Ibbott is convinced that their action was illegal. Nyerere was shocked on his return; he had not expected that this would be the outcome of the decision against the RDA, or that they would move so quickly and so brutally against it. But he did not reverse their action.[34]

Could Nyerere have done more?

The central committee decision against Nyerere and the RDA tells us how isolated he was at the top, not only without a committed core but hemmed in by those who hated the self-reliant grassroots and the strategy only they could carry out.

For the president to have an open disagreement with his party and government leaders on behalf of the RDA could have wide and unpredictable consequences. He had been bold before in defence of principle, but the RDA was small, the whole national and regional leadership was united against it—and thus against him. If he went to the people with this split in the leadership, would they support him? Or would they be discouraged and retreat from active participation? And if they supported him, would that result in civil war? Would there be opportunistic appeals to tribal, ethnic, or religious allegiances and conflict, especially between Africans and Arab and Asian Tanzanians? Would it trigger a coup or become an occasion for the cold war which he had kept out of Tanzania,[35] to divide the country he had worked so hard to keep together?[36] Could he take these risks?

Nyerere had worked for African unity all his political life, but this had failed. Without unity, African governments were much weaker. Tragedies had already afflicted country after country, the outcome of internal power struggles which the imperialists had seized on or directly organized to regain control and influence, often with the help of local elites. Patrice Lumumba had been murdered in Congo in 1961, Ahmed Ben Bella overthrown in Algeria in 1965, Kwame Nkrumah in Ghana in 1966, and the Biafran (Nigeria) war had started in 1967. Nyerere could not take a chance with the power balance in Tanzania and Africa generally.

Nyerere's speech on the fortieth anniversary of Ghana's independence explains what stood in the way of unity, and not only in Africa. Those of us in the independence movement who fought for the federation of the formerly British West Indies have lived through what he describes:

> [T]oo many of us had a vested interest in keeping Africa divided. Prior
> to the independence of Tanganyika I had been advocating that the East

African countries should federate and then achieve independence as
a single political unit. I had said publicly that I was willing to delay
Tanganyika's independence in order to enable all the three mainland
countries [Kenya, Tanganyika and Uganda] to achieve their independence together as a single federated State. I made the suggestion because
of my fear—proved correct by later events—that it would be very difficult to unite our countries if we let them achieve independence sepa-
rately. Once you multiply national anthems, national flags and national
passports, seats at the United Nations; and individuals entitled to a
21-gun salute, not to speak of a host of ministers and envoys, you would
have a whole army of powerful people with vested interests in keeping
Africa balkanized.[37]

So much was at stake that he seems to have deluded himself that *ujamaa*
could survive the destruction of the RDA, which was *ujamaa* in action, the
seeds of the *ujamaa* movement. The RDA went to the wall. It destroyed great
possibilities and broke many hearts, perhaps also Nyerere's.

In the mid-1970s, Nyerere was asked by a journalist what was his greatest success? He replied, "That we have survived." Asked the same question by
the same journalist in 1983, his reply was, "I think I would still give the same
answer."[38]

To this day, Tanzania, almost unique in Africa, while still poor, remains
free of wars or dictatorships, ethnic violence, or military coups. President
Nyerere's socialism, including his sharp refusal of any opportunistic attempts
to introduce racial or ethnic disparity of rights, must take much credit for
this.[39] In 2008, when republishing the "Arusha Declaration," a Ugandan woman
at our women's centre told us about Tanzania's invasion to save them and all
of East Africa from Idi Amin, who overthrew President Milton Obote and was
murdering and invading. "One of the soldiers asked me, please, could he have
a glass of water. I had never seen respectful soldiers like that. Tanzanians were
different." Nyerere was different.

Because of the specifics of time and place, the problems faced in impoverished
former colonies may not seem relevant to movements elsewhere. But look
again.

First, the battle against colonialism and the wars and proxy wars fought
for competing imperial interests are far from over. More than five million
people have been killed in the Congo, and yet this is hardly mentioned. The

genocide of Tamils in Sri Lanka is ongoing. We write not long after the latest (2014) slaughter in Gaza by Israel, which has occupied Palestine for almost seventy years.[40] Haiti, which gave us the first successful slave revolution, is moving towards yet another dictatorship under a brutal US-UN occupation.

Second, the same almost manic energy of those who form the hierarchy in ex-colonies is also a blight on every grassroots movement. Ambition, the great weapon of imperialism, has subverted struggles against all varieties of injustice—war, torture, every form of sexism, racism, exploitation, environmental devastation. . .—turning them into career options at the cost even of the planet's survival.

Ambition may appear to be merely a personal failing, but it is integral to capitalism. We are urged and trained to compete—for money, status, jobs, housing, everything. Nyerere knew that competition, with its few winners and millions of losers, would destroy Tanzanian society (as it has wrecked ours). Usually endemic, at this moment it is epidemic. Yet most of us have still to acknowledge the ambition that subverts us. Nyerere's alternative was *ujamaa*, which rests on the principles of communal equity and mutual accountability. In fact, whatever the particular context of our organizing for justice, the principles are the same. Indigenous societies today—from Asia to Latin America—have used similar communal principles to stand up to multinationals and all kinds of exploitation.

The RDA's history and the *ujamaa* principles they upheld can help us anywhere. Ralph Ibbott applied these when working with youngsters in working-class Greenock, Scotland, to brilliant effect.

In the decades since that more hopeful era, we have been told every day in a thousand ways, some subtle, some violent, that it would be foolish to rely for significant social change on people like those who made socialism in Ruvuma. In Ruvuma's story we glimpse what those of us with least resources, least rights, and least respect are able to accomplish. It is the single most important truth about our world, which we need in order not only to understand it but to change it.

Solveig Francis, Nina López, and I worked with Noreen and Ralph over the years (Noreen was a most gracious hostess to all three of us and our dogs.) This introduction reflects the views of all three of us. Nina's work editing, researching, and referencing was invaluable.

Notes

1   Ralph Ibbott, *Ujamaa: The Hidden Story of Tanzania's Socialist Villages* (London: Crossroads Books, 2014).
2   Britain had experience in partitioning colonies that wanted freedom; in 1921, they had partitioned Ireland, their oldest colony.
3   Ikamba Bunting, "The Heart of Africa" (1970 interview with Julius Nyerere), *New Internationalist* 309 (January 1999), accessed September 22, 2020, https://newint.org/features/1999/01/01/anticolonialism.
4   Julius Nyerere, introduction to *Freedom and Unity—Uhuru na Umoja: A Selection from Writings and Speeches, 1952–65* (Dar es Salaam: Oxford University Press, 1967), 1.
5   Shan van Vocht, "Socialism and Nationalism" (1897), in Peter Beresford-Ellis, ed., *James Connolly: Selected Writings* (London: Pluto Press, 1997), 121–24.
6   Introduction to Ralph Ibbott, *False Start in Africa* (London: Sphere Books, 1966), 20.
7   Ibid., 21.
8   René Dumont, *False Start in Africa* (London: Andre Deutsch, 1966).
9   Frantz Fanon, *Wretched of the Earth* (Harmondsworth, UK: Penguin Books, 1967 [1961]), 136, 138.
10   Cited in Cranford Pratt, *The Critical Phase in Tanzania 1945–1968* (Cambridge: Cambridge University Press, 1976), 110.
11   Kate Wenner, who worked in Litowa for a year, says: "Millinga . . . sometimes brought his [radio] along to *ujamaa* meetings. . . . When the news came on everyone hushed. . . . They wanted to hear news of Tanzania and the world"; Kate Wenner, *Shamba Letu* (Boston: Houghton Mifflin, 1970), 205.
12   Tanganyika, Legislative Council Official Report, 36th Session, vol. 1, cols 390–1, October 20, 1960, cited in Ibid., 85.
13   Ibid., 173.
14   He is referring to the policy of delaying independence until "the natives" were "ready for self-government," having learnt parliamentary democracy as practised in Westminster.
15   "*Ujamaa*—the Basis of African Socialism" (TANU pamphlet, 1962), in Nyerere, *Freedom and Unity*, 170–1.
16   Nyerere was sometimes criticized or even dismissed for not being a Marxist. Responding on one occasion, he is reported to have said, "If Marx had been born in Sumbawanga, he would have probably come out with the Arusha Declaration rather than *Das Kapital*!"; Issa G. Shivji, "The Mwalimu in Nyerere," October 16, 1999, 7, accessed November 24, 2020, https://www.academia.edu/5027998/The_Mwalimu_in_Nyerere, accessed October 15, 2020. The joke had an element of truth. Nyerere was closer to Marx than even he may have realized. They both were convinced that in the process of collectively transforming society people transform themselves. That is the basis of the *ujamaa* strategy.

    Marx's 1870s *Ethnological Notebooks* contain his research into pre-class and more recent societies with many communal or collective relationships. In his famous 1881 letter to Vera Zasulich, he said that in some circumstances these societies could bypass capitalism to become "the fulcrum of social regeneration"; see Teodor Shanin, ed., *Late Marx and the Russian Road: Marx and "the Peripheries of Capitalism"* (London: Routledge and Kegan Paul, 1983).

    Nyerere lived in a continent with many such societies; they had, of course, changed, but their communalism had still not been destroyed by imperialism. His strategy of *ujamaa* presumed that in the circumstances of that time the communal African village could become the fulcrum of Tanzania's social regeneration.

Marxist historian Walter Rodney, who worked for some years in Tanzania (and later became leader of a mass movement in his native Guyana), also notes the similarity between Nyerere's African socialism and Marx's view of the anti-capitalist potential of communal societies. Rodney dismisses the reduction of "African socialism" by Léopold Sédar Senghor and other African politicians to a "permanent co-existence of capitalist and supposedly socialist relations"; see Walter Rodney, "Tanzanian Ujamaa and Scientific Socialism," *African Review* 1, no. 4 (April 1972): 61–76.

17 Pratt, *The Critical Phase in Tanzania 1945–1968*, 117.

18 Julius Nyerere, "*Ujamaa*—the Basis of African Socialism," 166–67.

19 Julius Nyerere, "Socialism and Rural Development," in Julius Nyerere, *Freedom and Socialism—Uhuru na Ujamaa: A Selection from Writings and Speeches, 1965–1967* (Dar es Salaam: Oxford University Press, 1968), 339.

20 Ibid., 339–40.

21 Ibid., 341.

22 Ibid., 346.

23 Julius Nyerere, "The Arusha Declaration: Socialism and Self-Reliance," in Nyerere, *Freedom and Socialism*, 245; republished in Julius Nyerere, *The Arusha Declaration, Rediscovering Nyerere's Tanzania* (London: Crossroads Books, 2008).

24 Julius Nyerere, "After the Arusha Declaration," in Nyerere, *Freedom and Socialism*, 404.

25 Ibid., 407.

26 "An old wheel was struck with a short stick every morning at about 7:00 a.m. to muster the men for work. The married and older women were given a later time to start work on the farm crops so as to give them time for household chores, carrying water, washing, etc.: they went out about 9:00 a. m. or later"; Noreen Ibbott, *Mama Noreen—Story of a Mother* (UK: Lightening Source, 2015).

27 "Life was already becoming more satisfying; when the water came to the centre of the village it was wonderful"; ibid.

28 Kate Wenner was often asked about the Vietnam War: "How come Americans are spending so much money on a war in a country that doesn't belong to them? Why don't they worry about the race riots in America?" She "began to understand why the issue had become America against the entire Third World. . . . [T]he villages being bombed . . . were villages like Litowa, Liweta, Luhira, and Mtakanini. I knew that the people in the villages of Vietnam like the people in the villages of the RDA had no other source of livelihood but the lands. . . . Vietnam, the Vietnamese, their villages and houses, their farms—it became a new reality for me because of what I knew of Africa. It was frightening and senseless"; Wenner, *Shamba Letu*, 207–9.

29 Joining the village meant that, as well as participating in decision-making, his salary went to the village, where all shared the same standard of living.

30 Julius Nyerere, "Socialism and Rural Development," in Nyerere, *Freedom and Socialism*, 365.

31 Julius Nyerere, "Implementation of Rural Socialism," in Julius Nyerere, *Freedom and Development—Uhuru na Maendeleo: A Selection from Writings and Speeches, 1968–1973* (Dar es Salaam: Oxford University Press, 1973), 7.

32 Its original title was "The Arusha Declaration and TANU's Policy on Socialism and Self-Reliance."

33 "Is this what the citizens of this country worked for? . . . In order to maintain a top level of exploiters. . . . You are demanding a pound of flesh; everybody is demanding a pound of flesh except the poor peasant. What kind of a country are we building?"; cited in Pratt, *The Critical Phase in Tanzania 1945–1968*, 234. "These damn salaries. These are the salaries which build this kind of attitude in the educated people. . . . All of us, we belong to a single class of exploiters"; cited in ibid., 235.

34 The geography of Matetereka has helped it to survive as an *ujamaa* village to this day. The villagers were on hills where the newcomers forced in by villagization could not dilute their purpose and practice. In 1992, when the Ibbotts visited Tanzania, Matetereka welcomed them with a thrilling speech.

35 In 1964, Nyerere had faced an attempted coup based on the military's demand for Africanization and higher wages; it was quickly defeated. The army was disbanded, and a new one recruited from the TANU Youth League to begin with.

36 "We shall not allow our friends to choose our enemies for us"; Julius Nyerere, "The Union of Tanganyika and Zanzibar," in Nyerere, *Freedom and Unity*, 293.

37 Julius Nyerere: "Without Unity, There Is No Future For Africa,'" *New African*, July 26, 2012, accessed September 23, 2020, https://newafricanmagazine.com/3234; "Nyerere: 'Without Unity, There Is No Future for Africa,'" *New African*, May 3, 2013, accessed September 23, 2020, https://newafricanmagazine.com/3723.

38 Shivji, 1990, referring to an interview with Peter Enahoro, *Africa Now* 32, (December 1983): 101.

39 Julius Nyerere, "Socialism Is Not Racialism," in Nyerere, *Freedom and Socialism*, 257.

40 In the 1960s, Israel was known internationally for the kibbutz, a form of rural commune. Tanzania had recognized the State of Israel, but after its 1967 war against Egypt, Jordan, and Syria, President Nyerere condemned Israel: "The establishment of the State of Israel was an act of aggression against the Arab people . . . the United Nations which sanctioned her birth is, must be, unalterably opposed to territorial agrandisement by force or threat of force. . . . We cannot condone aggression on any pretext, nor accept victory in war as a justification for the exploitation of other lands, or government over other peoples"; Nyerere, "Policy on Foreign Affairs," *Freedom and Socialism*, 371–72. By 1973, many African governments had broken relations with Israel, including Tanzania. It expelled Israel's ambassador, cancelled all Israeli development programmes, and allowed the Palestine Liberation Organization to open an embassy in Dar es Salaam.

The Struggle of Prisoners
(2014–2020)

Prisoners Celebrate the Power of Their United Struggle (2014)

Il Manifesto, Italy, July 7, 2014; updated 2020.

A year ago, on July 8, thirty thousand prisoners across California went on hunger and work strike, the biggest prisoners' strike in US history. Their central demand was an end to long-term solitary confinement—people held in often windowless cubicles as small as six by seven feet, for months, years, even decades. Nineteen states impose long-term solitary confinement. California is one, with over ten thousand people deprived of human contact, often indefinitely.

Some strikers refused even water. One prisoner died after being denied medical help, but prison officials say he killed himself. This lie is from prison guards, who, with their union, greatly benefit financially from the solitary torture they oversee. Other unions have said nothing against this collusion with State repression.

How did thousands of prisoners, despite isolation from each other, organize together? Even more amazing, it was across racial, religious, and other divisions. Such unity is scarce anywhere. It was born in 2010, when all prisoners in Georgia refused to leave their cells to go to work. It was developed in the California hunger strike of 2011.

In August 2012, prisoners from California's Pelican Bay State Prison who had called for all three previous hunger strikes announced: "Beginning on October 10, 2012, all hostilities between our racial groups will officially cease." They had paved the way for the 2013 mass action to involve every prisoner and every prisoner's family. In California, this unity begins with bridging the "Black-Brown" divide—between African-Americans and Latinos (immigrants or their descendants from Mexico and Central and South America). A divide which has undermined the anti-racist and anti-deportation work of the movement. Even more astonishing was that prisoners who had been white supremacists had been turned around. They were part of the multiracial leading group who were all in solitary confinement cells in a single pod for years. The group had in some way read and discussed movement history, including the history of prisoners like Bobby Sands and Nelson Mandela.

Learning from this unity is the job of every movement outside.

The families, following the prisoners, were also organizing among themselves across race. Dolores Canales, whose son had been thirteen years in solitary, and other family members—almost all women—started California Families to Abolish Solitary Confinement. "Our organizing is all in our spare time, because we have families, jobs, etc." In the Bay Area of San Francisco, Marie Levin—whose brother is inside, and who is a member of Prisoner Hunger Strike Solidarity (a coalition of lawyers, advocates, and relatives)—demonstrated at street corners, parks, and universities with a mock solitary confinement cubicle to show the public what torture their taxes pay for. This was repeated in protests across the state.

The prisoners suspended their strike after fifty-eight days to avoid further deaths. But the organizing continues inside and outside. Besides this extraordinary unity, the strike has won: public government hearings on solitary confinement; the release from solitary of over five hundred people; extended visits with loved ones; access to canteen food (a crucial alternative to food contaminated by guards who piss and even defecate in it); and more.

Because the strike was called not only to improve prison conditions but as an "act of solidarity with oppressed people around the world," it got messages of support from people in many countries.[1] Palestinian prisoners with a history of fighting Israeli apartheid and of hunger strikes against the occupiers were among the first to send solidarity greetings.

The first anniversary will be marked in many places with events celebrating its victories, thus, strengthening every prisoners' rights movement. US events will highlight two Pennsylvania prison cases: the woman who has spent over thirty years inside for killing her attempted rapist,[2] as well as the Dallas 6, prisoners persecuted for publicizing the truth about the conditions they endure.

Ultimately, all movements for justice will have to acknowledge the clarity and direction coming from prisoners and FIPs—formerly incarcerated persons—of whom there are millions in the US in particular. They are giving in words and deeds a new meaning to the power of anti-racism. And their mothers, daughters, sisters, and wives who are fighting for loved ones are demanding that their justice work too, like all women's caring work, is acknowledged as political work that women do everywhere.

Notes

1   GWS and WoC GWS helped to coordinate "Hunger for Justice," an international day of action held on July 31, 2013, in solidarity with the California prisoners and for justice for Trayvon Martin, the unarmed Black teenager killed with impunity by a white vigilante. Close to one thousand organizations and individuals took part. UK actions included support for the hunger strikers in Guantanamo Bay and Harmondsworth Immigration Removal Centre.

2   Charmaine Pfender has now spent thirty-five years inside, and her mother Donna Hill is still campaigning for her release and for prisoners across Pennsylvania. She was eighteen when she shot and killed a man who was attempting to rape her. In 1985, she was sentenced to life without parole for this act of self-defence. Donna Hill works with the Women and Trans Prisoner Defense Committee, GWS, and Fight for Lifers West; see "Let's Get Free: The Women and Trans Prisoner Defense Committee," accessed November 25, 2020, womeninprisondefensecommittee.wordpress.com

     The Dallas 6 are now out. The last one to be released, Carrington Keys, came out in 2018, after nineteen years inside. His mother Shandre Delaney, spearheaded the campaign for their release, which the GWS and Payday men's network were deeply involved with. She is part of Women of Colour GWS and works with the Abolitionist Law Centre.

Women Prisoners: Housework Inside

(2020)

In 2011, some women in California prisons went on a rolling hunger strike in support of the men on strike. Several women would refuse food for a certain number of days (long enough to be counted by prison officials as a hunger strike). When they came off, another group would start their strike, so there were always women striking in solidarity with the men.

Women are not saved from mass incarceration in the "prison house of nations," as Mumia Abu-Jamal calls the US, and are, in fact, the fastest growing sector of people inside. While US women are 4 per cent of the world's women, they are 30 per cent of the world's women prisoners.[1] Yet little is generally known about the way they are treated, what their preoccupations are, and the struggles they have made and are making every day. Eighty per cent of them are mothers. Most have been victims of sexual violence for which they received no justice. Most are not inside for perpetrating violence, except in self-defence, but for "crimes of poverty," because they have mouths to feed and no decent wages or welfare benefits: sex work, shoplifting, minor fraud, and, of course, drugs.

The US "war on drugs," which has fuelled the mass incarceration of people of colour, including of women, has been exported to countries around the globe. Thailand, for example, imprisons more women per capita than any other country: 85 per cent of them for drug possession.

Organizations in our network do a lot of work with women and men in jail, prison, and detention.[2] So when Victoria Law, one of the few writers committed to women prisoners, came to London from New York, we organized a meeting for her.[3] The room was full with people eager to hear.

She pointed out that women of colour in the US have been and continue to be disproportionately brutalized and killed by police. But their names and stories are so often omitted in discussions about police violence that women of colour launched the #SayHerName campaign to draw attention to their experiences. The incarceration rate is also wildly racist: for Black women 3.7 times more and for Latina women 1.5 times more than that of white women.

We have always known that women don't cease to be housewives and mothers when they go to prison. The responsibilities of motherhood are never left behind; being denied the right to care for and protect their young is a sentence in itself, for both mothers and children. One UK mother trying to organize the children, the partner, and the dogs from her cell, told us: "It's a living hell."

Vikki, a mother herself and a woman of colour, made clear that a lot of the work and worry is to keep custody of the children, which is always under threat once you are inside, even for a short stretch.

She made visible the caring work women do for each other, which is never referred to: "Care is often overlooked and unrecognized by those who chronicle instances of organizing and resistance within US prisons. Instead, prison resistance and organizing is frequently defined through a more masculine lens."[4] So what she calls "collective care" must be counted as an important part of the struggle too.

We asked her who is organizing with women prisoners, bearing in mind that so many more women are now in government, the legal profession, academia, journalism, and even prison management. She confirmed what we had found, that support and advocacy, much of it informal, comes mainly from FIPs who have themselves been through the system and retain accountability to those still inside.[5]

In my experience, some of the most canny and politically intelligent people in the US, women and men, are the FIPs—they know how society really works, even when it has the sugar coatings of outside life.

Notes

1 See Prison Policy Initiative, accessed November 25, 2020, https://www.prisonpolicy.org/global/women/2018.html.
2 We have supported hunger strikes of women asylum seekers in detention, fought to prevent sex workers being sent down, to overturn the conviction of rape victims serving long prison sentences after being disbelieved and accused of perjury for reporting rape, and campaigned against racist convictions and solitary confinement.
3 Victoria Law, *Resistance Behind Bars: The Struggles of Incarcerated Women*, (Oakland: PM Press, 2012); see in particular "Barriers to Basic Care," 29–42, and "Mothers and Chidren," 43–58.

4   "Caring Collectively: 25 Years of Abolitionist Feminism," in *Abolition Journal*, special issue on abolitionist feminisms, accessed November 25, 2020, https://abolitionjournal.org/#journal.

5   FIP Susan Burton in Los Angeles is one example. She initiated and runs A New Way of Life, providing transitional homes, treatment, and legal advice to reunite mothers coming out of prison with their children.

Revisiting the Work of CLR James (2017–2019)

The Black Jacobins, Past and Present

(2017)

First published in *The Black Jacobins Reader*.[1]

In 1804, the independent republic of Haiti was born. Seizing on the revolution in France, the slaves had taken their freedom and had got revolutionary Paris to ratify it. But as the French Revolution's power waned, to prevent slavery's return the Haitians had to defeat the armies of Spain and Britain, as well as Napoleon. Amazingly, they did.

The Black Jacobins, published in 1938, was part of the massive working-class movement of the thirties in many countries, including in the British West Indies. Its impact has been overshadowed by, first, World War II, which it tried but failed to prevent (including trying to defeat Hitler in Spain 1936–1938), and then the movement of the sixties, which built on the thirties and the experience of this world war. The book was a contribution to the movement for colonial freedom—for Africa, first of all, when few considered this possible. (A quarter of a century later, Ian Smith of apartheid Rhodesia was still able to say he could not conceive of Black majority rule "for a thousand years.")

The book came from the pen of an anti-imperialist campaigner who was also a leader of the Trotskyist movement in Britain. Not long after, he began to break with the premise of Trotskyism.

By 1963, an exploding anti-imperialist movement and the civil rights movement in the US had created a new market for republication after years out of print.

Between 1938 and 1963, it was read and studied, first of all by colonials in the English-speaking and French-speaking Caribbean islands (in the translation by CLR's Trotskyist comrade Pierre Naville;[2] Frantz Fanon and Aimé Césaire from Martinique probably read it). Trinidadians told us in the late fifties that *Black Jacobins* had sustained them trying to build not only the movement for independence but an anti-capitalist youth movement. People from the Pan Africanist Congress of South Africa told us in the sixties that they had typed and copied sections for comrades to read clandestinely. It must have been known to people in the colonies wherever English was a second language. In 2011, when former Haitian president Jean-Bertrand Aristide returned home from exile in South Africa, he told me that *Black Jacobins* had put Haiti on the map; people didn't know where it was before. He also told me that former South African president Thabo Mbeki said he knew they would win against apartheid when he read *Black Jacobins.*

The book was called upon when the 2010 earthquake in Haiti, whose destructive power was increased manifold by dire poverty,[3] reignited interest in Haiti and its revolutionary past. Many who wanted to know who Haitians were seem to have turned to *Black Jacobins*, the classic history of the revolution the slaves made.

Later research has added substantially to our information and, therefore, our understanding of the revolution, but this has not challenged the book's classic status.

It's worth asking why.

First, CLR stands uncompromisingly with the slaves. Now we read about "partisan historical scholarship"; the historian was expected to be "neutral," especially seventy-five years ago; that is, not on the side of the subversives. In academia, few ignored that then or ignore it now. They did not commit themselves entirely to the slaves. Even today most historians find it hard to call the revolution anything more profound than a revolt or rebellion—not to demean the significance or the courage and organization demanded by every rebellion (and there have been many), but a revolution is qualitatively broader and deeper—it overthrows the State.

CLR has all the time in the world for anti-racist whites who loved the revolution and its leaders, but his point of reference, particularly in the first ten chapters, is the struggle of those who were wresting themselves away from being the property of others. The book recounts above all their determination to be free, whatever it took.

CLR doesn't glamorize; rather, he demands that we see the slaves' actions from their point of view:

> The slaves destroyed tirelessly. . . . And if they destroyed much it was
> because they had suffered much. They knew that as long as these

plantations stood, their lot would be to labour on them until they dropped. The only thing was to destroy them.[4]

Nor does CLR shield us from the terror and sadism of the "civilized" masters. But the catalogue of tortures rather than merely torturing the reader, deepens our appreciation of the former slaves' power to endure and overcome and their self-transformation from victim to protagonist. We are thrilled and inspired, learning from the Haitians' determination to be free what being human—and free—are about.

Second, Toussaint L'Ouverture possessed all the skills of leadership that the revolution needed. An uneducated, middle-aged Caribbean Creole when the revolution began, he was soon able to handle sophisticated European diplomats and potentates who foolishly thought they could manipulate him, because he was Black and had been a slave.

Much later, CLR liked to say that while the establishment's authorized version of US history was that Lincoln had freed the slaves, it was in fact the slaves who had freed Lincoln—presumably from his personal limitations and the conservative constraints of high office. Here CLR says, "Toussaint did not make the revolution. It was the revolution that made Toussaint." Then he adds, "And even that is not the whole truth."[5]

In other words, while the movement chooses and educates its leadership, the observer is unlikely to trace this ongoing process, however accurately events are recorded. We can be sure, however, that the great leader is never a "self-made man," free of the influence of those of us more lowly, as he or she is sometimes presented in an almost religious way. Leaders are a product of their individual talents and skills (and weaknesses) shaped by the power of the movement they lead in the course of social upheavals. The Haitian Jacobins chose and educated Toussaint, and he led them to where they had the will and determination to go—up to a point, which we touch on later.

This was groundbreaking considering that there were, in 1938—and still are—those organizations which claim that their vanguard leadership was crucial for a revolution's success. CLR had something to do with the movement breaking free of such dangerous delusions. On the other hand, trying to avoid betrayal, many believe leadership is unnecessary and inevitably holds the movement back. In Haiti, the slaves made the revolution, and Toussaint, one of them, played a vital role in their winning their freedom.

Third, CLR compares the revolutionary slaves with how class is traditionally defined. They were not proletarians,

[b]ut working and living together in gangs of hundreds on the huge sugar-factories which covered the North Plain, they were closer to a modern proletariat than any group of workers in existence at the time, and the rising was, therefore, a thoroughly prepared and organized mass movement.[6]

This is CLR the Marxist rejecting rigid definitions of class. It was those who did collective forced labour who ensured collective planning of the insurrection. The result is to open further the question of how to define who is working class long before this was on the movement's political agenda. What about not only unwaged slaves but others who don't sell their labour power on the market—subsistence farmers (often women), other unwaged women and men: Should they be excluded from definitions of who is a worker?

By the time he wrote the 1980 foreword, CLR was more confident in his assertion. By then some of us in the women's movement had helped to change the climate. And new research showed that the unwaged slaves were found to have made wage slave demands! "They wanted to have three days off from work or two and a half days or at least two days."[7] He is referring to Haitian historian Jean Fouchard who had also found evidence that as early as 1793 "black women dared to demand wages equal to those of the men."[8]

But there is more to learn about these revolutionaries.

In 1938, CLR knew that the revolution was spearheaded by the Maroons, the runaway slaves, some of whom formed their own alternative fortified societies, which lasted for years, even decades. (The Brazilian Quilombo dos Palmares lasted for almost a century.) CLR tells us about Mackandal, one of Haiti's great Maroon leaders, an enormously talented orator and organizer. Two things are of particular interest here. First, he was from Guinea—an African, not a Creole born in the Caribbean. Second, "He was fearless and though one-handed from an accident, had a fortitude of spirit which he knew how to preserve in the midst of the most cruel tortures."[9] He had built an organization of slaves over six years to prepare for the murder of the entire white plantocracy.

Fouchard confirmed that it was the Maroons who had led the Haitian Revolution. CLR had also made clear that the slave population were, like Mackandal, overwhelmingly African. "The enormous increase of slaves [due to a thriving economy and—not unconnected—to people being worked to death] was filling the colony with native Africans, more resentful, more intractable, more ready for rebellion than the creole Negro. Of the half-a-million slaves in the colony in 1789, more than two-thirds had been born in Africa."[10]

Fouchard's detailed research proves that the Africans who had made the Middle Passage were the dominant force among the Maroons. He is justifiably indignant that "those who have previously studied the Maroons have not considered the runaway new Negroes [that is, new to Haiti and slavery] with the attention they deserved yet they are the most significant expression of absolute refusal of the slavery they condemn." The new Negroes were "newly disembarked, ignorant of the language and the geography of the country" and thus "their necessary dependence for escape on accomplices."[11] That is, the Maroons must have organized to help those escaping—already revolutionary organizing.

Marcus Rediker indicates an early source of the slaves' collective rebellion. The slave ship was not only a chamber of horrors, a prison, a death trap, but a training ground. Rediker indicates some of the ways that "a multiethnic mass of several hundred Africans, thrown together . . . learnt to act collectively."[12] To do this, he says, they had to learn to cross language and culture divides among the various tribes and nations represented by the captive passengers. (It's worth mentioning that Africans often speak a number of languages, since villages and tribes may have their own languages, which their neighbours master, resulting in a general linguistic facility not known in Europe. We don't know if this is true in other parts of the non-industrialized world.) Those who were more likely to survive the Middle Passage were the strongest, possibly the more able, and may have learnt about organizing across divides. Wouldn't they most likely become runaways and join or form a Maroon encampment?

When CLR first read Fouchard's book with its new precise information, he was delighted. He thought it outdated *Black Jacobins*: "It lasted for thirty-five years. That's long enough for any history book!"

In chapter 11, the book takes a quite different turn. Slavery has been abolished, but Haiti is still a French colony and will soon face the attempt of post-revolutionary France to reimpose it. While the story of the revolution expresses the movement of the thirties, the story of post-slavery, pre-independent Haiti tells us what that movement had to confront.

CLR must present Toussaint's clash with those he had led to victory. As with so much else, Haiti faced earlier than others all the problems of shaping its course following the overthrow of the State. Theirs is also the story of what happens to the leader who, having led the revolution, believes he knows better than his people what is best for their future.

We are told that to restore order from the chaos and bloodletting after years of war, Toussaint "instituted a military dictatorship."[13] This is a shock. Worse follows. CLR tells us that Toussaint believed that the Haitian economy demanded the plantation system.

> The ultimate guarantee of freedom was the prosperity of agriculture. This was Toussaint's slogan. The danger was that the Blacks might slip into the practice of cultivating a small patch of land, producing just sufficient for their needs. He would not allow the old estates to be broken up.[14]

The 1930s faced Stalin's forced collectivization. How different was that from Toussaint reimposing the plantation system? In that decade also, Stalinism shocked the world into slow recognition that the very organization which had led the Soviet revolution was imposing forced labour. We must bear in mind that Trotskyism, from which CLR had not yet broken, characterized the Soviet Union as a workers' State.[15]

> He confined the Blacks to the plantation under rigid penalties. He was battling with the colossal task of transforming a slave population, after years of licence, into a community of free labourers and he was doing it in the only way he could see. On behalf of the labourers he saw to it that they were paid a quarter of the produce. This alone was sufficient to mark the change from the old to the new despotism.[16]

But it was despotism. After all, the revolution had begun by burning the plantations to the ground. Ultimately the labourers fought and won against the plantation. How much do we know of the society that then replaced it? We are told:

> Left to themselves, the Haitian peasantry resuscitated to a remarkable degree the lives they had lived in Africa. Their method of cultivation, their family relations and social practices, their drums, songs and music, such art as they practiced and above all their religion which became famous, Vodun.[17]

If this is so, the Africans were likely to reproduce the communal societies they had brought with them; they knew only this and the hated slavery. The general view at the time (and even today) was that communal village life was "primitive" and had to be superseded for there to be progress. In the 1960s, President Julius Nyerere of Tanzania had a different perspective. He characterized the village he had grown up in as "tribal socialism." It had weaknesses, he said, but with independence it could become the way Tanzania could develop, ending poverty and women's subordination, while bypassing capitalism.[18] Of course, we cannot say for sure, but it may well be that this was the course the population chose once they had won the right to do as they wished on the land.

But for Toussaint, the French, not the Africans, had "civilization." Once Toussaint and the Black population diverge, CLR has to choose his point of reference. It is not always the ex-slaves who provide his direction.

When CLR tells us that Toussaint "had no interests apart from theirs," that is, the labourers,[19] it is unclear whether this is what Toussaint thinks or whether CLR agrees. His later statement is unambiguous: "between Toussaint and his people there was no fundamental difference of outlook or of aim."[20]

CLR's restrained critique was, I think. not to risk undermining our appreciation for what Toussaint had accomplished despite acts that were "worse than errors." The revolution itself had powerful enemies, even at the distance of well over a century. He is more protective of Toussaint in 1938 than in the 1960s when he decided to revise his 1934 play about him, giving his nephew Moïse more of a role and enhancing his case against his uncle.

The crisis over imposing the plantation leads Toussaint into killing the leader who fought him on behalf of the labourers' movement: Moïse.

> Moïse . . . beloved by the blacks of the North for his ardent championship of them against the whites. He stood high in Toussaint's favour until he refused to carry out Toussaint's severe labour legislation in the North.[21]

It is clear from CLR's evidence that Moïse was the person Haiti needed post-slavery. Moïse sought to have unity among the Blacks and Mulattoes. It certainly seems that he was killed not only because he was the leader of a movement against Toussaint's plantation but also because of the superiority of his leadership over Toussaint's. CLR comments to underline the enormity of Toussaint's "crime" that "to shoot Moïse . . . was almost as if Lenin had had Trotsky shot for taking the side of the proletariat against the bourgeoisie."[22]

In the constitution Toussaint wrote and imposed, "he authorized the slave trade because the island needed people to cultivate it. When the Africans landed, however, they would be free men."[23] Commenting on the constitution, Moïse "called Toussaint an old fool. 'He thinks he is the king of San Domingo.'"[24]

It was ambition for power, a kind of madness which often afflicts those who have been put into positions of authority by the movement; this leads them to believe they have earned the right to impose their will.

Toussaint could not conceive of Haiti moving forward independent of what he calls French civilization; the African and Creole population could not move up from slavery without what the French had to teach them—though exactly what that was is not spelled out. He at first considers that Haiti would be a French colony and that the population would become French. We must assume that he was not thinking of Napoleon's imperialist France, which later attempted to reimpose slavery, but of the revolutionary population that agreed to abolish it.

Unlike Toussaint, who was ultimately kidnapped and murdered by the "civilized" French, CLR had a chance in the 1963 appendix to spell out his contempt for the Haitian elite which venerated "French civilization."

The term is at best unhelpful and usually dresses deep racism in respectability. Who is not civilized? When Mahatma Gandhi visited London in the 1930s, he was asked what he thought of Western civilization. His reply was filmed and became famous: "I think it would be a good idea." We can all agree.

Ten years after *Black Jacobins* was published, CLR, immersed in working-class organizing and, having broken with Trotskyism, completed a study of Hegel and Marx. In *Notes on Dialectics*,[25] he not only breaks with the vanguard party, but identifies and analyses the corruption in the new governing class, of which Toussaint was an example.[26] In this light, the delusions of grandeur Moïse describes is for CLR no longer merely a personal failing of Toussaint but a class characteristic. This enables us to call Toussaint on the class nature of his ambition, without either demeaning the great Haitian Revolution or his enormous contribution to making it.

Some of us feel strongly the need to acknowledge and support today's Black Jacobins. Actor-activist Danny Glover is a shining example. After the US-led coup that overthrew President Aristide, he wrote:

> The first time I went to Haiti was 30 years ago. . . . I'd read CLR James's *Black Jacobins* in college, about a country and a revolution I had never heard about. I wanted to see who these people were. Haiti did the unthinkable. . . . [I]t undermined the whole premise of white supremacy by overthrowing slavery. It was the first victory over slavery of Africans. And for that it has continued to be dismissed, beaten and just torn

apart.... [W]e have to find ways on every level to come to the aid of Haiti. My position is that President Aristide remains the duly elected president of Haiti, that position I will not waver from or be moved from.[27]

When I visited Haiti for the first time, I saw all the names of places that were associated with individuals, battles, events that I knew from the book. I also saw the revolution.

CLR had said that he could see the French Revolution in the faces of the fashion models from Paris. For the first time I understood what he meant. In Haiti, the revolution is on the faces even of the children. There is a dignity, a seriousness, a resilience, and an expectation of winning against almost insuperable odds. While there are those who explore the African roots in the customs, religion, etc., of modern Haiti, there seems little interest among those who write learned papers in exploring the revolutionary roots of who Haitians are now, the way their revolutionary impertinence has shaped them and their present struggle.

The indomitable spirit that won in 1804 defeated the murderous twentieth-century dictatorships of the Duvaliers (approved by Washington) after thirty years in 1986. It twice elected President Jean-Bertrand Aristide—a liberation theology priest who set out to raise Haiti "from destitution to poverty," built schools and hospitals, tried to regenerate agriculture, and raised the minimum wage—with 67 per cent of the vote in 1990 and 92 per cent in 2000. It steels the determination of the women I met who carry on fighting for justice against the rapes and murders of the 1991 and 2004 coups. It boycotted election after election when Aristide's Lavalas (flash flood) party was banned from standing (80 per cent of the electorate refused to vote at the US-led "selection" that put Martelly in power)—a level of mass organization we almost never see anywhere else. And it continues to campaign both for withdrawal of the UN troops that have occupied Haiti at the behest of the imperial powers since 2004 and for compensation for the UN-imported cholera that has killed nearly nine thousand people and infected more than eight hundred thousand.

Today's Jacobins are fighting today's imperialism: the US, Canada, France, the multinationals, the Clintons (who have "helped" by making a way for sweatshops paying the lowest minimum wage in the Western hemisphere), and others making deals with the tiny Haitian elite. The "international community" and "civil society," that conglomerate of NGOs which act for governments that have created or co-opted and now fund them, has been crucial to reimposing the deification of the market—which the slaves destroyed when they burned down the plantations and won back the land to cultivate for their own survival and happiness.

Despite occupation and repression, the murder and disappearance of many grassroots leaders like Lovinsky Pierre-Antoine, the Lavalas movement remains unbowed. Tens of thousands flood the streets to defend the Aristide family every time his freedom is under threat. They did this year [2017] when he was summoned to court on trumped-up charges.

Scandalously, in 2004, at the behest of the US and just before their coup, heads of State (except Thabo Mbeki of South Africa) snubbed Haiti's bicentenary celebrations. Even Latin American countries stayed away, despite their debt to revolutionary Haiti. As CLR points out in his appendix:

> Pétion, the ruler of Haiti, nursed back to health the sick and defeated Bolivar, gave him money, arms and a printing press to help in the campaign which ended in the freedom of the Five States.[28]

Only Venezuela and Caricom (the Caribbean Commission) opposed the UN occupation. But even they are now collaborating with Martelly, despite previous objections to electoral fraud and Martelly's attempts to reinstate dictatorship.

As the reader will see from the brief but potent contributions of Mumia Abu-Jamal and Russell "Maroon" Shoatz, two prisoner colleagues, this history book remains integral to present struggle, though this is often missing from commentaries that praise the book or its author. It offers an answer to the ultimate question in the mind of every struggler: Can we win against racism, against every form of slavery, against all the repressive powers that intend to be in charge of us forever? It replies: we did and we can again.

Postscript (2020)

In 1934, CLR wrote *Toussaint Louverture: The Story of the Only Successful Slave Revolt in History; a Play in Three Acts*. In 1936, it was performed at the Westminster Theatre, with Paul Robeson in the leading role. The original script was lost for many years and was recently found and published.[29] Act I, Scene 2, begins with the following stage direction:

> August 6th, 1791. The depths of a forest. A little clearing is dotted with groups of Negro slaves. They, the Negro slaves, are the most important characters in the play. Toussaint did not make the revolt. It was the revolt that made Toussaint.

Within the next decade CLR was to develop this conception of the role of the grassroots in political struggle and create a Marxist organization based on it. See "Striving for Clarity and Influence: The Political Legacy of CLR James."[30]

Notes

1   Charles Forsdick and Christian Høgsbjerg, eds., *The CLR James Archive* (Durham, NC: Duke University Press, 2017).
2   The cover had its author as "CRL James"—colonials were often treated carelessly.
3   The theft by NGOs ensured Haitians continue to live with the earthquake's impact.
4   CLR James, *The Black Jacobins: Toussaint L'Ouverture and the San Domingo Revolution* (London: Penguin, 2001 [1938]), 71.
5   Ibid., xix.
6   Ibid., 69.
7   Ibid., xvii.
8   Jean Fouchard, *Les Marrons de la Liberté* (Paris: Éditions de l'École, 1972), 355.
9   CLR James, *The Black Jacobins*, 16.
10 Ibid., 45.
11 Fouchard, *Les Marrons de la Liberté*, 395.
12 Marcus Rediker, *The Slave Ship: A Human History* (London: John Murray, 2007), 264–65.
13 CLR James, *The Black Jacobins*, 196.
14 Ibid.
15 He must already have questioned this view. He said that "the German comrades" had told him how wrong he was: that it was State capitalism.
16 CLR James, *The Black Jacobins*, 196.
17 Ibid., 307.
18 There were many communal societies on the African continent. They had, of course, changed over the years in a variety of ways—they were affected by the slave trade, when many villages were destroyed altogether. But even after European imperialism spread across the continent, the communalism of African societies survived, as Tanzania's *ujamaa* demonstrates; see Ralph Ibbott, *Ujamaa: The Hidden Story of Tanzania's Socialist Villages* (London: Crossroads Books, 2014); see Selma James, introduction to Ibbott, *Ujamaa*, 13–39, particularly footnote 15, for references, including to Marx's *Ethnological Notebooks* and the perspective of Walter Rodney.
19 CLR James, *The Black Jacobins*, 213.
20 Ibid., 233.
21 Ibid., 209.
22 Ibid., 231.
23 Ibid., 215.
24 Ibid., 216.
25 CLR James, *Notes on Dialectics: Hegel, Marx, Lenin* (London: Allison & Busby, 1980 [1948]). For anyone who wants to wrestle with a relevant passage of *Notes*: "We say that this cause seemed to have such a powerful effect because there was an effect waiting to be caused. The cause and the effect are in the substance of the thing."
26 This is not inevitable. It never happened to Fidel, with whom Toussaint is compared in the appendix.
27 Danny Glover, "Haiti and Venezuela—A Personal View," *Rise*, Summer–Fall 2004, 37.

28 CLR James, *The Black Jacobins*, 321; in fact, there were six States: Bolivia, Colombia, Ecuador, Peru, Panama, and Venezuela.

29 CLR James, *Toussaint Louverture: The Story of the Only Successful Slave Revolt in History; a Play in Three Acts* (Durham, NC: Duke University Press, 2012 [1934]).

30 Selma James, "Striving for Clarity and Influence: The Political Legacy of CLR James," in Selma James, *Sex, Race, and Class: The Perspective of Winning—A Selection of Writings 1952–2011* (Oakland: PM Press, 2012), 283.

Confronting Imperial Boundaries (2018)

Published in *Marxism, Colonialism, and Cricket: CLR James's* Beyond a Boundary.[1]

Georgetown, Guyana, May 19, 2016

Beyond a Boundary was published as the 1963 cricket season opened. Reviews, though not unfavourable, gave no hint that the book was in any way special. We had to wait until January 1964 and *Wisden Cricketers' Almanack* for a deeper appreciation. John Arlott, cricket's most distinguished (and anti-racist) broadcaster and commentator, wrote:

> 1963 has been marked by the publication of a cricket book so outstanding as to compel any reviewer to check his adjectives several times before he describes it and, since he is likely to be dealing in superlatives, to measure them carefully to avoid over-praise—which this book does not need. It is *Beyond a Boundary*. . . . [I]n the opinion of this reviewer, it is the finest book written about the game of cricket. . . . There may be a better book about any sport . . . if so, the present reviewer has not seen it.[2]

Years later, in *A Century of Wisden*, a compilation made up of "An Extract from Every Edition 1900–1999,"[3] Arlott's review, with its extraordinary claims, was the extract chosen from 1964, confirming the book's classic status.

It is hard to know from Arlott's review that *Beyond a Boundary* could not at first find a publisher. Those who published books on sports rejected it for sports fans; other publishers doubted that the general reading public would buy a book on cricket. How much these rejections had to do with refusal to consider a book by a West Indian who had the audacity to redefine cricket and its boundaries we will never know. We wondered at the time. It is worth recalling that cricket more than half a century ago was far more elitist on grounds of race as well as class (as we will see).

In desperation, CLR asked our friend George Lamming for help. Hutchinson had not long before published Lamming's *In the Castle of My Skin* (1953), a great novel.[4] Lamming used its succès d'estime to introduce this other Caribbean manuscript to Robert Lusty, Hutchinson's chair and managing director. To our relief, they accepted the manuscript. The title on the contract: *Who Only Cricket Know.*

Years later, we learnt that it was also Lamming who had renamed the book—almost. Hutchinson announced it was to be *Beyond the Boundary*, and we rejoiced. But then they changed "the" to "a" for no reason we could agree with. "The" challenges boundaries generally, not only those belonging to cricket.

It was a book CLR had to write. Devoted to the game since a child, he had studied over the decades the batting and bowling statistics, as well as cricket's literature. He was convinced he understood the game in ways many other commentators did not. He thought commentators often did not give a precise enough account of the play, favouring instead impressionistic flights of linguistic fancy. This aggravated him. He complained that similar imprecision had invaded literary criticism and much else.[5]

CLR had the contradictory advantage of being an outsider—a colonial—who was educated inside. He saw the game not only as it was played but also as it was lived. In his first period in England, he lived with Learie and Norma Constantine in "Red Nelson" in the north of England. Learie was playing in the Lancashire League, and this life and the cricket it produced are described in the book.

But the field of play that shaped him was the West Indies—a colonial society stratified by class and race. It offered few routes out of poverty and even fewer out of obscurity, even for the most talented in any direction. His unblinking description of the shades of status among the cricket clubs of his youth is reminiscent of the race hierarchy in pre-revolutionary Haiti, described in *The Black Jacobins*,[6] and it cuts like glass here too.

Because he was clever and was known early as a journalist and sportsman, CLR was invited to join the clubs of both the lighter- and the darker-skinned cricketers.[7] He confesses to regret having chosen the former:

> So it was that I became one of those dark men whose "surest sign of . . . having arrived is the fact that he keeps company with people lighter

in complexion than himself." My decision cost me a great deal . . . by cutting myself off from the popular side, [I] delayed my political development for years.[8]

It was the "popular side" in society generally with whom he was to spend most of the rest of his life.

Establishing the interconnection between cricket and divisions of race and class through his personal history, he paved the way for drawing out other connections. He could not claim cricket as an art without defining art, just as the social history of sports must lead to the ancient Greeks, who invented and organized the first Olympic Games. Three chapters that are devoted to re-evaluating the towering figure of W.G. Grace challenge, among much else, the respected liberal historians who never mention Grace, although the public had chosen this enormously talented cricketer as their hero.[9]

CLR's pursuit of the implications of each subject is far from academia's fragmentation of reality, which is pervasive nowadays and results in or from gross inaccuracy, prejudice, and worse. How much can be hidden by fragmentation? How much is misunderstood? What do we know of cricket, or anything, if it is severed from every other aspect of our life and struggle? What, indeed.

Beyond a Boundary was a long time coming. It had originally been planned much earlier and was nearly completed in 1958, before being finished in 1962. It was, all the same, right on time for the 1960s. This was the decade when massive movements challenged almost every authority, prejudice, and relationship and broke through cordons, fences, and barriers of many kinds. It was a decade that saw the assertion of many previously ignored rights and needs, even transforming musical taste—that same year, the Beatles rose to international stardom. People had greater expectations and more open minds and were more ready to be active on their own behalf than they had been for years.

Since the 1940s, CLR, a Marxist who saw history as a process involving everyone from the bottom up, had been trying to figure out how to address the power relation between working-class people and intellectuals, especially within the anti-capitalist movement to which he was committed. He was convinced that those of us who were considered politically backward were better equipped to change the world than the formally educated. We knew far more than we were credited with and were at least as capable of understanding anything once it was made accessible. For him, appreciating this and acting on it was what being a Marxist was all about. (*Notes on Dialectics* was CLR's attempt to make the dialectical materialism of Hegel available to those who had no training in philosophy.[10] It is soon to be republished after years out of print. CLR considered it his finest work.)

Living in the United States, he initiated a bold experiment: creating a political organization that was based on the experience, insights, and instincts of grassroots members and their networks rather than on those of formally educated people who invariably assume leadership.[11] Members were invited to write and speak publicly. They were also asked to read and comment on the political writing of intellectuals, including CLR himself. Working to understand the implications of people's comments and questions was political training for both intellectuals *and* workers, and the final edit was much more likely to be accessible to a wider audience and to be a better and more effective piece. *Mariners, Renegades and Castaways*,[12] CLR's analysis of Herman Melville's *Moby Dick*, was rewritten through this process.[13]

Thus, the man who wrote *Beyond a Boundary*, a great teacher, had the habit of making information and sophisticated concepts accessible to a non-academic audience. No wonder the book's unfamiliar subjects and connections have proved themselves to be accessible to a remarkably wide variety of readers.

Addressing the non-specialist, often "uneducated" but interested audience was a practice that was being adopted by others in that same period. One commentator, for example, has noted that the literary critic Frank Kermode (1919–2010) "wrote in the introduction to [his book *Continuities*, published in 1968][14] that any literary journalism that was able to satisfy non-specialist interests 'without loss of intellectual integrity' was 'more demanding than most of what passes for scholarship.' He was to continue to think this, and to write wonderfully well in this form."[15] Here too the implication is that assuming the non-specialist as part of the audience increases the quality of the work.

Motown, the famous 1960s music label from Detroit, worked out a musical form that would sell Black music to a white audience. They called this "crossover" and thus named the social process of moving beyond the boundaries that confine us to our own sector. Motown music had its own validity, although some of the original quality was bypassed. Can the "crossover" process happen for a mass audience maintaining or even raising rather than lowering the quality of the work?

Again, in 1963, as we waited for the arrival of *Beyond a Boundary* from the printer, the following massive class crossover was reported in the press. On January 20, the *Sunday Times* announced that "the new young gladiators

of BBC Television [had just] made their entry . . . to take over key positions."
They were trained and led by Grace Wyndham Goldie, who spelled out a new
job description for the producers of TV programmes:

> I have a great belief in the intelligence of the audience. When a producer
> fails with a programme and says it was because it was over the heads of
> the audience, I tell him it is he who has failed. . . . There is a confusion
> that the informed are mature and the uninformed are immature. Often
> it is quite the opposite. I like to think our audiences are mature people
> who want to be informed.[16]

This anti-elitism that gainfully employs the educated to make accessible
what they know to the rest of us—never levelling down or talking down and
certainly not dumbing down—produced the most remarkable television. The
most memorable was the brilliant and irreverent *That Was the Week That Was*,
still talked about, although most of the tapes have been mysteriously wiped.
A satirical look at the week's news, it was enormously popular with everyone
but the government.

When the manuscript was nearly complete, CLR was invited to return to
Trinidad after twenty-six years away. He worked with others for four years
to bring the English-speaking Caribbean together in a federation, so that
the coming independence would be stronger and based on popular power.
Independence of a sort came, but the federation failed. What stayed federated
was the cricket team. No one dared suggest otherwise.

But this great cricketing nation, with a primarily Afro- and Indo-
Caribbean population, had always been captained by a white man, and many
seethed with resentment. This had to change. Moreover, there was a cricket
precedent for moving such elitism aside. In England, in the 1950s, the game
was still divided by class, between professionals (the players) and amateurs
(the gentlemen). "Gentlemen v. Players" was an annual fixture. As late as 1958,
the Marylebone Cricket Club (MCC), cricket's international governing body,
affirmed its "wish to preserve in first-class cricket the leadership [read, cap-
taincy] and general approach to the game internationally associated with
the Amateur player." Len Hutton, a professional who many believed to be the
finest batsman in England and maybe in the world at that time, was part of
the England team of 1953 that toured Australia. He was called to substitute
as captain and did so well that he brought home the Ashes.[17] There was no
avoiding it: Hutton had to be made the first professional to captain England.

(Nevertheless, the distinction between gentlemen and players was not abolished until 1962.)

CLR told this story (among many others) to my son (Sam Weinstein, referred to in *Beyond a Boundary* as "the son of the house"), who became his cricket mate from when he was six. They would relish the way MCC, once it had been well and truly beaten, had gone to meet Hutton on his return at Southampton dock with an MCC tie—his passport to membership of the "Kremlin of cricket," as one West Indian was heard to call it. The overthrow of elite captaincy had happened in England. It could happen again, in the West Indies.

Everyone knew who the captain of the West Indies team should be. Frank Worrell was a great batsman, a great cricketing mind, an extraordinary human being, a natural leader. But Worrell, though middle-class, was Black. CLR seized the time. He set out to lift the lower orders to their rightful place, at least within the boundary of Caribbean cricket. He opened the campaign to make Worrell captain. Now editor of the *Nation*, the newspaper of Trinidad's nationalist party, he had the support of a mass anti-colonial movement. Every issue had articles, front-page editorials, cricket facts. The penultimate chapter of *Beyond a Boundary* describes something of the campaign. It also analyses the cause of a bottle-throwing incident during the Test series of 1960; this was provoked by "local anti-nationalist people [who] were doing their best to help the Englishmen defeat and disgrace the local players."[18] The crowd's furious response strengthened the Worrell campaign. Some of these "anti-nationalist people" thought challenging the racism that had always dominated cricket would lead to "communism."

We won, of course, and the day after Worrell was declared captain, Prime Minister Eric Williams opened his party's annual conference with an address that aimed to placate the "anti-communists" who were attacking CLR. He said, "If CLR James took it upon his individual self to wage a campaign for Worrell as captain of the West Indies team . . ." That was all I heard. Williams's words were drowned in a roar of applause and jubilation; a small but significant piece of the imperial past had crumbled. CLR saw and heard the approbation as we sat at the back of the hall. But he was not invited to the front.[19]

Like Sir Len Hutton, Worrell (who was also knighted) captained in Australia. The West Indies played such cricket and were such a team in a remarkable series, which included the famous "tied Test," that when they left for home, many thousands of Aussies came into the streets to wish them a genuinely fond farewell.

Soon after *Beyond a Boundary* appeared, despite calls to "keep politics out of sports," the anti-apartheid boycott of South Africa swept across every sport and every continent. In 1967, Muhammad Ali refused to be drafted into the US Army for the Vietnam War, although the price was giving up his brilliant boxing career. Widely acknowledged as "the greatest," Ali had demanded an answer to the question, "Why should they ask me to put on a uniform and go ten thousand miles from home and drop bombs and bullets on brown people in Vietnam while so-called Negro people in Louisville are treated like dogs and denied simple human rights?"[20] A year later, in 1968, a Black Power salute from the Olympic podium in Mexico City shook the world. Nowadays, political campaigns in sports (including against sexism) hardly startle. Alas, what sportspeople of colour have to contend with on the playing field is still often disconnected from injustice a few steps beyond sporting boundaries—from stop and search and racial profiling to benefit cuts to disabled people camouflaged with hard-won Paralympics praise. The Palestinians, as part of their resistance to Israeli occupation and to defend their footballers who "have been shot, beaten, bombed, and incarcerated along with their fellow citizens," have been pressing FIFA to expel Israel from international soccer.[21]

Beyond a Boundary has opened the way for more wide-ranging sports journalism. It also inspired Joseph O'Neill to write the best-selling novel *Netherland*,[22] dissecting American society after 9/11 using the cricket community brought by Caribbean immigrants to New York. The Indian film *Lagaan* (2001),[23] about a cricket match, is a wonderful example of the beauty and truth that can emanate from a judicious and artistic mix of cricket, class struggle, and anti-imperialism. Eduardo Galeano's splendid book on football, *Soccer in Sun and Shadow*,[24] also places every World Cup in its contemporary political and historical context.

My favourite chapter of *Beyond a Boundary* (part of which I typed many times—no computers then to input corrections in successive drafts) has always been "The Most Unkindest Cut." It reminds us that CLR was also a novelist. It is the tragic story of Wilton St Hill, who deserved to be chosen for a side that toured England but was left out; a story told with great compassion of one of many lives shattered by transparent but inescapable injustice.

As one would expect, Caribbean people were delighted that one of theirs had told the English about the game that the English had invented and carried around the world along with the Empire, but that others—once called "lesser breeds without the Law"[25]—had adopted and adapted as their own. But the book goes well beyond that boundary, as all kinds of people love it—in particular, grassroots people, who are gratified to see their passions and pre-occupations respected, explored, and celebrated.

Notes

1   David Featherstone, Christopher Gair, Christian Høgsbjerg, and Andrew Smith, eds., *Marxism, Colonialism, and Cricket: CLR James's Beyond a Boundary* (Durham, NC: Duke University Press, 2018).
2   John Arlott, review of *Beyond a Boundary*, in Norman Preston, ed., *Wisden Cricketers' Almanack 1964*, 993.
3   Chris Lane, ed., *A Century of Wisden: An Extract from Every Edition 1900–1999* (London: John Wisden & Co Ltd, 2000).
4   George Lamming, *In the Castle of My Skin* (London: Michael Joseph, 1953).
5   It was F.R. Leavis's critical focus on the text that CLR admired and trusted, despite Leavis's snobbish narrow-mindedness.
6   CLR James, *The Black Jacobins: Toussaint L'Ouverture and the San Domingo Revolution* (London: Penguin, 2001 [1938]).
7   The East Indian population of Trinidad was not visible in the cricket hierarchy of race and class at that time. The first East Indian cricketer who was part of the West Indies team was the Trinidadian Sonny Ramadhin, who, together with the Jamaican Alf Valentine, demolished the English batting on the tour of England of 1950. The first Indigenous player we know of, the Dominican Adam Sanford, emerged with the West Indies team in 2002.
8   CLR James, *Beyond a Boundary* (Durham, NC: Duke University Press, 2013 [1963]), 53.
9   A recent book by Richard Tomlinson, *Amazing Grace: The Man Who Was W.G.* (London: Little, Brown, 2015), shows how the establishment had to pay Grace because he was so popular but used this imperative to retain the class division in cricket. *Beyond a Boundary* may well have helped inspire such recent re-examinations of Grace.
10   CLR James, *Notes on Dialectics: Hegel, Marx, Lenin* (London: Allison & Busby, 1980 [1948]).
11   For a description of this aspect of the Johnson-Forest Tendency, as this organization was called, see Selma James, "Striving for Clarify and Influence," in Selma James, *Sex, Race, and Class: The Perspective of Winning—A Selection of Writings 1952–2011* (Oakland: PM Press, 2012).
12   CLR James, *Mariners, Renegades and Castaways: The Story of Herman Melville and the World We Live In* (London: Allison and Busby, 1985 [1953]).
13   *Moby Dick* had particular relevance to a working-class audience. It deals with the relation between the crew and their "monomaniac commander" who leads them to the bottom of the ocean. *Mariners, Renegades and Castaways* aimed to reach readers who may never have read *Moby Dick*, let alone a critique of it; *Mariners, Renegades and Castaways* was sold in factories for $1 as part of CLR's campaign to prevent his deportation from the United States during the McCarthy period.
14   Frank Kermode, *Continuities* (London: Routledge & Kegan Paul, 1968).
15   John Mullan, "Sir Frank Kermode Obituary," *Guardian*, August 18, 2010, accessed September 24, 2020, https://www.theguardian.com/books/2010/aug/18/sir-frank-kermode-obituary.
16   I was told by one of her producers on the flagship daily *Today* program that Grace Wyndham Goldie was a Tory. Irrelevant. More to the point, she had worked for the

Workers Education Association giving classes to miners on the medium of television. This must have helped shape her respect for the popular audience.

17 The Ashes is a Test cricket series played between England and Australia, usually biennially. Following Australia's defeat of England in 1882, a mock obituary in the *Sporting Times* announced the death and subsequent cremation of English cricket. Subsequent meetings between the teams have thus been represented as a battle for ownership of these original "ashes."

18 CLR James, *Beyond a Boundary*, 227.

19 The full passage reads, "If CLR James took it upon his individual self to wage a campaign for Worrell as captain of the West Indies team and in so doing to give expression not only to the needs of the game but also to the sentiments of the people, we know as well as he that it is the *Nation* and the [People's National Movement] to whom the people will give the praise"; James, *Beyond a Boundary*, 241; also see CLR James, *Party Politics in the West Indies* (privately published, printed in San Juan, TT: Vedic Enterprises,1962). Here Williams tried to undermine CLR, while taking credit for what he had achieved. This was the first salvo of a political attack aimed at distancing himself from CLR, his once close ally. The defining issue was the US base at Chaguaramas, which the independence movement wanted back. Unknown to CLR, Williams had made a deal with the US, details of which began to emerge later that same day.

20 Mike Marqusee, *Redemption Song: Muhammad Ali and the Spirit of the Sixties* (London: Verso, 2005), 214.

21 "We call on FIFA to Suspend the Israeli Football Association" (letter), *Guardian*, May 15, 2015, accessed September 29, 2020, https://www.theguardian.com/world/2015/may/15/call-on-fifa-suspend-israel-football-association.

22 Joseph O'Neil, *Netherland* (New York: Pantheon Books, 2008).

23 Ashutosh Gowariker, dir., *Lagaan: Once upon a Time in India* (Mumbai, IN: Aamir Khan Productions, 2011).

24 Eduardo Galeano, *Soccer in Sun and Shadow* (London: Verso, 1998).

25 Rudyard Kipling, "Recessional" (*1897*), accessed September 24, 2020, https://www.poetryfoundation.org/poems/46780/recessional.

Beyond Boundaries—A Talk with Selma James on Her Political Activities and Years with CLR James (2019)

with Ron Augustin

Published in *Monthly Review*, September 1, 2019; later expanded.

When CLR James died thirty years ago, he had become one of the most considered theoreticians in what was called Black Studies at universities across the US, the UK, and the Caribbean. In his native Trinidad and Tobago, James is still well-known for his brilliant interpretation of cricket in Beyond a Boundary, *first published in 1963. However, his life and thinking as a revolutionary involved in struggles and debates throughout an important period in the history of the left are widely ignored or forgotten today.*

In 1932, at the age of thirty-one, James left Trinidad for Britain, where he got involved in the international "left opposition" around Leon Trotsky and the anti-colonial International African Service Bureau. "I arrived in England intending to make my way as a writer of fiction, but the world went political and I went with it." From 1938, he spent fifteen very active years in the US, where, eventually, through what was known as the "Johnson-Forest Tendency" or "Johnsonites," he broke with the Trotskyist movement. As a Marxist, he continued to advocate the emancipation of Black people and to encourage an independent voice for women.

Expelled from the US in 1953, he returned to Britain, from where he travelled extensively to Africa, the Caribbean, Canada, and the US, writing, lecturing, and advising the various anti-colonial and anti-imperialist movements of those days. In what may be termed the Black movement of the 1960s and 1970s, "CLR," short for Cyril Lionel Robert, or Nello for friends and relatives, was a popular and influential speaker.

Selma James, a Jewish working-class woman born Selma Deitch in Brooklyn, New York, in 1930, joined CLR James in the UK in January 1955. They married in 1956 and were together for almost 30 years, each with their own political activities but also sharing important struggles. Founder of the International Wages for

Housework Campaign, Selma James co-authored, with Mariarosa Dalla Costa, the women's movement classic The Power of Women and the Subversion of the Community.[1] *Today, Selma James is the coordinator of the Global Women's Strike, an international network of grassroots women's initiatives. She is based at the Crossroads Women's Centre, home to more than fifteen different groups in the heart of London's Kentish Town, a few streets away from where Karl Marx lived with his family for more than ten years. As alive and kicking as many people could only wish for, Selma James is also an active member of the International Jewish Anti-Zionist Network and has been involved in work with her friend Mumia Abu-Jamal and other political prisoners when visiting the US.*

In an interview with Ron Augustin at her home in London, she speaks of her years with CLR James and their political activities.

How did the two of you get to know each other?

My sister was working as his secretary. She was already in his organization, the Johnson-Forest Tendency [pseudonym for CLR (Johnson) and Raya Dunayevskaya (Forest); Grace Chin Lee (later Grace Boggs) and others were also members], a minority within the Workers Party, and she brought her kid sister to meet him. That would have been 1943 or 1944, when I was thirteen or fourteen. I joined the Workers Party Youth Group in 1945 and was soon part of Johnson-Forest.

In 1949 or 1950, people started to tell CLR that I, in Los Angeles, had these ideas on women, and he invited me to have lunch with him when I came to New York. He said, "They tell me that you have ideas on 'the woman question.'" And I said, "Yes." And he said, "You know, what is needed is a theory that embraces millions of women." It had never crossed my mind before, but I immediately said, "Yes, I know," because as soon as he said it, I did know. And he said, "Do you have that?" And I said, "Oh, yes." I had no doubt that this was the case. And he said, "Alright." So we sat down and I spoke, I don't know for how long, a half hour or forty-five minutes. He said nothing. He listened intently to all that I said and nodded appropriately. And then I said, "That's it." And he got up and started to pace back and forth, saying, "This is really something. I mean, this is really something. You have to write this." I didn't know how to do that. But later he seemed to incorporate some of what I had said into his view.

Fundamentally, I was saying that housewives are part of the working class and that their work (what is now called reproductive work) is integral to the way capitalist production is organized and describing how this determined the way women and men and children related to each other in the family (the language I used was much less sophisticated than that). He later asked me to do a pamphlet on women based on what I'd told him. He told everybody, "Leave her alone. Do not tell her what to say. Let her do it herself." And I did it, and it was successful, in the sense that all kinds of people read it and liked it, including my neighbours and the people I worked with in the factory, and even my mother. We called it *A Woman's Place*.[2]

In 1951, CLR came to Los Angeles on a lecture tour, and we got involved. That same year, Johnson-Forest made a final split from Trotskyism.[3]

I saw him before he was detained in Ellis Island by McCarthyism, and we corresponded while he was in detention. He also asked me to read the first draft of his book on Herman Melville, which became *Mariners, Renegades and Castaways*,[4] part of his case against deportation. Then, in 1952, I went back East to type *Mariners* as it was rewritten and also to attend Johnson-Forest's "third layer" school for the leadership to learn from its working-class members.[5] I was in New York when CLR was released from Ellis Island, and we were together from then. He had to leave the US the next year, and my son and I joined him in January 1955.

You each had a child already, and you were very young compared to him. How did that determine your life?

He was very respectful of mothers and of children. He knew that I had a child and that was a commitment he had to make, and he was quite prepared to make it. He and my son Sam had known each other in the US, and after a while they became very close. He also stayed in contact with his own son Nob (CLR Jr.), for whom he wrote stories, and he would draw a picture on the envelopes of a man's face with a pipe and a hat, so that before he could read Nob would know that these letters were for him from his father.

He was a political animal. What about you?

I was already one too. I grew up in the movement of the 1930s, with the Spanish Revolution and the campaign to free the Scottsboro Boys.[6] My truck driver father helped found a branch of the Teamsters union in Brooklyn. He used to listen to Hitler's speeches with a clenched jaw, he knew what was coming. His language had been Yiddish, but he understood German, because he was born in Poland, the Austro-Hungarian Empire at that time. He never learnt to write but taught himself to read the *Daily Worker*. My mother quit school when she was twelve to work in a paper box factory. She told me stories later, including breaking the lock when a family had been put on the street and moving them back in, and, with me in one arm, going into Home Relief, being thrown out and going in through another door to fight for people to get welfare (known as Home Relief at that time).

I was committed to Johnson-Forest. It was a different way of looking at the world from the rest of the left. Working-class people were central, not backward ones to be led but the source of the revolution. I was in the movement, and I never thought that I should be doing something else. My commitment was much the same as his. But I was an American working-class girl, and he was a European intellectual and an anti-imperialist colonial. I never remember finding the age difference problematic. I think the class difference between us was the greater gap, though my instinctive responses to all kinds of things interested him greatly, and I learnt from him every day.

You would describe him more as an intellectual, although he had no formal academic background?
He had an educated and well-stocked mind. He had always read voraciously and carefully. He would read one book several times. I think he probably would learn some books by heart. I gathered, finally, that this was a way he would concentrate on developing his own ideas. He would finish a book and go back to particular sections until he had conquered what the author was saying and, therefore, incorporated it into his own thinking or rejected it, or both. At different points there would be different subjects he concentrated on. He was well beyond the restraints of university.

The person he was in Britain was not the person he had been in the United States. That has to be said. In Britain, there was an anti-imperialist movement and the class struggle and a Labour Party. In the US, race was central to class politics, and the struggle against US imperialism was much more fragmented than the pervasive focused struggle against the British Empire. It felt like an entirely different context. Also, when we work in an organization we are very different people, and when he was in Britain without Johnson-Forest he was much more of an individual. You can't do the same work or be the same person if you don't have an organizational framework within the movement.

I also missed an organizational framework. And the left in the UK seemed out of date and out of touch, especially to my generation. That was not a framework for either of us. Some in the left were lovely people, and they liked *Correspondence*, the newspaper that we'd been putting out in the US. One of them, when I first met him, said, "Ah, you're Selma, you know we read the woman's page of *Correspondence* first, that's our favourite section." It connected politics with people's personal lives and that was something new to them.

Does that mean that the first years after you came to the UK you were rather isolated?

Yes, I was. I went to work in a factory similar to the one I had worked in in the United States. I wanted to know what British society was about and to find my connections. I was an immigrant, and it takes a couple of years for any immigrant, no matter who you are, to settle in. I had to work hard to find my feet. CLR knew Britain, because he had lived in Britain as a British colonial before he went to the United States. That was an entirely foreign life to me, and I had to find and make my own life, and I did.

One night when I got home from work, CLR had a comrade with him who was not an intellectual and was very clever (though his views on women did not bear examination). I announced that the heating had gone out in the factory that day, and we women had to wait for hours in the cloakroom for it to be repaired (which we didn't care about, because we weren't working but gossiping and being paid for it). Alan said, "And I know just what happened then. Every woman told the story of factories where she'd worked where the heating went off and what management did and what the women did. By the end you got the whole history of problems with heating in factories in north London." I was stunned. That's exactly what had happened. I understood for the first time that that's one way the history of the movement is conveyed from one group of workers to the next and even one generation to the next. It is part of the informal class education we give each other. Johnson-Forest repudiated the vanguard party, which was justified by the view that the party had consciousness and the working class didn't. Our view was that working-class struggle brings us consciousness. And here was an example of our consciousness being collectively raised in the cloakroom.

One of the things CLR told me when I got here was that Stalinism proclaimed that the working class in the US was backward—they had all been bought by cars, refrigerators, and washing machines. Therefore, the Communist Parties were the only alternative to US imperialism. CLR felt it was our job to explain that the working-class movement in the US was powerful even though we didn't have a Labour Party, and, therefore, Stalinism was not the only option. (Don't forget there were mass Communist Parties all over Europe at that time.)

Also, it took us a while to get to know each other, since we had never lived in the same city before I came to England. CLR was different in England.

He told me once that he was never completely relaxed in England; he was more comfortable even on the continent—despite it being largely white and racist, it was not the British Empire and the particular antagonism that he had always lived with.

I was shocked by the unself-conscious racism (the shoe polish was called "Nigger Brown") and the absence of people of colour in Britain and the rest of Europe in ways that he took for granted. The European left then, despite being anti-imperialist, hadn't come to terms with the importance of race in the class hierarchy internationally. But it finally had to when, in the last few years, the people crossed the Mediterranean in dinghies, risking and many losing their lives to escape wars, dictatorships, and ecological devastation. It was amazing to see how much that changed Europe. Millions have now understood that their own movement for liberation and to defeat the new fascism depends on supporting immigrants' right to stay and to make a claim on the accumulated wealth, which they have suffered so much to create through centuries of imperialism.

Before leaving for Trinidad in 1958, in the run-up to that country's independence, and after your return to Britain in 1962, you had both left behind a certain political practice. Did you look for new political avenues?
I became immersed in the anti-racist and anti-war movements, and later in the women's movement. CLR went on with his writing and with cricket, and we were both involved with the Caribbean diaspora. But the left was not very interested in what CLR had to offer. And it was mutual.

Before he was deported from the US, what CLR, and all of Johnson-Forest, had been engaged in was putting into practice what he had worked out as a new political and organizational perspective which left the vanguard party behind. This was the return to Marx, after Stalinism had corrupted the left by echoing in the vanguard party capitalist forms of management and repression. The vanguard party, we were told, made the revolution in 1917, and since then we all had to form a vanguard party to make the revolution. The fact that the party was out of Lenin's control and resulted in Stalinism was not considered. Even Trotskyism, the prime enemy of Stalinism, formed a vanguard party where the intelligentsia were in charge. Johnson-Forest was based on the rejection of a vanguard and experimented with new ways of organizing within the working-class movement, almost two decades before the mass movements of the 1960s undermined the whole hierarchical concept of a vanguard.

That's what CLR contributed more than any other one thing: creating a new kind of working-class organization where the autonomy of Black people and of women was integral to our political focus, the way our organization was structured, and our relationships. We were trying to build an organization based on the power of the grassroots and the end of the domination of intellectuals over working-class people. My work about women was encouraged by that. People don't talk about "intellectuals" now; rather they speak about academics and professionals who are embedded in universities or NGOs; that is, they are employed by institutions rather than being freelance as they had been. They are far more integral to the way society is managed than intellectuals were fifty years ago.

In industry, for example, auto in Detroit, our people did not engage in competition with other left organizations for union posts. We were not trying to become union bureaucrats to "lead the workers"; we were involved instead in trying to strengthen the struggle. We put out a newspaper that working-class people wrote and helped edit. (How many people knew that workers often had picket lines in front of union offices in Detroit and elsewhere? What does this mean about their evaluation of their union?)

When CLR came back to England, he continued to try to lead the US organization with long letters from abroad (which I typed).

When did it become clear to you that, in fact, Johnson-Forest was over?
It became clear to me in the 1960s, because the organization hobbled along, and then Martin Glaberman, who was keeping it going in the United States, wanted to put a motion forward before members that it should be dissolved. I voted for that, and CLR voted against it.

It was obvious to me that Johnson-Forest was falling behind where the new movements were leading, including the connection between industrial countries and the "Third World." But the years of Johnson-Forest, the return to Marx, had pointed the way, no question. Johnson-Forest could not go further in that form. But what Johnson-Forest stood for and worked for have been my political perspective ever since, enriched by all kinds of struggles and campaigning. Many more people have rediscovered it in recent years.

In 1958, CLR got this invitation from the new West Indian Federation.
Yes, we were in Spain. We had gone there so CLR could finish what became *Beyond a Boundary* and not spend a lot of money.[7] The West Indies were celebrating the federation of the islands in preparation for independence,[8] and he

was invited. When he went, he was asked to stay and work for the Federation, and he wanted to do the work. I joined him in British Guiana (now Guyana) around June 1958, and then we continued to Trinidad. CLR enjoyed being home a great deal. I also loved the West Indies.

CLR was secretary of the West Indian Federal Labour Party and editor of the *Nation*.[9] I also worked on the *Nation*. Eric Williams, his old student and then chief minister, would come to see CLR at all times of the day or night. He would come and pick him up from the office, and he would say, "I have to deal with the post office" or the phone company or MI5 or something. "What do you think I should do?" He would take out his notebook (he was the most extraordinary note taker, with a beautiful handwriting, always using the fountain pen that I admired), and he would take notes on everything CLR said. "Tell them this and tell them that," etc. CLR enjoyed it enormously; it was something to pay back to the country which gave him birth. It was anti-imperialist, but it also was a lot of fun.

But politically there was not much in common between him and Williams, was there?
Well, looking back when I was no longer so ignorant, I finally understood that all differences could be blurred in the nationalist movement, especially if you are working in or around the rarefied and disconnected atmosphere of governments. CLR wasn't a nationalist, and I certainly wasn't. But we were definitely for the West Indies against the British Empire, we were for the Federation of the West Indies to gain independence. At that moment in time, the basic differences between CLR and Williams were never articulated. Because you were beating the hell out of the empire, fundamentally, and that's what you had always wanted to do. But, of course, the differences ultimately emerged.

One day Williams came to tell us that the British representative had refused to hand over control of the police. Once Williams had left, CLR said to me as a joke, "What would *you* do?" "I would tell them to go to hell, take the police, take it all." And then a couple of hours later, Williams called and said, "I told them to take it all, and as soon as I told them that, they said 'Alright you can have the police.'" They knew he had a movement behind him! We had a good laugh.

That's how it was at that moment in time. That was 1958–1959. The Bandung Conference, which united the colonies and former colonies to take a non-aligned political position, had happened in 1955. Ghana became independent in 1957, the first African country to win independence. The anti-imperialist movement was the biggest movement the world has ever seen. In the words of cricket, we were on a winning wicket; it seemed to us that there was not a lot you could do wrong.

How wrong can you get! The politicians in the English-speaking Caribbean were avoiding the serious problems which the society faced, except one: a federation of the islands. At a certain point, CLR and I had a disagreement on Williams. I had seen clear signs that Williams didn't care if the West Indian Federation survived, and I told CLR that all Williams wanted was to be king of Trinidad. CLR hadn't seen that, but he later acknowledged it.[10] Trinidad had oil, which meant an income independent of other islands. The politicians generally were more interested in their own power than in bringing the populations together. Norman Manley of Jamaica was different, but Jamaica voted him down and the Federation ended.

CLR and I were deeply disappointed when the Federation fell apart. We knew it was a major defeat. The politicians had not explained to the people what was at stake and how joining forces and resources would give each of the islands much more bargaining power against the monster neighbour to the north. Independence would not be held back, but it would be a flag-and-national-anthem independence, with the personally ambitious in charge and ready to make a deal, paving the way for an updated brand of imperialism.

Years later, I saw how Hugo Chávez, who was a tremendous and truly revolutionary leader, was sabotaged in Venezuela by the same ambitious types. Later still, when I edited and introduced a book on the socialist villages in Tanzania under Julius Nyerere,[11] another fantastic and revolutionary leader, it was again clear how much the personally ambitious in his own government undermined all he was trying to do. By then, I knew that achieving State power blinded most people to everything else that should have mattered; they became entirely manipulable by the same forces the movement had overthrown—the imperial powers and their multinationals.

Nyerere said that independence was the "preliminary goal" which would give the movement, backed by the new independent State, the power to transform the society structurally.[12] But for the nationalists independence was the only goal. They took over the old colonial State—nothing changed except the personnel at the top. The issues that mattered in the West Indies, the question of what kind of economy to have (that is, what is produced by whom in the city and in the countryside, and how the wealth is to be distributed, how trade is to be organized, etc.), the racial split in the population between those of African and Indian descent, and how the Amerindians were finally to be acknowledged, none of this was ever seriously tackled.

Why did you leave the Caribbean in the end?
CLR could not earn his living there (and I certainly couldn't). Williams made a deal with the US and dissociated himself from CLR almost overnight. The movement wanted the US military base out of Chaguaramas, and Williams made some compromise. CLR went back to cricket journalism in England. By then he was not well, following a car accident in Jamaica. We were deeply upset when the outcome was individual independence as opposed to a West Indian Federation, but we were glad to have done the work. At some point CLR went back to Trinidad to report cricket, and Williams put him under house arrest for some weeks, and then he was released.

Once we got back to England, apart from CLR finishing *Beyond a Boundary* and preparing a new edition of *The Black Jacobins*,[13] there was already an anti-racist movement coming together which I was very much part of. By 1965, I was a founding member and organizing secretary of the Campaign Against Racial Discrimination.

When *Beyond a Boundary* came out in 1963, was that a kind of turning point?
It was for him. It had the most extraordinary review in *Wisden*,[14] which is the annual cricket bible. It was soon headed to be a classic, which is now translated into a number of languages—unusual to say the least for a book on cricket. Wherever he went, when CLR opened his mouth, people came to me and said things like, "Mrs. James, your husband is a poet." And then *The Black Jacobins* was republished with a new appendix, "From Toussaint L'Ouverture to Fidel Castro." He began to get invitations to speak and then to teach in the US—Black students in the universities had gone to the authorities to say they wanted him to be allowed back into the US. He did lectures, and then taught Black history courses for some years at Federal City College, which then became the University of the District of Columbia.

When CLR returned to Britain in 1953, he was active in the anti-colonial and Pan-African struggle, continuing his earlier involvement in the International African Service Bureau. Is there a link with his later contacts in Africa?
When I joined him in the UK in 1955, he was involved with Mbiyu Koinange, who was Kenyan, at the time of the Mau Mau, and CLR, along with Grace Boggs,

helped publish a book called *The People of Kenya Speak for Themselves*,[15] about the education that a woman called Njery was developing at the grassroots. This was one way of counteracting what the British government was doing and saying against the movement in Kenya. The repression was horrendous, widespread torture and detention camps. Mbiyu used to come regularly to the house and get help with writing letters to the Colonial Office and the newspapers, which is some of what CLR had been doing in the 1930s before leaving for the United States. Our friends George and Dorothy Padmore, his colleagues in the 1930s, continued to be central to the anti-imperialist struggle worldwide.

CLR was invited to Ghana's independence celebration in 1957. We both went in 1960 when Ghana became a republic. He met Nyerere in Tanzania and was deeply impressed, especially with the "Arusha Declaration," which he later wrote about in a new edition of *History of Pan-African Revolt*.[16] In 1968, CLR attended a Black Writers Conference in Canada, which was a memorable occasion. That's when Walter Rodney was prevented from returning to Jamaica to take up his post at the university. There were demonstrations in Jamaica, where people died in the clashes with police, and in London, where a number of us were arrested for protesting in support.

In the same period, CLR also spoke at a conference in Cuba about intellectual workers. He did some support work for prisoners in South Africa. He also broadcast on a free radio that the Pan Africanist Congress had organized. PAC was not connected with the Communist Party, as the ANC was, and had a most remarkable leader who died on Robben Island—his name was Robert Sobukwe. Later, CLR was involved in supporting the Grenada Revolution.

CLR would always do what the movement asked, but he didn't himself try to build or join any organization in Britain.

Can we say that he was quite involved in the Black movement at the time?
He was a big support for the Black students. He certainly gave them a historical framework. CLR was an extraordinary historian, by which I mean not merely did he make sense of history, but he was able to make it accessible to anyone, academic or not academic. People learnt a lot at his hand. He was not only appreciated as a speaker, he was appreciated as an educator and as someone who gave meaning and perspective to the movement activities people were involved in. His conception of Black history was an anti-racist conception which every committed person could be nourished by. When I visited him on my own lecture tour in the US, I could see that the students really loved him.

At the Dialectics of Liberation Congress in London 1967, where CLR intervened in support of Stokely Carmichael and Black Power, he referred to the fact that the movement needed more knowledge of where it stands in history and where it's going. Is that something you remember from those days?

I took those things for granted. I knew that CLR had a political perspective based on history. From 1968, he was on and off in Chicago, Washington, DC, Montréal, other places. He always stressed the self-activity of the oppressed, and that this was the driving force of history, and he thought it was the job of Marxists to convey that, especially to those in the movement—they had to look for it, encourage it, and base all they did on it. Writing *The Black Jacobins* and what the Haitian slaves were able to organize to liberate themselves educated him in world history. He'd show that events were a response to what the movement demanded and fought for. Aside from Marx, there was nowhere else you could get that perspective then, and I suspect it is still rare now.

Can you say something about his life in Britain?

A lot of CLR's life was study. He would produce extraordinary new insights into everything that he touched. He did a study of Michelangelo's frescoes and statues which showed the class politics of the great artist—Michelangelo had been in charge of the armaments in the uprising against the Medici. I don't know if that was ever written up, but it is quite brilliant. Recently, I saw an article of his which I hadn't known about on the action painter Jackson Pollock, something completely new and different.

In the sixties, we had a study group once a week of young people from the West Indies and one or two others. I was part of that. Everyone took a turn at presenting their interests or what they had been studying. I presented on women. Walter Rodney sometimes attended. CLR would spend hours every week advising students, who came and said, "I'm doing this thesis," and he would say, "Your weakness is that. I would suggest you look at this." They would leave with a much broader view of their subject than they had had. But what benefit did the movement get from this work? Most of them were in academia to build their careers not to change the world. There are always exceptions, and Walter Rodney was a stunning example: his thesis was politically useful and historically creative, and he went back to the Caribbean to make available to grassroots people what he knew. He led the movement in Guyana in the seventies.

CLR also spent a lot of time and thought promoting the writers from the English-speaking Caribbean, especially Wilson Harris and George Lamming.

From what he published in those years, the main topics seem to centre around creativity, the artist in society, Marxism and culture, also some articles on Nkrumah, Padmore, etc., but no "return" to the Marxist classics, so to speak, or to the New Left's discussions of the late 1960s and 1970s.
He had completed the work of studying and writing about Hegel and Marx in 1948. We called his manuscript the Nevada Document, and the typescript was circulated among some of us. (At the time, he was in Nevada getting a divorce and working as a janitor, the only job he, as a Black man, could get.) It was first published in 1980 as *Notes on Dialectics: Hegel, Marx, Lenin.*[17] It is a great book which helps train your mind to think in an anti-capitalist way, dialectically—about everything, beginning with day-to-day politics. You learn always to begin with the movement of the exploited: its strivings, its forms of organization, the new forms its enemy takes in response, and the ways the movement reorganizes in order to deal with that. He said *Notes* was his best written work, and I agree. Whether you agree with everything in it or not is irrelevant. It is the attempt to make the dialectic accessible to people like me who want and need to know but are not trained to read and understand Hegel. It is always enlightening and sometimes beautiful. It is a scandal that it has been out of print for almost forty years and tells us how little regard there is for Marx's methods, and, by the way, for CLR's.[18]

CLR spent his last years studying decisive moments of class conflict. When he was in the US, he had done work on the Civil War and the struggle against slavery; the abolitionist movement was the basis of Johnson-Forest's anti-racism. But now he concentrated on the French Revolution and the great struggles in the Low Countries in the Middle Ages.

CLR was interested in everything that was going on and always incorporated new information into his wide body of knowledge. In the 1960s, in the UK, a man called Beeching had a plan to cut the rail lines that were not "economic." One day I moved a pile of books and there was the Beeching report, annotated. I could not imagine why CLR had read it in such detail, but it was something that was going on in the society, and he wanted to know.

He saw every phenomenon as part of a widening pattern. Each addition gave greater clarity to the rest. He was able to do that. And he always asked the right questions. You told him something, and he asked you a question which made you review everything that you had just thought you knew all about.

Sometimes it reinforced you: "Yes, I was right all along." But sometimes you had to say, "I have to look at it again." He could always do that.

CLR studied Lenin and Lenin's "conclusion" in his last three essays, "Better Fewer but Better," "On Co-operation," and "How We Should Reorganise the Workers' and Peasants' Inspection."[19] He thought that the political mistakes that Trotsky made were revealed in the trade union debate in volume 9 of Lenin's *Collected Works*.[20] He knew that the central political issue was the self-activity of the working class striving for power against the planners and managers in society generally and within the movement. He was always looking for ways to identify self-activity and the forces against it, including within working-class organizations such as the unions and political parties of the left.

Wasn't he also looking for new forms of organization?
In some way, forms of organization are always quite similar: collectivity, cooperation, self-activity, all in the service of autonomy from all the forces and agents of repression. What changes is the sectors that come together, how comprehensive are their demands, what other sectors of society they can bring to their side, and what they are ready to do to win. Whether it was factory committees or peasants' collectives or a slave rebellion or a movement for civil rights or a women's movement against rape or for pay equity or an anti-war soldiers' movement or the Palestinian Great March of Return or a prisoners' hunger strike or fighting to keep the land from the clutches of multinationals that will exploit and pollute it and rob you of your means of survival and your community . . . Whatever it is, whenever it is, people everywhere find themselves building organizations that aim to have these qualities. I learnt this from things that CLR would read to me or tell me about. What he wanted to find out, for example, was what individuals of what sector/s had initiated the organization/s behind events, as opposed to who might have been credited with it, and what sectors came into the movement when. Freedom is always what we strive for, whoever we are and whatever is the immediate goal of the struggle.

But the context of all organizing is the specific balance of power between the movement you are trying to form and the State. Most countries have suffered dictatorships or are living under dictatorships of one form or another right now. To organize in this environment requires not only enormous courage but a great awareness of where the population is at and what struggles different sectors are waging on whatever level. It also requires great imagination in working out how to bring people together without bringing the full force of the State against you. When we hear the news of this country or that where the movement has exploded, we are never told in any detail what repression they face and what they have been able to accomplish despite that. If you organize internationally you learn to ask the right questions.

The question for us was not what organization, the question was who is going to form it and when, and who is going to try to take it over and "lead it" to enhance their own power, and whether we will be able to defeat them. Ultimately, the question is how much of our freedom we have the power to demand. What happens now, increasingly, in most struggles, is that different sectors speak up to ensure that they become visible and are included, broadening what the whole movement stands for and what it demands: women, the nationalities, the races, the ages, the disabled, the subsistence farmers, the sweatshop workers, the sexual choices and identities, the prisoners, the veterans, the children . . . CLR does not spell this out but opens the way for what the movements have articulated in action. For him, our job as anti-capitalists is to see that even before organizations of struggle announce themselves, their direction is welcomed, encouraged, protected, advertised, built on. He saw that to want to use and/or be in charge of such organizations of rebellion for one's own purposes rather than be an integral part of them, was itself the enemy. That's also what *Notes* is about.

Hadn't that been exactly the point in the analyses of the Johnsonites?
Of course. Johnson-Forest was an organization rather than a party aiming to take power "on behalf of the working class." CLR was convinced of what Johnsonites could accomplish. Lenin had published *What Is to Be Done* in 1902,[21] saying that the working class could not achieve revolutionary consciousness, that the intellectuals had to bring it from outside, and the left stuck with that. CLR insisted that Lenin later regretted writing that. But it was a lot of years later before Lenin fully understood all that was involved. He found out, because he led a revolution, and then had to lead a workers' State, despite the fact that the intellectuals who were supposed to bring consciousness to the working class hadn't even wanted to make the insurrection and were now managing and disciplining the working class. Before his death, in the last three articles mentioned above, Lenin proposed ways for workers to take charge of the economy.

For CLR, Trotskyism had not broken with Stalinism—the direction still came from the "vanguard" rather than from the workers and peasants.

Trotskyism had based itself on raising the consciousness of workers, but Marx had a much more realistic view. Early on he said:

> Both for the production on a mass scale of this communist conscious-
> ness, and for the success of the cause itself, the alteration of men on
> a mass scale is necessary, an alteration which can only take place in a
> practical movement, a *revolution*; the revolution is necessary, therefore,
> not only because the *ruling* class cannot be overthrown in any other
> way, but also because the class *overthrowing* it can only in a revolution
> succeed in ridding itself of all the muck of ages and become fitted to
> found society anew.[22]

Martin Glaberman used to say with glee after reading this quote to me: "So it's not communist consciousness that makes the revolution but the revolution that makes communist consciousness!"

CLR didn't understand this when he joined the movement in the mid-1930s, but researching for *The Black Jacobins* what the slaves accomplished in Haiti taught him a lot. By 1948, he was able to grasp Hegel and return to Marx. He spelled it all out in *Notes on Dialectics*. He then said, "Okay, now we have to build an organization that is not trying to be a vanguard, where working-class members are the transmission belt with the working class outside. They must shape what the organization stands for, what it does, and how it does it." And that was the Johnson-Forest Tendency when it split from both wings of US Trotskyism in 1951.

To ensure workers' power it's not enough to put working-class people in leadership positions. That's a way to manipulate and even corrupt good comrades by pulling them away from their power base so they're entirely under the influence of the "educated." CLR was proposing something far more profound: an organization that fuses movement experience with an anti-vanguard theoretical perspective. It reinforced you against the capitalist habit of becoming a vanguard over others. As a young member, I was able to read or listen to the organizational speeches that CLR would make laying down the organization's problems and principles as we developed them. Not this question or that question but *the* question of how to organize internally and with the public as one continuum. These speeches must be somewhere in his papers and should be published and read today as a historical moment of an organization working out its anti-vanguard principles. I remember CLR in the 1950s dictating a letter to Grace Boggs, whose training was in philosophy, saying, "Pay as much attention to the organization as you do to Hegel." And this has always stayed with me. That means that the internal structure of your organization, or, rather, what you strive for it to be, is an embodiment of what you stand for. You cannot achieve it under capitalism but working to achieve it enhances all you are striving together to do.

CLR is often credited with making the case for Black autonomy. How did this relate to the movements of the 1960s?
In the 1940s, even in the 1930s, he had established "the independent validity of the Negro struggle," that is that you couldn't prioritize the struggle of "workers" (i.e., white workers) over the struggle against racism (i.e., Black workers). This is what we Johnsonites had all been educated to understand. Establishing the autonomy of the Black struggle also gave validity to the autonomous struggles of other sectors.

Once you establish the "independent validity of the Negro struggle," it is not difficult, with the massive Black movement of the 1950s and 1960s in the US, to move from "independent validity" to Black people as a sector of the working class and their anti-racist struggle as integral to the struggle of the class. This is no less true because some Black people in the movement are from other classes. Within every movement—people of colour, women, children, every sector—the class struggle rages between moving up in capitalism and destroying the capitalist hierarchy.

I made the short leap from "independent validity" to the Black movement as a working-class movement in 1972, in the introduction to *Power of Women and the Subversion of the Community*. Once the Black movement is acknowledged as a working-class movement rather than a "special interest," the potential for racism within the movement is undermined. Women speak for the whole class, as Black people speak for the whole class, as each sector making its own power felt against the capitalist hierarchy speaks for the whole class—each broadens what the class struggle aims to achieve. The Poor People's Campaign, a new mass movement in the US, calls this coming together of sectors "fusion."

The issues that women raise are also unifying issues within the whole movement.

The Wages for Housework Campaign had begun to redefine the working class from what most of the left had understood it to be, when we said that unwaged housewives were part of that class. Redefining Black people and housewives as sectors of the working class, broke with the left fixation that the definition of working class was workers, mainly white men, in industry—at the "point of production." This was not only a sexist but a racist definition which excluded most of the Global South, most women, and most people of colour in societies divided by race. This grossly underestimated the power of our enemy, on the one hand, and our potential power, on the other.

From the mid-1960s, you have been continuously active in the anti-racist and women's movements. More than fifty years later, you're still in the midst of political campaigns, the Global Women's Strike network, and your cherished Crossroads Women's Centre. What do you consider your most important political experience?
Building the WFH Campaign and the Global Women's Strike which it coordinates has been hard work but exciting and satisfying, as working creatively with others to change the world always is. Especially on an international level. The principles I learnt in Johnson-Forest have been my starting point and the Campaign people have embraced them. They have been collectively developed and in fact transformed by beginning with women and the struggles of many different sectors we have been involved with in a number of countries. We were creating an anti-capitalist organization, which was rooted in working-class struggle, beginning with women. We had no models. We knew only what we wanted to avoid. The membership was not a means to an end, but the means and the end. All who participated learnt much about the movement, about the world, and about themselves.

It is no easy matter to think and act internationally. We are talking about a working relationship not token solidarity. Luckily, we now have Skype, Zoom, and other technology that does not eat the whole budget. But even this doesn't guarantee a working relationship. Yet we, all of us, are dependent on that working relationship which we strive for but still eludes us given language barriers, time zones, and each particular frame of reference.

What we put forward about unwaged caring work, starting with *A Woman's Place* in 1952,[23] is much more acknowledged everywhere today as a crucial part of what the grassroots must stand for to oppose capital's destructive market and military.

All the autonomous organizations which are part of our network are involved with some or all of that, and with their own specific anti-racist, anti-discriminatory demands.

I've also been changed by meeting the movement we had been working with in Haiti. In 2011, President Jean-Bertrand Aristide and his wife and colleague Mildred Trouillot came back from exile and asked that I be one of the people welcoming them. My association with *Black Jacobins* took on a deeper meaning for me—a commitment to the Haitian struggle which to this day risks everything to defend that great revolution, renewing what we owe to it.

One final word. CLR was asked what he thought of "what Selma is doing with wages for housework." He gave his usual brilliant answer: "You can't be against it." By which he could only mean that he was not going into the arguments, but that there was no way that anti-capitalist people could oppose women, who reproduced the whole human race but were unwaged, building a movement to demand that the State pay them for their work.

Notes

1 Mariarosa Dalla Costa and Selma James, *The Power of Women and the Subversion of the Community* (Bristol, UK: Falling Walls Press, 1975).

2 Selma James, "A Woman's Place," in Selma James, *Sex, Race, and Class: The Perspective of Winning—A Selection of Writings 1952–2011* (Oakland: PM Press, 2012), 13–31.

3 Johnson-Forest had tried to get the Workers Party and the Socialist Workers Party back together, but we left the WP after its refusal and joined the SWP in 1947.

4 CLR James, *Mariners, Renegades and Castaways: The Story of Herman Melville and the World We Live In* (London: Allison and Busby, 1985 [1953]).

5 See Selma James, "Striving for Clarity and Influence: The Political Legacy of CLR James," in Selma James, *Sex, Race, and Class*, 283–96.

6 The Scottsboro Boys were nine Black teenagers falsely accused of raping two white women aboard a train near Scottsboro, Alabama, in 1931.

7 CLR James, *Beyond a Boundary* (Durham, NC: Duke University Press, 2013 [1963]).

8 Ten English-speaking islands which were colonies of the British Empire became the Federation of the West Indies in preparation for independence. Agitation began in Jamaica, the biggest island, for it to "go it alone." A referendum was held in Jamaica to decide whether or not to stay in the Federation, and the population voted the Federation down. Once Jamaica was gone, Trinidad and Tobago, the second largest, also left, and the Federation collapsed.

9 The *Nation* was the newspaper of Trinidad and Tobago's People's National Movement, Eric Williams's party.

10 In 1961, after the break with Eric Williams, CLR wrote: "One of my close personal associates never trusted the bona fides of [Williams's] politics. I used to hear regularly: 'He is not the man you think he is.' 'All this federation business, he is sticking to it only because you are there.' 'All he wants is to sit on a little throne and be king of Trinidad.' . . . 'It should be noted that my wife has political reservations about Dr. Williams, as all people of our training and outlook have of all bourgeois politicians'"; CLR James, *Party Politics in the West Indies*, 159. This was the first book ever published in Trinidad—Walter Annamunthodo and Vedic, the press where Walter worked, helped me to publish it.

11 Ralph Ibbott, *Ujamaa: The Hidden Story of Tanzania's Socialist Villages* (London: Crossroads Books, 2014).

12 Julius Nyerere, introduction to *Freedom and Unity—Uhuru na Umoja: A Selection from Writings and Speeches, 1952–65* (Dar es Salaam: Oxford University Press, 1967), 1.

13 CLR James, *The Black Jacobins*.

14 Arlott, review of *Beyond a Boundary*, in Preston, *Wisden Cricketers' Almanack 1964*; also see "Confronting Imperial Boundaries," 146–54, this volume.

15 Mbiyu Koinange, *The People of Kenya Speak for Themselves* (Detroit: Kenya Publication Fund, 1955).

16 CLR James, *History of Pan-African Revolt* (Oakland: PM Press, 2012 [1938]).

17 CLR James, *Notes on Dialectics: Hegel, Marx, Lenin* (London: Allison & Busby, 1980 [1948]).

18 A new expanded edition is being prepared by Dr. Robert Hill for publication by Duke University Press in 2021.

19 Vladimir Ilyich Lenin, "Better Fewer but Better" (1923), in V.I. Lenin, *Collected Works*, vol. 33, 2nd ed. (Moscow: Progress Publishers, 1965), accessed September 25, 2020, https://www.marxists.org/archive/lenin/works/1923/mar/02.htm; Vladimir Ilyich Lenin, "On Co-operation" (1923), in ibid., accessed September 25, 2020, https://www.marxists.org/archive/lenin/works/1923/jan/06.htm; Vladimir Ilyich Lenin, "How We Should Reorganise the Workers' and Peasants' Inspection," in ibid., accessed September 25, 2020, https://marxists.catbull.com/archive/lenin/works/1923/jan/23.htm.

20 V.I. Lenin, *Collected Works*, vol. 9 (June–November 1905), 2nd ed. (Moscow: Progress Publishers, 1965), accessed September 25, 2020, https://www.marxists.org/archive/lenin/works/cw/volume09.htm.

21 Vladimir Ilyich Lenin, "What Is to Be Done" (1902), in V.I. Lenin, *Collected Works*, vol. 1 (Moscow: Foreign Language Publishing House, 1961), accessed September 25, 2020, https://www.marxists.org/archive/lenin/works/1901/witbd.

22 Karl Marx and Frederick Engels, *The German Ideology* (Moscow: Progress Publishers, 1968), accessed September 25, 2020, https://www.marxists.org/archive/marx/works/download/Marx_The_German_Ideology.pdf.

23 Selma James, "A Woman's Place," in Selma James, *Sex, Race, and Class*, 13–31.

The Grassroots Labour Movement
That Shook Britain
(2015–2020)

Introduction

It's always been our premise that we cannot make any fundamental changes, or even keep changes that we are able to win, unless we build a powerful movement which embraces many sectors active on their own behalf. (With the internet and other technology, such a movement can become international from the start, wherever it originates.)

A movement announced itself in the UK in 2015 to win a socialist Labour government. In 2019, it was defeated. It is worth recording how we experienced it, how it changed us, and how the landscape has changed.

In July 2015, having lost the general election to the Tories,[1] the Labour Party set out to elect a new leader. The left-wing group of MPs put forward Jeremy Corbyn—"It was his turn." Corbyn, like his close ally John McDonnell who had stood in previous leadership elections, was well-known as a principled backbencher with a distinguished anti-war, anti-imperialist, anti-racist track record. The movement Corbyn's candidacy immediately called forth took everyone by surprise.

The letter below was our first statement of support for Corbyn, published on August 18, 2015, in the *Guardian*, whose editorial had backed the right-winger Yvette Cooper for leader.[2]

To everyone's astonishment, especially Corbyn's and McDonnell's, Corbyn went on to win by a landslide—he got more votes than the other three candidates put together. The Parliamentary Labour Party, which is mainly right-wing, was shocked at being defeated and set out to remove him. I deal with this in the second piece, which I wrote in my blog a year later.

Corbyn's leadership was defined by unrelenting attacks from inside and outside the party, including fabricated and malicious allegations of anti-semitism against him and his supporters. Those of us who are Jewish had a particular responsibility to discredit these attackers and to enable anyone to organize against Israeli apartheid and murder without fear of being labelled antisemitic. Three of us composed an open letter to the Board of Deputies of British Jews, a leader of the witch-hunt.

The fourth piece is my open letter in support of MP Chris Williamson, which was published in the *Morning Star*, the movement daily. I met Chris at a meeting of Momentum, the organization created to harness the power of the movement that got Corbyn elected leader. He had been invited to speak about his campaign for mandatory reselection—something the membership was pressing for. He faced great hostility from the Parliamentary Labour Party and was suspended for criticizing the party's handling of the antisemitism allegations. After an investigation he was reinstated, but then resuspended two days later. Despite winning in the high court against his suspension, he was blocked from standing as a Labour candidate in the general election. He resigned and stood as an independent but lost to the Tories (as did the official Labour candidate.)

The concluding piece aims to evaluate why we lost and how the grassroots movements that have emerged since are further reshaping the political landscape for all of us.

Notes

1   The right-wing Conservative Party is often referred to as the Tory Party or the Tories.
2   Selma James and Nina López, Global Women's Strike, "Yvette Cooper Supported Sexist Austerity; Jeremy Corbyn Has Always Opposed It," 178–79, this volume.

Yvette Cooper Supported Sexist Austerity; Jeremy Corbyn Has Always Opposed It (2015)

with Nina López

Guardian, Letters, August 18, 2015

The Guardian endorses Yvette Cooper, since "a female leader would be a plus in itself." But Labour women lead the surge for Corbyn: 61 per cent want him as their first choice compared to 48 per cent of men, according to a YouGov survey.[1]

Corbyn's anti-austerity, anti-war, pro-welfare, labour rights, and environment programme rides on a wave of local campaigns, many initiated by women—against this or that hospital or library closure, welfare cut, zero-hours contract, eviction, deportation, death in police custody, the mass rape of children, the arms trade... Only 25 per cent of women supported the Iraq war, but most women MPs, including Cooper, voted for it.

Austerity is sexist, attacking carers first of all. Cuts in wages and welfare have targeted women—as waged workers in caring and public service jobs, as unwaged workers deprived of services. In 90 per cent of families the primary carer is a woman. Corbyn offers women 50 per cent of his shadow cabinet but also free childcare and the "recognition and valuing" of women's unremunerated caring work.

As Secretary of State for Work and Pensions in 2009, Cooper abolished Income Support and extended Labour's infamous Work Capability Assessment for sick and disabled people. The money that recognized unwaged caring work enabled mothers to leave violent men and disabled people to live independent lives, is now gone or under threat.

Professor Alison Wolf has attacked as a "betrayal of feminism" the "obsession" with women in boardrooms or in parliament, while the poorly paid women shift workers on whom "golden skirts" depend are ignored.[2]

John McDonnell, MP, who ensured Corbyn would run, was "ready to swim through vomit" to oppose the cut to tax credit for the third child. Better men against sexist austerity than women for it.

Notes

1   Will Dahlgreen, "With One Month to Go, Corbyn's Lead Increases," YouGov, August 10, 2015, accessed September 26, 2020, https://yougov.co.uk/topics/politics/articles-reports/2015/08/10/corbyn-pull-ahead.
2   Alison Wolf, "Feminists Today Are Too Obsessed with Their Own Elite, Metropolitan Lives," *Guardian,* January 21, 2015, accessed September 26, 2020, https://tinyurl.com/y3l5qz7o.

On Winning with Corbyn (2016)

When Jeremy Corbyn announced that he was anti-austerity, overnight he began to attract thousands who then joined Labour to vote for him as leader of the party. Some who had left in disgust at Blair's deadly wars rejoined. Membership doubled, becoming a political force. This was entirely unexpected, like an earthquake. It upset the whole structure of the party hierarchy and alarmed the Parliamentary Labour Party, who had never experienced such pressure from the public. Labour MPs, like every three-year-old, had to learn to share—in this case share power with the membership. It was a first. Most hadn't become MPs for that!

That was the beginning of the end of credibility for MPs who had been careful not to go "too far," that is, from the Tories: against cuts, privatization, and war. They had been trained by Tony Blair to make policy on the basis of what the media, and Murdoch in particular, would find acceptable. If we bear this in mind, we may be shocked to realize that Murdoch and the 1% he speaks for were governing through Blair-led MPs. Who in fact was involved in making the decisions on policy we don't know, but it was not ad hoc.

Our movement has thrown a wrench into the Blair legacy, which had never been fully confronted.

Corbyn's principled policies are based on an updated Welfare State properly funded and workers' and other human rights defended internationally. All of this we have been told is outdated and a throwback practically to cavemen. But, in fact, we never stopped believing in it. The proof is that people came running when it was offered. It was new only to a generation which has never experienced the Welfare State as it was before Thatcher. That Welfare State had given us the right not to starve and never to have to beg. You were not demonized as a scrounger if you asked for help; it was your right. Despite many injustices, it was better than what we had known and have known since. It was won by the post-war working-class movement, people who had defeated Hitler and would not settle for less.

What seems really new in what Corbyn proposes is how the public and the party should relate. The leadership that came forward from the campaign to get Corbyn elected created Momentum, which many of us hope can be a kind of transmission belt between the party and the wider movement, an attempt to begin to involve the public in decision-making.[1]

Not all the MPs who oppose Corbyn are Blairites, but they and their backers (who are they?) prioritize making policies that win elections for themselves and their outside interests rather than for their constituents. So 172 MPs, without ever mentioning what Corbyn stands for or what they think of it, opposed him with a secret vote of no confidence (one later rejoined the shadow cabinet and was welcomed back). They say he can't win elections, despite him having won a number which they had tried to sabotage (including with wild charges of widespread antisemitism in the Labour Party).[2] They failed to distract voters, and Labour mayors were elected in Bristol, Liverpool, London, and Salford. Corbyn and company were particularly proud of a Black mayor in Bristol, which had been a major slave trade port.

On July 10, Andrew Marr asked Jeremy Corbyn, "Is the victory of the left inside the Labour Party more important than winning the next general election?"[3] Corbyn answered, "What's most important is to change how politics is done in this country."

Marr's question assumed that Corbyn had to choose between his principles and winning elections. But principles and winning are one with the Corbyn movement. That's what that movement has glimpsed and is excited by.

Corbyn and McDonnell have told us over and over that the population must be involved in making policy, otherwise nothing can change. There is a way in which we always knew that, but it seemed a fantasy when you looked at our reality. What Corbyn calls "the new politics" has now brought membership of the Labour Party to half a million, and growing every day. The MPs are frantically trying to destroy this movement, which they take as their enemy.

We have been trained, especially in the last four decades, to believe that we cannot change the economic and political framework, that we have to accept it no matter how blatant the lies and the life-threatening policies based on them. This has damaged us in ways we'll be discovering as we reclaim our own experience—it is not only the policies which attack us; we also lose the habit of insisting on the truth about our own reality. We hold back from spelling out what we know best, because it has been so much work to go against the official tide.

We have been divided on gender, on race, on nationality, on age, on disability, on sexual preference, on income, on immigration status, on parenting, on religion, on prison record, on every conceivable aspect of our lives. Our education system teaches us from the earliest age to compete with each other. Building a movement, we find out what power we can generate together. We finally begin to grasp that nobody wants less, needs less, or deserves less than anybody else. We can refuse to compete.

Since we have come together even this far, we have brought on our movement the wrath of the whole establishment. Those professing democracy are appalled when they finally see it coming into action. Can this democracy win? It had better.

Notes

1   As we read this now, we are even more aware of how crucial it is for the movement to impose its will. It has not done that yet, in part because of the attacks on Corbyn by the media, the right-wing Labour MPs, and the conservatism of most trade unions which impose themselves on Labour's grassroots.
2   In August 2015, when it first looked like Corbyn would win the Labour leadership election, Israel appointed Mark Regev as ambassador to the UK; he had been the chief spokesman for the prime minister.
3   *The Andrew Marr Show* is a weekly current affairs programme on BBC television.

Standing with Palestinians (2018)

Open Letter to the Board of Deputies of British Jews from Jewish People in the UK

with Michael Kalmanovitz, Sam Weinstein, and 102 others

We are appalled that the Board of Deputies (BoD), which claims to be "the voice of British Jews," has once again attempted to justify the massacre of unarmed Palestinian people by the Israeli military. You issued a throwaway tweet on March 31 and a full statement on May 15,[1] followed by a comment opposing the World Health Organization fact-finding mission into the health needs of the occupied territories on May 24.[2]

As you know, on March 30, when Israel began its latest attack, Palestinians were commemorating Land Day.[3] It was the launch of their Great March of Return demanding the right to go back to their homeland and an end to the blockade of Gaza. The March continued until May 15, the seventieth anniversary of the Nakba, when three-quarters of a million Palestinians were ethnically cleansed from their land: hundreds of towns and villages were depopulated and destroyed to make way for the State of Israel.

Since March 30, 123 Palestinians, including children, women, medics, and journalists wearing vests marked PRESS, have been killed, many shot in the back, and 13,600 have been maimed or injured by live ammunition, tear gas, and firebombs.[4] For six weeks, the killings continued, day after day, and, on May 14, when the US moved its embassy to Jerusalem, despite "overwhelming global opposition," another massacre: 60 people killed and 2,771 maimed and wounded. The Israeli use of illegal "dumdum" bullets, which expand after entering the body, was clearly intended to cause not only greater pain but permanent disabilities.[5]

Your statement justifying this massacre prompted over five hundred Jewish Zionists to write to outgoing President Jonathan Arkush and President-elect Marie van der Zyl,[6] protesting that the BoD had "deeply misrepresented" their views by relieving Israel of all responsibility for the deaths caused by their snipers.[7]

The BoD is doing its best to hide that Jews are divided over Israel's ongoing repression and slaughter of the Palestinian people, which many of us, like most people everywhere in the world, including a number of Zionists, are outraged by. So much for the BoD "speaking for all Jews"! You are so determined to defend Israel that you have even accused Jewish organizations and individuals of "antisemitism" because they support Palestinian rights and have campaigned for their expulsion from the Labour Party.

This is not the first time the BoD has condoned murder, claiming to speak on behalf of Jewish people in the UK. The BoD publicly supported pro-Israel rallies during the bombing of Gaza in 2008–2009 and 2014 that killed thousands of Palestinian women, children, and men. It has consistently supported a regime that is widely considered guilty of war crimes and the racist crime of apartheid.[8] You are now saying that opposition to Israel's actions is antisemitic, thus demanding that Israel should be the only government in the world exempt from criticism.

In recent years, the BoD has been uncritical of Israel and pro-Tory, contrary to the great Jewish working-class tradition of struggling for social justice in every situation. Arkush declared his political allegiance when, on June 9, 2017, he mourned the Tory prime minister's failure to win an outright majority at the general election as a "loss" for the Jewish community and described the Tory alliance with the extreme right-wing, homophobic, antiabortion Democratic Unionist Party in the North of Ireland as "positive news" and the DUP as "exceptionally warm and friendly."[9] The Tories that Arkush supports are aligned in Europe with right-wing political parties that honour Nazi collaborators and Islamophobes. Arkush also celebrated the election of Trump, undeterred by his racist, Islamophobic, and antisemitic campaign.

Your identification with the Israeli government could prove even more frightening. Governments and people around the world fear that the wrecking of the agreement with Iran by Netanyahu and Trump (the heads of two nuclear powers) may start yet another war, repeating the horrors of Afghanistan, Iraq, Libya, and Syria. You may find yourself not only supporting the destruction of Iran but urging the risk of nuclear war.

As Jewish people, we are distraught that the Nazi Holocaust has been, and continues to be, used to justify the brutal occupation of another people who played no part in our historic persecution and to indulge in warmongering.

We reclaim our tradition of struggling for social justice for all by echoing the call by Jamal Juma, coordinator of the Palestinian Grassroots Anti-Apartheid Wall Campaign and the Land Defence Coalition:

> It is time for the world to stop standing in implicit or explicit complicity with Israeli apartheid and to join us in nonviolent action by taking up the Palestinian call for boycotts, divestment and sanctions until Israel respects international law and human rights.[10]

Signed by 105 people, including a number of prominent individuals.[11]

Notes

1. Board of Deputies, "Board of Deputies Reacts to Violent Scenes and Loss of Life at Israel-Gaza Border," May 15, 2018, accessed September 26, 2020, https://www.bod.org.uk/board-of-deputies-reacts-to-violent-scenes-and-loss-of-life-at-israel-gaza-border.
2. "Board of Deputies Applauds UK Government Stand on World Health Organisation," Board of Deputies of British Jews, May 24, 2018, accessed September 26, 2020, https://www.bod.org.uk/board-of-deputies-applauds-uk-government-stand-on-world-health-organisation.
3. Land Day is the annual remembrance of the 1976 general strike protesting Israeli land theft from Palestinian citizens of Israel, when six unarmed Palestinians were killed, a hundred wounded, and hundreds arrested.
4. MEE staff, "Twitter Hits Back at Israeli Attempt to Smear Slain Gaza Medic Razan al-Najjar," Middle East Eye, June 8, 2018, accessed October 8, 2020, https://www.middleeasteye.net/news/twitter-hits-back-israeli-attempt-smear-slain gaza-medic-razan-al-najjar.
5. "MSF Teams in Gaza Observe Unusually Severe and Devastating Gunshot Injuries," Médecins Sans Frontières, April 19, 2018, accessed September 26, 2020, https://tinyurl.com/y2gzqgm4.
6. We note that van der Zyl's suitability to be president of BoD has been questioned by victims/survivors of child sexual abuse, who accuse her of "abandoning" them in their efforts to eradicate this crime from Jewish institutions.
7. Yachad: Together for Israel, Together for Peace, accessed September 26, 2020, https://yachad.e-activist.com/page/24544/petition/1?ea.tracking.id=c2186023
8. *Israeli Practices towards the Palestinian People and the Question of Apartheid, Palestine and the Israeli Occupation* no. 1 (Beirut: United Nations, 2017), accessed September 26, 2020, https://electronicintifada.net/sites/default/files/2017-03/un_apartheid_report_15_march_english_final_.pdf.
9. Raoul Wootliff, "UK Jewish Leader: Election Result a 'Loss' for Community, and Israel," *Times of Israel*, June 9, 2017, accessed September 26, 2020, https://www.timesofisrael.com/uk-jewish-leader-election-result-a-loss-for-community-and-israel.
10. Cited in Jamal Juma, "Why the Time Is Right for Action to Help Palestine," *National*, April 23, 2018, accessed September 26, 2020, https://www.thenational.scot/news/16176594.time-right-action-help-palestine.

11   "Open Letter to the Board of Deputies of British Jews from Jewish People in the UK," IJAN UK, June 11, 2018, accessed September 26, 2020, https://www.facebook.com/ AfterGazaMassacre/posts/200767647231085.

We Are in the Midst of an Anti-Left Witch-Hunt (2019)

Open Letter to Chris Williamson

Morning Star, December 9, 2019

Dear Chris,

I read your statement in support of Jeremy Corbyn and your article in the *Morning Star* and was struck by your honesty, clarity, and determination to win for Labour in this election.

Though I wish you were running as an official party candidate, I am well aware of why you are running as an independent.

Many of us have to hold our tongues about the malicious fabricated attacks on the Labour leadership, which have often gone unchallenged and have resulted, therefore, in wildly unjustified suspensions and expulsions like yours. Otherwise, we risk being suspended just when we are needed to fight for Labour in the election. (This, of course, is the intention of the attacks.)

I'm delighted to hear that many party members in your constituency are backing your candidacy in order to get a Corbyn victory based on Labour's terrific manifesto, which outlines a new start for Labour, for working-class people, and for the country as a whole. In fact, it's a new start for the planet when we consider Labour's programme for immediately and massively funding measures to address the climate crisis.

We thank you for campaigning for a Corbyn-led government that we desperately need. We are terrified of what might happen to the National Health Service (NHS), the climate emergency, and rights of all kinds if Johnson is elected.

He is pro–fossil fuels, pro–hostile environment, pro-austerity, pro–arming the Saudi and Israeli governments, pro–occupation of Palestine, and a friend of the racist, antisemitic, Islamophobic far right in Europe—the list is endless.

A deal with Donald Trump, the sexist, racist climate change denier, would destroy the NHS and our possibilities to stop climate change.

They are genocidally and suicidally greedy for money and power and don't care that over fifty million people in Africa (the equivalent of three-quarters of the UK population) are already going hungry because of previously unheard of climate catastrophes, or even that unprecedented numbers of people in Britain are being flooded or surviving on foodbanks. Even Dominic Cummings has spelled this out, saying Tory MPs "don't care about these poor people, they don't care about the NHS."[1]

I want to tell you a few things about recent Jewish history which have been censored by apartheid Israel. One big event that has been misrepresented is the Battle of Cable Street.[2] The East End of London had Irish and Jewish immigrants. The Irish Catholics were likely to be dockers and the European Jews sweatshop workers, for example, in the garment industry. They had a good understanding and supported each other. When the fascist Blackshirts attempted to march through the East End, the Irish and the Jews fought alongside each other and drove the fascists out. Those who represented Jewish nationalism rather than traditional Jewish internationalism told the Jewish community to stay home. But the Jewish working class came out with their Irish comrades and won the day. On the eightieth anniversary of that great victory, the Israeli ambassador, who had been the spokesman for the bombing of Gaza that killed over two thousand people, tried to claim the Battle of Cable Street for Israel.

I grew up in the US in the thirties when the Nazis came to power in Germany. Among the first to be put in concentration camps were Jewish people, not only because they were Jewish but because they were trade unionists, socialists, communists, anti-war, anti-Nazi, lesbian, and gay.

There was a tradition among Jews, wherever we were in the world, that we stood with every underdog, every fighter for freedom, every struggler against racism and other discrimination. To quote Marek Edelman, one of the leaders of the Warsaw Ghetto uprising, "To be a Jew means always being with the oppressed and never the oppressors."

Imperialist and militarist Israel has hidden that history and replaced it with political alliances with dictators and far-right regimes, beginning with Trump, Viktor Orbán, etc., and charges of antisemitism against anyone left-wing. The latest is their connection with the genocidal Myanmar regime, which they helped arm and train, which raped, tortured, and even burned alive Rohingya people, driving hundreds of thousands out of their homes and out of their country. Israel's ambassador to Myanmar tweeted "Good luck" to Aung San Suu Kyi, who is testifying at the International Court of Human Rights on behalf of the military which committed these atrocities.[3] The mainstream media has censored out any reference to this alliance.

How is it possible that we can even consider the views on antisemitism or any other human rights issue from supporters of such a barbaric apartheid regime?

Haaretz, the most truthful Israeli daily newspaper, has published an article by one of its editors saying that there has been a "contract" on Corbyn since his election as leader of the Labour Party.[4] Anyone who cares about Jewish people anywhere should take this very seriously.

There has also been a "contract" against you, Chris, as a vocal, effective, and principled supporter of Corbyn and his policies. It is scandalous that you have been denied a platform, as venues cancelled meetings where you were to speak following threats and false accusations of antisemitism. And when Greg Philo of Glasgow University Media Group and other academics showed how much the biased media has been allowed to influence public opinion on the basis of lies and misinformation, they also were denied a venue to issue the book with their findings by Waterstones bookshop.[5] Professor Philo said, "The next step is book burning."

We are in the midst of a witch-hunt where the witch-hunters attacking both the Labour leadership and the hundreds of thousands who elected them are both inside and outside the party, supported by the corporate media, beginning with the Murdoch press and extending to the BBC and the *Guardian*.

Much like the fifties in the US under Joe McCarthy, attacks are launched against anyone who speaks up, lies are presented as truths, accusations equal evidence, and denial proves guilt. I lost my job in a factory because they knew I was a socialist, and the man I came to England to marry, CLR James, had been deported for being an anti-Stalinist socialist.

There's one letter that won't make headlines. It is from Rabbi Mayer Weinberger on behalf of the executive board of the United European Jews. He "totally rejects and condemns" comments that British Jews are "gripped by anxiety" at the thought of a Labour government, saying that "such assertions are due to propaganda with a political and ideological agenda." He thanks Corbyn for his "acts of solidarity for the Jewish community over many years."[6] Subsequently, he and his family have been threatened with harm.

How much do people believe the lies of the Tory media? We won't know until the election. But we do know that many people know the difference between what the media tells them and their own reality, and your campaign strengthens them and all of us to stick to our guns and work for a Corbyn victory.

Power to the people against the exploiters, the polluters, and the warmongers.

Notes

1 Film footage of Boris Johnson's closest adviser saying this was shown during the election campaign; see Michael Gove, *Andrew Marr Show* (transcript), November 24, 2019, accessed September 26, 2020, http://news.bbc.co.uk/1/shared/bsp/hi/pdfs/24111901.pdf.

2 On Sunday, October 4, 1936, the working class in the East End of London famously clashed with the Metropolitan Police, who were protecting Oswald Mosley's British Union of Fascists marching in Cable Street.

3 "Good Luck in Your Genocide Trial" (editorial), *Haaretz*, November 29, 2019, accessed September 26, 2020, https://www.haaretz.com/opinion/editorial/good-luck-in-your-genocide-trial-1.8196994; "Israel has issued a gag order against the country's High Court, which will now be forced to keep secret details of its ruling on a petition against arms sales to Myanmar"; "Israel Court Gagged, Details of Ruling on Arms Sales to Myanmar Remain Secret," Middle East Monitor, September 27, 2017, accessed September 26, 2020, https://tinyurl.com/ybale7gp.https://tinyurl.com/ybale7gp.

4 Gideon Levy, "Opinion: The Contract on Corbyn," *Haaretz*, November 28, 2019, accessed September 26, 2020, https://www.haaretz.com/opinion/.premium-the-contract-on-corbyn-1.8192769.

5 Greg Philo, Mike Berry, Justin Schlosberg, Antony Lerman, and David Miller, *Bad News for Labour: Antisemitism, the Party and Public Belief* (London: Pluto Press, 2019).

6 Rabbi Mayer Weinberger, "Pan European Jewish Organisation Sends Letter of Support to Corbyn," SKWAWKBOX, November 27, 2019, accessed September 26, 2020, https://skwawkbox.org/2019/11/27/pan-european-jewish-organisation-sends-letter-of-support-to-corbyn; Rabbi Weinberger's attached letter on United European Jews letterhead is dated November 26, 2019.

Why the Movement Lost the Election and What Followed (2020)

with Nina López

In December 2019, Boris Johnson won the general election, and our hopes for a socialist government evaporated. But we had got very near in 2017, and in 2019 we had hoped, despite predictions, that we could win. We now have to come to terms with what defeated us at the polls.

In June 2016, the Tory government held a referendum to decide whether or not the UK should remain in the European Union. The government had campaigned to remain and expected to win. But the leave vote, driven by extreme right-wing forces within and beyond the Tory party, won and the prime minister resigned.

Jeremy Corbyn, like most Labour MPs, had campaigned hard for "remain." He bore no responsibility for Brexit, but Labour MPs found it convenient to put the blame on Corbyn in order to push him out. They passed a vote of no confidence which triggered a second leadership election, less than a year after he'd won the first. This time against one candidate.

One hundred and thirty thousand were disqualified from voting by a party bureaucracy hostile to Corbyn. The membership was furious at this new attempt to reverse their original decision. They voted for Corbyn again by an even larger majority.

Surely, now the road was clear for the transformation of the party by a change of personnel in parliament and in the party machinery at last reflecting the will of the members. They expected their leadership to use the power they had given it to draw a line under Blair's New Labour and clean out the party of the Blairites who had colluded with the Tories against Corbyn.

This didn't happen. Instead, the attacks on Corbyn continued. The media, quoting some of his own MPs, accused him of being unelectable and, in the same breath, dangerous were he to be elected! (He was called a "terrorist" who had connections with the IRA and was "friends" with Hamas.) The opinion polls seemed to confirm that the public shared these views.

Believing the polls, in 2017, the Tories called a snap general election to finish up with Corbyn. But despite all predictions, Labour nearly won, destroying the Tory majority in parliament.

Corbyn's resilience and a radical manifesto that promised to reverse austerity and to renationalize all major services, from the railways to water and the post office, but above all to reverse the creeping privatization of the NHS and to return to free university education by abolishing tuition fees and reinstating student grants had inspired millions of voters. That summer, Glastonbury, the UK's biggest music festival, resonated to the refrain of "Oh, Jeremy Corbyn!"

Corbyn seemed unassailable now.

The membership had been organizing for some time to demand mandatory reselection of MPs—an issue that had dogged the Labour Party almost from its beginnings. Under Tony Blair, candidates were parachuted into constituencies from headquarters to the fury of local Labour voters.

At the 2018 party conference, mandatory reselection was finally on the agenda, and the expectation was that it would win, changing everything. At last, some of Labour's right-wing MPs would be replaced and the rest would be under manners.

But in the name of pulling people together, that is of keeping the right-wing MPs on board, a compromise was worked out at the top—including the heads of some unions which had previously supported mandatory reselection. The membership was faced with a watered-down motion that thwarted their widely expressed will. The majority of members voted against it, but this was not enough to defeat the union bloc vote. We were all gutted.

Once again, the right-wing MPs were protected. As a result, they went for the jugular. All along their weapon of choice against the Labour membership, which was overwhelmingly anti-racist and pro-Palestinian, had been the charge of antisemitism: led by the Zionists, orchestrated by the media, and confirmed in interview after interview by Labour's anti-Corbyn MPs. There were weeks, especially before elections, when every newscast and bulletin would headline Corbyn's "problem with antisemitism."

Corbyn was accused of enabling and even supporting antisemites within the party. Despite a long anti-imperialist and anti-racist track record, Corbyn and McDonnell never tackled this politically. They never publicly questioned the motivations of those attacking them—right-wing Labour MPs, Tories, and

Zionist organizations acting for Israel (and Trump) against the Palestinians. They never called on or even referred to those Jewish members who repudiated the charge of antisemitism. Worse: they publicly disagreed with those who spoke out, apologizing for crimes that neither they nor the membership had committed. It was painful, frightening and mystifying to watch the leadership submit to the enemy. It strengthened the right-wing in every constituency against Corbynistas—people censored themselves to avoid "making it worse" for a leadership under siege which seemed unable or unwilling to defend itself but also to avoid being a target themselves and then disowned by the leadership.

Yet the evidence of collusion between right-wing MPs and the Israeli embassy was known at least since January 2017. An Al Jazeera covert investigation, "The Lobby,"[1] had exposed Israeli interference in British politics, including the embassy's close connection with the Jewish Labour Movement and Labour Party MPs who were accusing Corbyn of antisemitism. (The official in charge of this subversion boasted of having a million pounds to pay for MPs' junkets to Israel.) Unbelievably this was never pursued.

Instead the right-wing was allowed to call the shots. The major Zionist organizations and newspapers demanded that Corbyn should go, and even had demonstrations in front of parliament, which many Labour MPs attended.

In 2018, Corbyn was pressed to adopt the full IHRA definition of antisemitism,[2] which aims to silence criticism of Israel and criminalize the Palestinian-led BDS (boycott, divestment, and sanctions) movement. Corbyn had resisted, wanting Labour's National Executive Committee (NEC) to adopt an additional statement that said:

> It cannot be considered racist to treat Israel like any other State or assess its conduct against the standards of international law. Nor should it be regarded as antisemitic to describe Israel, its policies or the circumstances around its foundation as racist.[3]

Twenty-four Palestinian trade unions, organizations, and networks representing the majority in Palestinian civil society appealed to Labour and its affiliated trade unions to reject IHRA as an attempt to

> erase Palestinian history, demonize solidarity with the Palestinian struggle for freedom, justice and equality, suppress freedom of expression, and shield Israel's far-right regime. . .
>
> We expect [social-justice oriented political parties, like Labour, and progressive trade unions] to help us in the struggle against apartheid

and for equal rights of all humans irrespective of identity. Is this too much to expect?[4]

Members from seventeen London Momentum groups called a rally, including Jewish anti-Zionists, Palestinians, and many others, outside Labour HQ during the NEC's deliberations.

The NEC, including the head of Momentum, ignored the Palestinian appeal and the party members demonstrating and rejected Corbyn's statement. The full IHRA, with all its examples, was agreed by consensus—there was no vote. It became Labour policy, further emboldening the (Zionist) right-wing. As in the 1960s, when Labour Prime Minister Harold Wilson called Ian Smith, the PM of apartheid Rhodesia, "our kith and kin," the Labour Party supported apartheid.

The Momentum membership was undermined and bypassed by its leadership who, instead of attacking the right-wing Zionists who were attacking Corbyn, attacked the left-wing Jews who were defending him. Momentum was reduced to an electoral machine (as the membership generally had been before Corbyn), far from the transmission belt between the party and the wider movement which some of us worked for. Encouraging people to put themselves forward for local government or parliamentary positions became the focus. Though filling positions is necessary for any party aiming to govern, making this the focus attracts the ambitious rather than the principled.

A witch-hunt was launched against any member, especially Jewish members, who supported Palestinians and opposed Israeli apartheid. Some were forced to resign, others were suspended or expelled.[5] At least one constituency which had organized to get rid of its hated right-wing MP received a call from the leader's office demanding they drop it, and its officers, including a Jewish chair, were later investigated for antisemitism.

Days before the 2019 general election, the UK Chief Rabbi (supported by the Archbishop of Canterbury) told Jews not to vote Labour, because they would be in danger under a Corbyn government. (He had previously welcomed Boris Johnson into Downing Street, despite Johnson's Islamophobic, antisemitic, racist, and sexist record.) [6] The Chief Rabbi later spoke against Bernie Sanders, advising Zionists in the US to do what "Jews of the United Kingdom have done [against Corbyn] . . . and the results are there to be seen."[7]

Many on the left have blamed Labour's defeat on Brexit. Boris Johnson succeeded in making "Get Brexit done" central to the 2019 election, and Labour could not win on that basis.

That's a fact. But it is the four years of unrelenting daily attacks from Labour's right-wing that reinforced Tory power, proving fatal in undermining Corbyn's credibility and strength of purpose. Many were MPs who had supported Blair's wars, privatizations, anti-immigration laws, and welfare cuts (including against single mothers and people with disabilities), who had stood with the Tories on defending Israeli apartheid and on arming Saudi Arabia against Yemen. These Tories within Labour had based their political lives on preventing the direction the party had taken under Corbyn.

Their mantra that Corbyn "is not a leader,"[8] amplified by the Tory and even the liberal media, and Corbyn's refusal to decisively reject the charge of antisemitism made him look weak and guilty. Much of the electorate became increasingly convinced that they shouldn't vote for him.

This, the most principled and honest politician, was dismissed, because "If his own MPs don't trust him, how can we?" The most pro–working class, pro–climate justice manifesto, full of policies which were popular and carefully costed, was voted down as wishful thinking and untrustworthy, since Corbyn was "useless."

Boris Johnson, on the other hand, was upper-class, brash, arrogant, ruthlessly ambitious, a proven liar, and an open racist—a leader. The Tories loved him.

Of course, the media manipulated the electorate. And now, like Trump did in the US, they can manipulate through social media as well—a whole new level of technology with which to distort reality.

Three months after the election was lost, an 850-page report was leaked detailing how the party's central office had sabotaged Labour's chances of winning the 2017 election—losing by a mere 2,500 votes![9] Heartbreaking.

The report exposed the most vile racism and sexism in Labour's headquarters, especially against Black women MPs on the left, by some of those making accusations of antisemitism. Why had they been allowed to get away with it?

The hundreds of thousands who came into the party to support a socialist leadership were ready for something new and worked for it. We were convinced we could win. Corbyn and McDonnell had been shown not to be personally ambitious—a rare quality in politics—and could be called on to use their position as MPs to back the movement anywhere. Why then, when they had the power of the mass membership, did they apologize to the defenders of Israeli apartheid, which they had always opposed? Why did they discourage pro-Palestinian members, including Jewish ones, from taking on the Israeli agents? Did it have anything to do with some unions' historic connections with Israeli unions?[10] Did they really think that the only way to keep the party together was to give in to the right-wing?

Whatever the reasons, the movement was bypassed and no explanation was ever given to it.

It is painful to face that Labour lost the 2019 general election, since winning could have changed so much, not only in the UK but in the world balance of class power. Of course, if socialism had won, the reactionary forces nationally and internationally would have sabotaged every attempt to implement the manifesto.[11] But a movement could have defeated them. And the movement in a number of countries would have been strengthened against extreme right-wing governments.

Instead, State power has shifted to the right in the UK and in the Labour Party. Labour's new leader was voted in after presenting himself as a safe pair of hands who would retain the most popular manifesto policies. (We never believed it.) Most importantly he has the media's approval. At the moment of Labour's electoral defeat, this seemed to many to be more important than what the party would now stand for. Soon after being elected, he reversed a party conference decision condemning the occupation of Kashmir in order to back India's racist prime minister. When the Black Lives Matter protests began, he called them not a movement but a "moment," and declared that his "support for the police is very, very strong."[12] He has demonstrated this by instructing his MPs not to oppose the "licence to kill" bill, which allows agents and informants to commit any crime—rape, torture, murder—with impunity not only in the name of national security but UK economic interests.[13] On a list of fifty world Zionist influencers it turns out he is fourteenth.[14] He organized for Labour to pay hundreds of thousands of pounds to staff who had sued the party after being accused of undermining Corbyn's leadership and the 2017 election, despite legal advice that the party had a strong case.

Some of the members who joined Labour for Corbyn have left in disgust. Others have stayed in "to fight." In or out, we maintain connections with the serious people we have worked with in the party.[15]

Since the Global Women's Strike and Payday are non-party political, why did some of us join Labour? Because in the UK a grassroots movement appeared almost overnight to elect a socialist government—we could not stand outside of that movement. It was led by two politicians with whom we'd had working relationships. (This was especially true of John McDonnell.) They had both formally welcomed the creation of the International Jewish Anti-Zionist Network (IJAN); Corbyn had chaired a meeting in parliament called by IJAN, with an Auschwitz survivor who was an IJAN member and a Palestinian academic speaking from Gaza;[16] both had consistently helped to stop deportations; Corbyn had intervened to stay the hand of the Mexican army threatening a Oaxaca rural community (some of us were there and had called him); McDonnell had supported sex workers' campaign for decriminalization, defended the benefits of people with disabilities, single mothers, and asylum seekers.

We have always used the State against the State, that is, used whatever official power we can connect with to advance the movement without compromising our principles. (This requires that we ourselves don't wish to be the State.)

Our international network was excited to be part of fighting for a real socialist government in the UK—it represented the possibility of some support and protection for us. In the same way, we were excited at Bernie Sanders' campaign for the Democratic nomination in the US, which had also called forth a movement.

Some people debate whether engaging with parliamentary democracy is useful or a waste of time or even a corrupting influence. For us, it depends on the situation, not on a fixed ideology: Would it help build the movement at that particular moment? Our non-party campaigning work never changed direction and, if anything, grew when some of us joined Labour.

We don't regret engaging with the Labour Party as we did, though losing this movement battle has been very hard, since we came so near to winning and so much was at stake.

A Boris Johnson government is catastrophic, especially when the Labour leadership is as pro-Israeli apartheid as the Tories, thus aligning the UK, government and opposition, with the extreme right.

The world was then faced with the coronavirus pandemic, which has killed more than one million people and is being used to widen the powers of governments. In the UK, emergency laws were passed that allow local government to withdraw services from children, disabled, and elderly people without parliamentary accountability—now the most vulnerable have even fewer rights.[17]

Discussions about the causes of the crisis go well beyond the virus. Finally, we are hearing about how our immune systems have been undermined by the air we breathe, the food we eat, the houses we live in, the work we do, the poverty we suffer, the low wages we get, and the racism and discrimination we meet and confront at every level, which explains why people of colour are twice as likely to die from Covid-19. The pandemic has confirmed that governments, whatever they say, don't care how many of us live or die, especially if we are elderly, disabled and/or the "wrong" race. It also confirmed that we are deeply dependent on carers; that if we want to prioritize life, we must prioritize those who care for life—and not only during a pandemic. This is a new awareness, but it is still to be realized in cash for those who do this work.

Just as unexpected was the Black Lives Matter movement which burst out in the US and spread around the world. First of all, in support of Black lives, rapidly extending to Brown, Indigenous, Palestinian, and Haitians lives . . . then against every racial injustice and increasingly *any* injustice anywhere. In the UK and elsewhere, the true history of slavery, empire, and police violence is being spelt out as never before.[18]

Women have been in the majority in many of the demonstrations. In the US, as the repression escalated, women came in as mothers to stand between the federal troops and the protestors. They said, "When George Floyd called for his mama, he was calling for all mamas." This is not the first time women, the carers, have played this protective role.[19]

Black women undoubtedly led the mobilization that defeated Trump at the polls—a victory that has changed what we can hope for. In the UK, young women of colour have been at the forefront of demonstrations, some already trained by their participation in the school climate strikes of the past two years.[20] Greta Thunberg, who started the school strikes in Sweden, welcomed the Black Lives Matter movement: "People are starting to find their voice, to sort of understand that they can actually have an impact." For many young people, and increasingly for other sectors, climate justice and racial justice are inseparable. Many millions for whom Greta Thunberg is a point of reference will agree with her view that: "The climate and ecological crisis cannot be solved within today's political and economic system. . . . That isn't an opinion. That's a fact."[21]

Movements are bursting out in many places, feeding each other, reshaping politics and possibilities for the clashes we are destined to face.

Notes

1   Al Jazeera Investigative Unit, "The Lobby: Young Friends of Israel, part 1," January 10, 2017, accessed September 26, 2020, https://www.aljazeera.com/investigations/thelobby.

2   In 2016, the International Holocaust Remembrance Alliance issued a controversial "working definition" of antisemitism, which various governments have adopted. Even Kenneth Stern, the man who drafted it, has condemned its use to curb political and free speech. The definition includes several examples conflating criticism of Israel with antisemitism.

3   Dan Sabbagh, "Labour Adopts IHRA Definition in Full," *Guardian*, September 4, 2018, accessed October 8, 2020, https://www.theguardian.com/politics/2018/sep/04/labour-adopts-ihra-antisemitism-definition-in-full.

4   "Labour Must Reject Biased IHRA Definition That Stifles Advocacy for Palestinian Rights," August 28, 2018, accessed October 8, 2020, https://www.opendemocracy.net/en/opendemocracyuk/labour-must-reject-biased-ihra-definition-that-stifles-advocacy.

5   Among them, tellingly, the famous and popular former London mayor Ken Livingstone, a strong and important Corbyn ally, Jackie Walker, a Black Jewish woman, and MP Chris Williamson.

6   Boris Johnson's record of bigotry, antisemitism, and far-right politics is well-documented; "Boris Johnson's Record of Bigotry, Antisemitism and Far-Right Politics Must Not Be Forgotten" (letter), *Guardian*, December 11, 2019, accessed September 26, 2020, https://tinyurl.com/yyf4lyfv; the letter was signed by twenty-four prominent people.

7   Mathilde Frot, "Chief Rabbi Ephraim Mirvis Calls for Unity against Antisemitism in AIPAC Speech," *Jewish News*, March 4, 2020, accessed September 26, 2020, https://tinyurl.com/y3qbm3w7.

8   He had, of course, done what a leader is supposed to do: built Labour into the largest political party by far in Europe.

9   John McDonnell, "The Revelations in the Leaked Labour Report Are a Genuine Scandal," *Guardian*, April 21, 2020, accessed September 26, 2020, https://tinyurl.com/y8jq6jmp. It had been previously claimed that Corbyn had lost by 2,227 votes; Harriet Agerholm, "Jeremy Corbyn Was Just 2,227 Votes from Chance to Be Prime Minister," *Independent*, June 9, 2017, accessed October 8, 2020, https://tinyurl.com/y7yxj99z.

10   Some union leaders did speak out against the antisemitism allegations, notably Mark Serwotka, general secretary of the Public and Commercial Services Union and a strong Corbyn ally. Days after being elected president of the Trades Union Congress (TUC), he told a Palestine Solidarity Campaign meeting: "[I]nstead of being on the front foot, denouncing [Israeli] atrocities . . . we have had a summer of asking ourselves whether leading Labour movement people are in any way anti-Semitic. . . . I'm not a conspiracy theorist, but I'll tell you what—one of the best forms of actually trying to hide from the atrocities that you are committing is to go on the offensive and to actually create a story that does not exist for people on this platform, the trade union movement or for the leader of the Labour Party"; Benjamin Kentish, "Labour Antisemitism Row Was Created to 'Distract from Atrocities,' Trade Union Boss Suggests," *Independent*, September 13, 2018, accessed October 10, 2020, https://tinyurl.com/yaq12axx. Two years later the TUC voted against Israeli annexation of Palestinian land in the West Bank and called for an end to Israeli apartheid—a historic move. But by then Corbyn was no longer a threat since he was no longer leader of the Labour Party.

11   That's what they did with Labour's 1945–1951 government, but they could not stop the creation of the NHS and the rest of the Welfare State.

12   BBC Breakfast, June 29, 2020; Kuba Shand-Baptiste, "Keir Starmer's Dismissal of Defunding the Police Has Lost Him Black Support. The Problem Is, I Don't Know if He Cares?" *Independent*, July 1, 2020, accessed September 26, 2020, https://tinyurl.com/y3yj48ar.

13   Lizzie Dearden, "MPs Vote against Attempt to Ban Undercover Agents from Committing Murder, Torture and Rape," *Independent*, October 15, 2020, accessed October 18, 2020, https://tinyurl.com/yywml67v.

14   "Top 50 Zionist Influencers," Social Lite Creative LLC, accessed September 26, 2020, top50proisraelinfluencers.com.

15   In their letter of resignation, two colleagues from Women of Colour GWS wrote: "We won't campaign for a party where people of colour and anti-racists, and our movements, are maligned and attacked. We resign with immediate effect. We will continue to work with all anti-racist, anti-sexist, anti-capitalist members in the party. We need each other to build a strong enough movement to win the changes we have all been fighting for"; "Why We Are Resigning from the Labour Party (24 July)," Women of Colour Network, accessed October 15, 2020, https://womenofcolournetwork.wordpress.com/2020/07/24/why-we-are-resigning-from-the-labour-party-24-july.

16   The meeting "Never Again—For Anyone," with Dr. Hajo Meyer and Dr. Haidar Eid was held on January 27, 2010, Holocaust Memorial Day. It was part of a tour organized jointly with Scottish Palestine Solidarity Campaign.

17   The Coronavirus Act 2020 reduced the State's legal obligation to safeguard elderly and disabled people and children and introduced government impunity. Baroness Hale, retired head of the Supreme Court, criticized Parliament for "surrender[ing] control to the government at a crucial time" of "sweeping" powers and "draconian" regulations. See Owen Bowcott, Heather Stewart, and Andrew Sparrow, "Parliament Surrendered Role over Covid Emergency Laws, Says Lady Hale," *Guardian*, September 20, 2020, accessed October 15, 2020, https://tinyurl.com/y4ekr9xe.

18   For example, we are hearing for the first time that the UK payment for slave owners' loss of their human property did not end until 2015! Even Churchill, the establishment's venerated war hero, is being called on his genocidal racism, which caused the death of millions during India's famine. Lots more will emerge about the barbaric empires of "European civilization."

19   In 1936–1937, in Flint, Michigan, General Motors was the first plant to be hit by a sit-down strike. Genora Dollinger describes how she led the women to protect the strikers against police teargas. "I appealed to the women . . . 'Break through those police lines and come down here and stand beside your husbands and your brothers and your uncles and your sweethearts.' In the dusk, I could barely see one woman walking down the battle zone. And as soon as that happened there were other women who followed down, then more men. And there was a big roar of victory. From that night, I decided that women could form an emergency brigade and every time there was a threatened battle, we could make a difference. . . . After GM workers organized, Chrysler followed, then Ford, then the rubber workers, then the glass workers, then steel was organized. And all these formed the Congress of Industrial Organizations. These initials, CIO, stood for power"; Susan Rosenthal, "Striking Flint: Genora (Johnson) Dollinger Remembers the 1936–37 General Motors Sit-Down Strike . . . as Told to Susan Rosenthal," *Socialist Review* 191 (November 1995), accessed September 26, 2020, https://www.marxists.org/history/etol/newspape/amersocialist/genora.htm.

During the trial of the Mangrove Nine in London, in 1971, there was a Black women's march against police harassment of supporters outside the court; this ended the harassment.

In the Bronx, a Black Families Matter march accused the Administration for Children's Services of acting as an arm of the police, using poverty to take children from their mothers.

20 Jessica Murray and Aamna Mohdin, "It Was Empowering': Teen BLM Activists on Learning the Ropes at School Climate Strikes," *Guardian*, August 11, 2020, accessed September 26, 2020, https://tinyurl.com/y6392wc8.

21 Jessica Murray, "'Tipping point': Greta Thunberg Hails Black Lives Matter Protests," *Guardian*, June 20, 2020, accessed September 26, 2020, https://www.theguardian.com/environment/2020/jun/20/tipping-point-greta-thunberg-hails-black-lives-matter-protests.

Sex, Race, Class . . . and Autonomy
(2020)

The Organizational Strategy of Autonomy

The Wages for Housework Campaign (WFH) has within it a number of different sectors which have their own autonomous organizations but share a political perspective and organizing principles. Each sector represents itself, and at the same time it also represents the whole Campaign.

Looking back at our history, we can trace how we came to create this kind of campaigning organization. It was not planned but developed as our campaigning developed.

The WFH Campaign began on the assumption that almost all women did unwaged housework, but there are widely differing levels of social power, incomes, workloads, etc. among us, which must be addressed organizationally if we are to work together. So anti-racism, like anti-sexism and the undermining of all power relations, was integral to the Campaign from its very beginning. Divisions of race, nationality, income, Global South and Global North, urban/rural, age, genders, sexuality, disabilities, (il)legality . . . and any combination of these—the more such divisions are addressed, internally and working with others, the less we are divided by them, and the more the power of each sector becomes a power for all.

We also began as an international network in a few countries. Most people are not aware of how racist are our assumptions when we are divided nationally and linguistically. We worked hard to take full account of the struggles for autonomy of other sectors, including nationalities. In the UK, for example, London dominates not only Wales, Scotland, and the North of Ireland, but even the North of England. Even the awareness of this lifts us. Like everything we attempt, our striving enhances our effort.

Soon after we came together as a campaign, I saw that you can begin anywhere, with any sector, and embrace every sector.

By the time we began in March 1972, we had all seen massive liberation movements in the Global South and among different sectors in the North: Black, welfare rights (led by Black mothers), women, gay, waged workers, students, people with disabilities. . .[1] People from different movements temporarily came together internationally, for example, against the Vietnam War and against apartheid in Southern Africa. But other than that, there were clashes between sectors (even left organizations were often furious when women members took their autonomy, for example), and competition for prominence and resources.

Race Today, a Black movement publication in the UK, which had just been taken over by the grassroots, published "Sex, Race, and Class" in its January 1974 issue,[2] proclaiming on its entire cover: "Power to the sisters!" In it, I was making the case for autonomy, including Black women's autonomy, while attacking separatism as an expression of competition between sectors. Working in the anti-racist and anti-imperialist movements—always prioritizing women—had been an education for me. Every movement, it seemed, had tensions within it between various sectors; there was clearly class conflict and other power relations which were undermining but rarely acknowledged— between the waged (mostly men) and the unwaged (mostly women), between the higher and the lower waged, between the industrial world (mostly waged) and the non-industrial world (mostly unwaged) . . .[3]

To drive the movement forward, the autonomy of different sectors was crucial so that the more socially powerful within the movement could not assume dominance over the less powerful, hiding the leadership that comes from the more grassroots experience. We could strive for unity by ensuring that each sector visibly contributed its experience, tactics and possibilities, thus refusing to be dominated by others. (Horizontalism is no substitute for autonomy; it presumes that power relations can be abolished either by goodwill or by democratic voting—if only! They are too deep-rooted in the very structure of capitalism to be so easily overcome.)

To be in the WFH Campaign you had to stand for autonomy of every (grassroots) sector—and with time this became almost instinctive among us.

Lesbian Women

In 1975, I got a call from Toronto WFH Campaign to say that a group of lesbian women thought Wages for Housework was the political perspective they agreed with and asked could they join as a group?

At that time the Women's Liberation Movement in the UK and US were often openly hostile to lesbian women. Some of the most prominent feminists thought that associating Women's Liberation with lesbians would discredit the feminist cause and lessen its power rather than build it.[4] At the same time, lesbian separatism was strong, and many lesbian women wanted nothing to do with straight women, whom they considered to be sleeping with the enemy; some even objected to male children being allowed in childcare.

Without thinking much about it, we assumed that everyone had the right to choose who they slept with and, in any case, lesbian or not, as women we were all in a power relation with men and the society generally. In our discussions of the Toronto lesbians' proposal, one woman expressed a view, which others shared: lesbian women are a power for straight women, because men will know we have another option.

Lesbian women were, of course, more likely to be independent of men. For example, they didn't have to convince husbands or boyfriends that they had a right to be politically active. That explained why a few years later so many of the women at Greenham Common Women's Peace Camp and other feminist initiatives were lesbian.

At the same time, lesbian women were more vulnerable to persecution for breaking the mould by rejecting men as partners. (Some men would say that what lesbians needed was to be raped, as that would set them straight.) And if the authorities found out that you, as a mother, were lesbian, especially if you were in a lesbian relationship, they could take your children into care on the grounds that you were an "unfit" mother or give them to the father who might be furious at having been left—and for a woman! Nobody in the Campaign thought twice about defending the right of a lesbian mother—or any mother—to her own children.[5] We not only gave birth to them but cared for them, worried about them and fought for them; they belonged with us, whatever our sexuality.

Our unequivocal support for lesbian mothers was an important part of what had attracted the lesbian women in Toronto to want to be with us. We also made clear that women who were bisexual were welcome in our international network.

Women in the WFH Campaign (in Toronto, London, Italy, and the US) thought it would be great if the lesbian women joined as a group—it was a new and exciting departure. Some of the Toronto women visited London in July 1975 for our first international conference, and a couple of romances soon began. What emerged from these discussions was that Wages for Housework was also a lesbian perspective, since the wages we were demanding for the work that we were all doing was our passport to being able to live our own sexuality. Other women who had not considered lesbianism were ready to, once they had the power of an organization.

So it was that the first organization to be autonomous within the Campaign was Lesbians for Wages for Housework, which they renamed Wages Due Lesbians (WDL). Our badge said, "Coming Out in Millions with Wages for Housework," by which we meant that if women had financial independence many more of us would be with women.

Problems arose when the new WDL made decisions without reference to other sectors in the Campaign and what else the Campaign stood for and was fighting for. That was not our view of autonomy. While we would not tolerate any anti-lesbian sentiments or attacks, we could not allow any sector to ignore the interests of any other sector. We understood autonomy to mean that within the perspective we shared, lesbian women would have their view on every issue and express it within the Campaign, as everybody else did. It was not a competition for power or influence. We aimed not to reorganize the order of the hierarchy but to undermine it, beginning with refusing it in our political relationships within the Campaign.

The question always was that each of us had to be accountable to all of us. To concentrate on your own situation could never mean that you did not consider the impact you could be having on what others faced and were struggling for and against. We argued it out and concluded that for any sector to prioritize their needs over the needs of any other sector was separatism, not autonomy.

In 1976, the Canadian government wanted to freeze the Baby Bonus, what in the UK was called Family Allowance and later Child Benefit. The Toronto Campaign designed a beautiful folded petition which included a sheet with a statement from a lesbian mother about why she wanted the Baby Bonus and how that money was helpful in her living a lesbian life. Going door to door, women could read it or ignore it, but it was available to them. The Campaign women noticed that some women were very interested in it; they were likely to be lesbian mothers who were still in the closet or mothers who were considering lesbianism.

In both London and Toronto, we had street events where one of the speakers identified herself as lesbian. In the mid-seventies that was still unusual, but we had no problem with the audience. It was our job, lesbian or straight, to make clear that whatever our sexuality we suffered similarly as women and could work together. Lesbian or straight, we both got lower pay than men, for example.

We had seen that at different moments the struggle of a particular sector is everybody's priority because it is urgent to all of us for that sector to win over the powers that be. In 1988, the UK government under Thatcher tried to turn the clock back by introducing Section 28 of the Local Government Act, which banned the teaching "of homosexuality as a pretended family," thus threatening the jobs of lesbian and gay teachers, witch-hunting students, and cutting services. Wages Due Lesbians took the lead in bringing the UK WFH Campaign into the movement that ultimately defeated Thatcher's legislation.[6]

The important principle which was established was that whatever our sector, whatever discrimination or other disadvantage our sectors suffered and we concentrated on opposing, we wanted the money for all of us for work all of us were doing, and we needed each other in order to win. At the same time, the specific discriminations raised by any sector within the Campaign were incorporated into what the whole Campaign stood against.

Day to day, each organization acts as a point of reference on their struggle for the whole Campaign.

The principles established when WDL came in served us well when, in 1975, two other sectors asked to be autonomous organizations within the Campaign.

Sex Workers

The first was the English Collective of Prostitutes (ECP)—women sex workers who were responding to the massive occupation of churches by sex workers in France and some parts of Switzerland.[7] Not long after, a group of Black sex workers founded the New York Prostitutes Collective, which became multiracial and national and changed its name to the US Prostitutes Collective (US PROS).

We were faced once again with having to distinguish autonomy from separatism. The target of the struggle of sex workers was criminalization, which gave the police a licence for constant persecution and prosecution. It was what the whole Campaign had to learn about and stand against. (I in particular, since the ECP had asked me to be their spokeswoman as none of the sex workers could be public at the time.) The burning injustice of criminalization became the occasion for some sex workers to claim "special" status which would absolve them of the need to be accountable—that is, to take the rest of us into account. We discussed it, and sex worker members soon agreed with what we were saying, since they felt more powerful and protected if they had the backing of the rest of the Campaign for their struggle for decriminalization, which was new at the time. Some of the sex workers were women of colour and/or lesbian, which enhanced both WDL and ECP/US PROS. They now relate to a number of sex worker organizations, especially Empower in Thailand.[8]

Black Women

In 1975, Black Women for Wages for Housework (BWWFH) was formed and joined the Campaign.[9] At that time, in the UK, many people of colour who organized against racism, including, for example, immigrants from Asia, the Caribbean, and Turkey identified as Black.

The question of how women of different races were to work together despite the power relations among us in a racist society, that is what the WFH Campaign had addressed from its very inception in 1972 and what we continue to work out collectively and ongoingly.

The formation of BWWFH within the Campaign represented a break with the de facto white ghetto which generally characterized the women's movement in Europe and North America at that time. It also represented a challenge to various racial divisions among women of colour. In most societies, the class hierarchy takes the form of divisions of sex, race, ethnicity, language, immigration status, sexuality, etc. In her anthology, Andaiye (from Guyana) summed up the tragic impact of race divisions: they "have derailed the struggle of Guyanese people for much of the past sixty years."[10] (See "The Uses of Autonomy" below.) Similar statements could describe many other movements in the world. It is a central issue most movements face. From the beginning BWWFH worked to bring together people of colour who are the majority of people internationally. In the UK, members were both of African and Indian descent; in the US, one member was Native American.

The two women who formed BWWFH, both of African descent, one a lesbian and the other an immigrant from the Caribbean, were soon able to act as spokeswomen for the whole Campaign.[11]

By this time, we were more experienced, and we understood autonomy much more concretely, so separatism was not the problem it had been. The Black women had considered joining because the autonomy the Campaign offered was a guarantee of both anti-racism as well as anti-sexism—we stood with women (of any colour) against sexism (of any colour), and we stood with women and men of colour against racism anywhere, beginning of course within the Campaign.

We had to explore what it meant in practice for WFH to be anti-racist. The white women had to learn to notice and identify racism, which was (and is) pervasive but often disguised or denied, and how to expose and oppose it. This was daily useful, especially for a campaign determined to be international. We also learnt to distinguish between those people of colour who were committed to anti-racism and those who used the rhetoric of anti-racism to play power games, fuel separatism, narrow nationalism, and/or advance their careers. These distinctions were paralleled in every sector, and learning to spot and oppose them was an important part of our political education.

One of the functions of our autonomous organizations was to urge and protect the autonomy of the movements they belonged to from separatism.

The existence of BWWFH ensured that the whole Campaign was committed to anti-racism. We were known for insisting on anti-racism, and sometimes were hated for it.

Soon after BWWFH was formed, predictably, there was a split on race in WFH. It came to a head in 1977 in New York and reverberated in Italy (see Margaret Prescod's introduction to this volume).

Women with Disabilities

Women with visible and invisible disabilities—WinVisible—formed their own autonomous group in 1984, enriching the Campaign's perspective in every country, as other sectors had done earlier. Coping with disability is work in itself, but an inaccessible society adds work which is avoidable and infuriating, confining people and limiting participation and other possibilities. (If they can send a man to the moon, they can make public transport accessible!) Disabled women, especially those who are mothers, also do caring work for others. As with every discrimination, low status makes life harder and less satisfying—it is a crime against humanity. The autonomy of the disability rights movement made visible that disabled people are a sector of millions. The Bhopal gas disaster in India in 1984 exposed how much disabilities are the result of negligence—industrial, environmental, medicinal (like Thalidomide prescribed to pregnant women)—and war.[12]

WinVisible brought together women across visible and invisible disabilities and addressed the power relations between those needing care and support and those who provide care within the family or in institutions, unwaged or for (low) wages. WinVisible made the case that disabled people have a right to support and financial independence; it has focused on defending benefits and independent living.

Payday Men

From early on, we have worked closely with men who share our perspective on payment for caring work and on autonomy. We have always said that the money to pay for unwaged caring work should come first of all from military budgets, starting with the biggest—the US. So the WFH Campaign always had an anti-war and anti-militarist perspective.

Payday, a network of men, was formed in 1976. They have focused on supporting conscientious objectors, refuseniks, and whistle-blowers against war and occupation, as well as on prisoners fighting miscarriages of justice and solitary confinement. Their first statement was in support of Women Against Rape. They are also part of Support Not Separation, speaking out against men who deny domestic violence in order to avoid prosecution and take children from their mothers (see below.)

Global Women's Strike

In 1999, we called a global women's strike for International Women's Day 2000. Women in many countries responded and took action on March 8. As a result, we became known as the Global Women's Strike (GWS), which is coordinated by the WFH Campaign. This is also when Wages Due Lesbians updated their name to Queer Strike (lesbian, bi, trans in the GWS), and Black Women for Wages for Housework became known as Women of Colour GWS. GWS groups are now based in UK (1972), US (1973), India (1992), Ireland (2000), Peru (2008), and Thailand (2015), and we relate to women and men in a number of other countries.

Creating this new kind of organization and network built on the autonomy of sectors within the working class finding ways to work together productively, including across national and language boundaries and barriers, has been a collective process which broadens all the time as different countries and sectors become involved. Wages for Housework is, therefore, much more than a demand or an academic theory—it is an international organizing strategy, from the bottom up.

Others Based at the Crossroads Women's Centres

The Campaign's perspective on women's unwaged work of caregiving, on financial dependence, and on organizing autonomously has also helped shape other groups based at the Crossroads Women's Centres, the first of which opened in London in 1975.

In 1977, a UK guardsman was given a mere six-month suspended sentence for rape so that it wouldn't ruin his "promising army career." There was an outcry. Women Against Rape (WAR),[13] which had formed the previous year, decided to hold a public rape trial in Trafalgar Square, central London, putting the criminal justice system, the government, and industry in the dock: "You uphold men's power over us in order to uphold your power over everyone."

I was not in WAR but was asked to chair the open meetings to organize the trial. When rape in marriage was raised, some women objected: it was "widening the issue" and discrediting the case against rape, which was identified as perpetrated by a stranger in a dark street. Highlighting women's financial dependence on men as central to rape, WAR wrote: "Rape like charity begins at home and spills out into the streets."[14] It was the first organization that confronted rape within the family and by men known to the victim, which has since proven to be the most common rape of all. WAR campaigned for fifteen years to win the criminalization of rape in marriage in the UK. It also uniquely spoke out against racist sexual assault, including by police and others in authority. It campaigns for non-discriminatory compensation for rape survivors and for recognition of rape as a form of torture and, therefore, grounds for political asylum. It has opposed the prosecution of rape victims disbelieved by police. WAR has stood against the charge of rape being used by the State to silence and imprison those who expose war crimes, including rape and murder.[15]

Black Women's Rape Action Project was started by BWWFH in 1991 to defend women against racist and sexual violence and to support rape survivors facing deportation. It worked closely with WAR, and they've now merged.

Legal Action for Women (LAW), a grassroots legal service, was started by the ECP after its church occupation in 1982 to defend sex workers from "police illegality and racism."[16] LAW is open to all women (and their loved ones) whatever their legal need.

Single Mothers' Self-Defence works with mothers whose welfare benefits are threatened.

In the US, the Every Mother Is a Working Mother Network was formed, and it coordinates Give Us Back Our Children in Philadelphia and Los Angeles to fight alongside mothers whose children have been taken or are threatened with removal by local government departments on spurious and discriminatory grounds.[17] About ten years later, LAW in London formed Support Not Separation, a coalition of organizations doing similar work in the UK. As in the US, poverty is used as an excuse to accuse mothers of neglect, especially if they are single mothers, women of colour, have a disability, and/or are victims of domestic violence.

From the beginning the autonomous organizations have campaigned against deportation. In 2002, asylum seekers who began to meet at our Centre in London formed the All African Women's Group (AAWG), which works closely with LAW, WAR, and WoC to support hunger strikers in detention to get the women out and the detention centres closed. In 2019, Global Women Against Deportation was formed to coordinate the anti-deportation work and end the State-imposed destitution of asylum seekers. Many deportations have been stopped, even at the airport.

Finding good accountable lawyers is a major problem faced by every sector. The groups work hard to build relationships with lawyers and other professionals of whatever gender, who are dedicated to fighting for justice and respectful of the grassroots.[18]

All of the organizations in the Campaign share the principle of collective self-help and mutual accountability, that is, campaigning with women and their loved ones not only for them, if they are ready to fight against the injustice they are suffering. Every group looks for women's financial and other entitlements in every struggle—welfare benefits, compensation, pay equity, housing, and any other resources. Each draws on the information and experience of other groups. Denial of financial entitlement is almost always key to the injustice.

We win more often than we lose because we never give up, and we are known for this. We also count and try to publicize every success—not only what resources we won but what we learnt, who we met, what sectors we brought together.

Autonomy is the best we can do for every individual member to be respected and considered when decisions are being made about what to do and how to do it. If we, in any organization, are not respectful of our own membership, we will never respect the public or the class we say we are accountable to.

This holistic approach to organizing has attracted alternative practitioners, especially of homeopathy and the Alexander Technique, to offer their skills and knowledge to our centers and networks.

Much has changed since we began in 1972. In some countries, especially of the North, lesbian women are less persecuted, and some are even integral to the power structure.[19] (We're aware that this can change.) A number of AAWG members are running away from persecution on sexuality grounds, often the legacy of British imperialism.[20] Trans women, especially women of colour and/or sex workers, bear the brunt of violent attacks and murder[21]—being a woman and, worse, the "wrong kind of woman" is again a source of discrimination in all areas of life and of rejection, even by other women. As with lesbianism, racism, sex work, and rape in marriage before it, some feminists are hostile, even bitterly hostile, to trans women. Their separatism adds fuel to the male violence against women which they reject for themselves.[22]

The hierarchy has shifted. The establishment is no longer almost exclusively white, male, upper-class, and straight. But it is no less exploitative, repressive, and psychopathic. As Queer Strike puts it: "No to pink capitalism!" Or any capitalism.

Notes

1   The gay movement grew into today's LGBTQ+ movement.

2   *Race Today* was edited by Darcus Howe. (I helped with the work, especially at the beginning.) "Sex, Race and Class" was republished as a pamphlet jointly by *Race Today* and Falling Wall Press (1975), and in Selma James, *Sex, Race, and Class* (Oakland: PM Press, 2012), 92–101

3   That was forty years ago. There have been important shifts internationally since the majority of the population that lived by subsistence farming was forced off the land and into the city where they are more dependent on finding waged work, and many more women have gone out to work and are now waged.

4   In 1969, Betty Friedan, president of the National Organization of Women (NOW) and author of *The Feminine Mystique*, (New York: W.W. Norton, 1963), referred to lesbian women as the "Lavender Menace."

5   In London, we were involved with a single mother of four who asked the State to take her children for a month or two when she was fleeing domestic violence. The local authority offered to rehouse her in a one-bedroom flat, and then refused to give the children back because the flat was too small for all of them. After months of public campaigning, mother and children were reunited and a larger flat secured. From this case we learnt a lot about fighting for women's right to our own children and the power of the State against the mother.

6   Wages Due Lesbians, *Policing the Bedroom and How to Refuse It*, (London: Crossroads Books, 1991).

7   They called themselves the French Collective of Prostitutes, and the ECP took its name from that; see Selma James, "Hookers in the House of the Lord," in Selma James, *Sex, Race, and Class*, 110.

8   The Empower Foundation was started in 1985.

9   International Black Women for Wages for Housework was one of the WFH Campaign organizations which got consultative status with the United Nations.

10   Alissa Trotz, ed., *The Point Is to Change the World: Selected Writings of Andaiye* (London: Pluto Press, 2020), x.

11   Creating an organization based on the autonomy of different sectors was worked out collectively many years before "intersectionality" made the legal case that Black women face both sexism and racism. The term intersectionality has become widely used to describe overlapping sectors and discriminations.

12 Testifying before a US congressional committee, a Payday member said that every industrial job he had ever done had left him with some disability or scar.

13 Women Against Rape at our centre in the UK is not related to Women Against Rape in the US.

14 Ruth Hall, "When Rape, Like Charity, Begins at Home," *Guardian*, August 1, 1977, accessed January 2, 2021, http://againstrape.net/wp-content/uploads/2018/05/1977-When-rape-like-charity-begins-at-home.jpg.

15 See Katrin Axelsson and Lisa Longstaff, "We Are Women Against Rape but We Do Not Want Assange Extradited," *Guardian*, August 23, 2012, accessed November 26, 2020, https://www.theguardian.com/commentisfree/2012/aug/23/women-against-rape-julian-assange; Lisa Longstaff, "Unpublished Letter on Arrest of Assange," in Tariq Ali and Margaret Kunstler, eds., *In Defense of Julian Assange* (New York: OR Books, 2019).

16 Selma James, "Hookers in the House of the Lord," 110.

17 Both Legal Action for Women and Every Mother Is a Working Mother Network have published self-help guides which are available on line.

18 We mourn the loss of my friend Ian Macdonald QC. I had known him since 1965. He was always available to any group at our London Centre who needed help and advice. He was what we call "a movement lawyer." He had been a key to the Mangrove Nine defendants winning their historic trial against police racism. In 2016, we held a benefit for Haiti where Altheia Jones-LeCointe, one of the defendants who had represented herself, and Ian told the story of the trial. The filming of that meeting, "The Mangrove Nine: How We Won," is available. There is also now a major film; Steve McQueen, dir., *Mangrove* (London: BBC Films, 2020).

19 In the past few years, the women's movement internationally has centred on the rape and murder of women. How many of the victims are murdered because of their sexuality we don't know.

20 There is now evidence that it was the imperial powers which introduced homophobia into African society; Val Kalende, for Think Africa Press, "Africa: Homophobia Is a Legacy of Colonialism," *Guardian*, 30 April 30, 2014, accessed October 15, 2020, https://www.theguardian.com/world/2014/apr/30/africa-homophobia-legacy-colonialism.

21 "TMM Update Trans Day of Remembrance 2019," Trans Respect versus Transphobia, accessed September 26, 2020, https://transrespect.org/en/tmm-update-trans-day-of-remembrance-2019. "They talk about the murders of trans people but it is trans women and travestis who are dying and have the highest poverty. It is femicide, it is transfemicide. . . . The murders and the violence they come also from the police and military. . . . And this violence it is most for the Afro-Brazilian women. They are attacked more because they are Black"; "Natalia, a Trans Sex Worker" (interview), accessed January 12, 2020, https://prostitutescollective.net/interview-natalia-a-migrant-trans-sex-worker.

22 Some are aligned with fundamentalist Christian and other misogynist, anti–sex worker, and anti-gay organizations and are usually well-funded. The US State Department/USAID insists on opposition to prostitution, which they equate with sex trafficking, as a condition for receiving a grant, especially in the case of groups outside the US. How much is this influencing at least some of those who take an anti–sex worker position?

Andaiye: The Uses of Autonomy

Andaiye (1942–2019) was a founder of Red Thread, an organization of grass-roots women across the race divides in Guyana, and a member of Women of Colour GWS. Her death was the loss of a dedicated anti-racist, a valued sister, and a friend we loved.

She changed her name to the Swahili Andaiye, which means "a daughter comes home," when she returned in 1978 from teaching in New York to join the new Working People's Alliance (WPA). The WPA, led by Walter Rodney until his assassination by the Guyanese government in 1980, spearheaded a great multiracial working-class movement. It was Walter who, after reading *The Power of Women and the Subversion of the Community*, had proposed the inclusion of "housewives whose role in production is obscured by lack of a wage" in the WPA's definition of the working class.

Andaiye's anthology *The Point Is to Change the World* makes clear that what most excited her about the Wages for Housework perspective was the analysis in the 1974 *Sex, Race and Class* pamphlet of what Marx calls "a hierarchy of labour powers." She quotes:

> A hierarchy of labour powers and a scale of wages to correspond. Racism and sexism training us to develop and acquire certain capabilities at the expense of all others. Then these acquired capabilities are taken to be our nature and fix our functions for life, and fix also the quality of our mutual relations. So planting cane or tea is not a job for white people and changing nappies is not a job for men and beating children is not violence. Race, sex, age, nation, each an indispensable element of the international division of labour.[1]

She relates two events that propelled her towards the women's movement in about 1985.

The first in 1982, was a reencounter with the International Wages for Housework Campaign . . . whose basic organizing principle is the autonomy of sectors with different levels of power, including sectors of women with different levels of power.[2]

The second . . . came in 1983 as I looked at the internal struggles of the New Jewel Movement [in Grenada] and asked, "where are the women from the National Women's Organization?" . . . [T]he NWO had no independent influence it could exercise on the internal struggle which destroyed the New Jewel Movement, because this "mass organization" of women had no autonomy from the party.

These two moments (the spectacle of the NWO's impotence; the re-encounter with the Wages for Housework Campaign) were a turning point for me—the one, demonstrating the need for women to organize autonomously from men because they have different levels of power, and the other, applying the principle of autonomous organizing among women because we, too, have different levels of power among our different sectors.[3]

It was through these eyes that Andaiye looked again at her experience in the Guyanese movement. She recounts a great struggle led by housewives in 1982–1983, over the government's ban of the basic staples of the diet of both the Afro- and Indo-Guyanese working class: wheat flour and split peas.[4] A high point followed the arrest of twenty-four bauxite workers who had been part of a march against the ban, when

nearly two thousand housewives and children stormed the Wismar/Mackenzie police station demanding their release, faced down the riot squad, and forced the jailers to free them.[5]

Two things stand out: first, the protagonists are referred to as "housewives" rather than the generic women to credit this usually neglected sector of the working class; second, the housewives came together across the two races which had been in conflict and encouraged the men—the Bauxite workers in Linden (almost all Afro-Guyanese) and the sugar workers in the countryside (almost all Indo-Guyanese)—to follow their example.

Andaiye makes a critique of her own organization, the WPA. She says that, though entirely supportive and active for the housewives, the WPA had not treated their autonomy with the respect it deserved and that was needed to help drive the movement forward.

Instead of moving towards and reinforcing the self-activity of the housewives, the WPA Women's Section organized at best parallel activities. . .

. . .Understanding and consciously recognizing the housewives in the food rebellion as the unwaged sector of the working class (as distinct from individuals), might have led us to organize a housewives committee, meeting autonomously and then meeting with sugar and bauxite workers in one unity committee, so that the sectors acknowledged and strengthened each other. Each would have been changed in ways we can't know.[6]

In another essay, Andaiye speaks about the two race-based organizations which abhorred racial violence and helped form the anti-racist, pro-working class WPA: the African Society for Cultural Relations with Independent Africa (ASCRIA) and the Indian Political Revolutionary Associates (IPRA). The WPA, with members from both these organizations, aimed to tackle the race antagonisms so they could get on with the business of the class struggle, which was in the interest of all races, including the Indigenous who lived in the interior and were the poorest people in Guyana. Once the WPA was formed, both organizations dissolved into it. With hindsight, Andaiye concludes:

In my view, if ASCRIA and IPRA had remained alive as autonomous political organizations within the WPA, they would not only have been positioned to help work against the renewed descent into race violence and the further entrenching of opposing race narratives, but to ensuring that the WPA remained a force in touch with and representing the separate and shared interests of Africans and Indians. . . . Working alongside a similarly autonomous organization of Indigenous peoples could have ensured that their interests were also properly addressed.[7]

No one can be sure that this would have worked. What is important is that she looked again at the race divides and how the anti-capitalist strategy of autonomy might have helped.

Recently, I spoke with Eusi Kwayana, a founder of ASCRIA and of the WPA, a close associate of Walter and Andaiye, and the only survivor of the multiracial grassroots government elected in 1953 and overthrown by a British invasion 133 days later. He is to this day, at age 95, the most trusted Caribbean political person.

Andaiye had discussed her conclusion with Eusi not long before she died. His response had been that there is no formula for dealing with racism, but this would have been worth trying.

Andaiye's anthology, published posthumously, is a great and unique gift to the movement.

Notes

1   Selma James, "Sex, Race, and Class," in Selma James, *Sex, Race, and Class: The Perspective of Winning—A Selection of Writings 1952–2011* (Oakland: PM Press, 2012), 96.
2   She had lived in New York in the 1970s and had been in a women's study group; the two founders of Black Women for Wages for Housework were also in that group. They met again in London in 1982.
3   Andaiye, "What Propelled Me towards the Women's Movement," in Alissa Trotz, ed., *The Point Is to Change the World: Selected Writings of Andaiye* (London: Pluto Press, 2020), 8–9.
4   Andaiye, "Housewives and Carers in the Guyanese Resistance of the Late 1970s and Early 1980s: Looking Back" (2010), in ibid., 134.
5   Ibid., 141.
6   Ibid., 146–47.
7   Andaiye, "Organizing within and against Race Divides," ibid., 94.

Unlocking the Power of the Movement

The form of autonomy we are describing is particular to our network. But even if it is not spelled out or if other words are used to describe it, autonomy is always central to working-class organizing.

Capital penetrates our initiatives in all kinds of ways, but primarily by using the hierarchy among us: the more powerful sectors socially and economically, or the more powerful within each sector, challenging and undermining the less powerful. We must remember that this power hierarchy is fundamental to capitalist society.

In 1973, the first paragraph of "Sex, Race and Class" ended with:

> [L]ocked within the contradiction between the discreet entity of sex or race and the totality of class is the greatest deterrent to working-class power and at the same time the creative energy to achieve that power.[1]

I never explained it because I didn't know how. Almost half a century later, it is easier to spell out what I was trying to say.

Many of us don't know how much we lose by being cut off from other sectors of people and the power they have to offer. This unawareness undermines our access to our own power and traps us into going it alone and even colluding with our enemy.

Autonomy, which stands against every form of separatism, has increasingly enabled us to embrace the interests of other sectors while never losing sight of the interests of our own. In this way, we arm ourselves against divide and rule.

Autonomy enables us to develop the political habit of identifying and acknowledging sectors in struggle that are points of reference for our own. This advances the process of rejecting the personal ambition and competition, within our own sector and between sectors, which have often corrupted the movement's purpose and resulted in dirty compromise and defeat.

Thus, autonomy is the necessary and potent strategy with which to identify the many faces of the State and confront each collectively wherever they appear. As we break out of the confinements of the hierarchy, the power of our movement is unlocked, and we assume possibilities that we could never consider before. The energy, creativity, and boldness which are released are truly joyous and liberating.

Notes

1   Selma James, "Sex, Race, and Class," in Selma James, *Sex, Race, and Class* (Oakland: PM Press, 2012), 92.

Index

Page numbers in *italic* refer to illustrations. "Passim" (literally "scattered") indicates intermittent discussion of a topic over a cluster of pages.

About the Authors

Selma James is an anti-sexist, anti-racist, and anti-capitalist campaigner and author. She was born in Brooklyn, New York, in 1930. Raised in a movement household, she joined CLR James's Johnson-Forest Tendency at fifteen, and in 1955 emigrated to London to marry CLR, who had been deported from the US during McCarthyism. From 1958 to 1962, she worked with him in the movement for independence and federation of the English-speaking Caribbean. In 1965, back in London, she was the first organizing secretary of the Campaign Against Racial Discrimination. In 1972, she founded the International Wages for Housework Campaign. She co-authored the classic *The Power of Women and the Subversion of the Community,* which launched the "domestic labour debate." She coined the word "unwaged" to describe the caring work women do; it has since entered the English language to describe all who work without wages, on the land, in the home, in the community. . . In 1975, she became the first spokeswoman for the English Collective of Prostitutes. In 2000, she helped launch the Global Women's Strike, which the Wages for Housework Campaign coordinates. She is a founding member of the International Jewish Anti-Zionist Network (2008). Her pathbreaking "Sex, Race and Class" (1974) on different sectors, waged and unwaged, Global South and Global North, working together on the basis of autonomy, was republished in her first anthology *Sex, Race, and Class: The Perspective of Winning* (PM Press, 2012). Other publications include: *The Rapist Who Pays the Rent* (co-author, Falling Wall Press, 1981), *The Ladies and the Mammies: Jane Austen & Jean Rhys* (Falling Wall Press, 1983), *Marx & Feminism* (Jubilee Group of Christian Socialists, 1983), *Strangers & Sisters: Women, Race and Immigration* (ed. and introduction, Falling Wall Press, 1985), *The Milk of Human Kindness: Defending Breastfeeding from the AIDS Industry and the Global Market* (co-author, Crossroads Books, 2002), *Jailhouse Lawyers* (ed. and introduction, Crossroads Books, 2011), *Ujamaa: The Hidden Story of*

Tanzania's Socialist Villages (ed. and introduction, Crossroads Books, 2014). She is a coordinator of the Care Income Now! campaign launched jointly with the Green New Deal for Europe in 2020. Selma James is a renowned public speaker, a mother, and a grandmother.

Margaret Prescod is the co-founder of Black Women for Wages for Housework and coordinator of Women of Color in the Global Women's Strike and an award-winning, nationally syndicated journalist on Pacifica Radio. She is founder of the Black Coalition Fighting Back Serial Murders and co-founder of Every Mother is a Working Mother Network. She is the author of *Black Women: Bringing It All Back Home* (Falling Wall Press, 1980). She is originally from Barbados. She is a mother and lives in Los Angeles.

Nina López is joint coordinator of the Global Women's Strike and founder of Legal Action for Women. Her writings and edited volumes include: *Some Mother's Daughter: The Hidden Movement of Prostitute Women against Violence* (Crossroads Books, 1999); *The Milk of Human Kindness* (co-author, Crossroads Books, 2002); and *Creating a Caring Economy: Nora Castañeda and the Women's Development Bank of Venezuela* (Crossroads Books, 2006). She is originally from Argentina. She is a mother and lives in London.

ABOUT PM PRESS

PM Press is an independent, radical publisher of books and
media to educate, entertain, and inspire. Founded in 2007
by a small group of people with decades of publishing,
media, and organizing experience, PM Press amplifies the
voices of radical authors, artists, and activists. Our aim is to
deliver bold political ideas and vital stories to all walks of life and arm the dreamers
to demand the impossible. We have sold millions of copies of our books, most
often one at a time, face to face. We're old enough to know what we're doing and
young enough to know what's at stake. Join us to create a better world.

PM Press
PO Box 23912
Oakland, CA 94623
www.pmpress.org

PM Press in Europe
europe@pmpress.org
www.pmpress.org.uk

FRIENDS OF PM PRESS

These are indisputably momentous times—the financial system is melting down globally and the Empire is stumbling. Now more than ever there is a vital need for radical ideas.

In the years since its founding—and on a mere shoestring— PM Press has risen to the formidable challenge of publishing and distributing knowledge and entertainment for the struggles ahead. With over 450 releases to date, we have published an impressive and stimulating array of literature, art, music, politics, and culture. Using every available medium, we've succeeded in connecting those hungry for ideas and information to those putting them into practice.

Friends of PM allows you to directly help impact, amplify, and revitalize the discourse and actions of radical writers, filmmakers, and artists. It provides us with a stable foundation from which we can build upon our early successes and provides a much-needed subsidy for the materials that can't necessarily pay their own way. You can help make that happen—and receive every new title automatically delivered to your door once a month—by joining as a Friend of PM Press. And, we'll throw in a free T-shirt when you sign up.

Here are your options:

- **$30 a month** Get all books and pamphlets plus 50% discount on all webstore purchases

- **$40 a month** Get all PM Press releases (including CDs and DVDs) plus 50% discount on all webstore purchases

- **$100 a month** Superstar—Everything plus PM merchandise, free downloads, and 50% discount on all webstore purchases

For those who can't afford $30 or more a month, we have **Sustainer Rates** at $15, $10, and $5. Sustainers get a free PM Press T-shirt and a 50% discount on all purchases from our website.

Your Visa or Mastercard will be billed once a month, until you tell us to stop. Or until our efforts succeed in bringing the revolution around. Or the financial meltdown of Capital makes plastic redundant. Whichever comes first.

Sex, Race, and Class—The Perspective of Winning: A Selection of Writings 1952-2011

Selma James
With a foreword by Marcus Rediker
and an introduction by Nina López

ISBN: 978-1-60486-454-0
$20.00   320 pages

In 1972 Selma James set out a new political perspective.
Her starting point was the millions of unwaged women who, working in the home and on the land, were not seen as "workers" and their struggles viewed as outside of the class struggle. Based on her political training in the Johnson-Forest Tendency, founded by her late husband C.L.R. James, on movement experience South and North, and on a respectful study of Marx, she redefined the working class to include sectors previously dismissed as "marginal."

For James, the class struggle presents itself as the conflict between the reproduction and survival of the human race, and the domination of the market with its exploitation, wars, and ecological devastation. She sums up her strategy for change as "Invest in Caring not Killing."

This selection, spanning six decades, traces the development of this perspective in the course of building an international campaigning network. It includes excerpts from the classic *The Power of Women and the Subversion of the Community* which launched the "domestic labor debate," the exciting "Hookers in the House of the Lord" which describes a church occupation by sex workers, an incisive review of the C.L.R. James masterpiece *The Black Jacobins*, a reappraisal of the novels of Jean Rhys and of the leadership of Julius Nyerere, the groundbreaking "Marx and Feminism," and more.

The writing is lucid and without jargon. The ideas, never abstract, spring from the experience of organising, from trying to make sense of the successes and the setbacks, and from the need to find a way forward.

"It's time to acknowledge James's path-breaking analysis: from 1972 she reinterpreted the capitalist economy to show that it rests on the usually invisible unwaged caring work of women."
—Dr. Peggy Antrobus, feminist, author of *The Global Women's Movement: Origins, Issues and Strategies*

"For clarity and commitment to Haiti's revolutionary legacy . . . Selma is a sister after my own heart."
—Danny Glover, actor and activist

A New Notion:
Two Works by C. L. R. James
"Every Cook Can Govern" and
"The Invading Socialist Society"

Edited by Noel Ignatiev

ISBN: 978-1-60486-047-4
$16.95   160 pages

C. L. R. James was a leading figure in the independence
movement in the West Indies, and the black and
working-class movements in both Britain and the United States. As a major
contributor to Marxist and revolutionary theory, his project was to discover,
document, and elaborate the aspects of working-class activity that constitute
the revolution in today's world. In this volume, Noel Ignatiev, author of *How the
Irish Became White*, provides an extensive introduction to James' life and thought,
before presenting two critical works that together illustrate the tremendous
breadth and depth of James' worldview. "The Invading Socialist Society," for James
the fundamental document of his political tendency, shows clearly the power of
James's political acumen and its relevance in today's world with a clarity of analysis
that anticipated future events to a remarkable extent. "Every Cook Can Govern," is
a short and eminently readable piece counterpoising direct with representative
democracy, and getting to the heart of how we should relate to one another.
Together these two works represent the principal themes that run through James's
life: implacable hostility toward all "condescending saviors" of the working class,
and undying faith in the power of ordinary people to build a new world.

*"It would take a person with great confidence, and good judgment, to select from the
substantial writings of C. L. R. James just two items to represent the 'principal themes'
in James' life and thought. Fortunately, Noel Ignatiev is such a person. With a concise,
but thorough introduction, Ignatiev sets the stage and C. L. R. James does the rest. In
these often confusing times one way to keep one's head on straight and to chart a
clear path to the future is to engage the analytical methods and theoretical insights of
C. L. R. James. What you hold in your hands is an excellent starting point."*
— John H. Bracey Jr., professor of African-American Studies at the University of
Massachusetts–Amherst and co-editor of *Strangers & Neighbors: Relations Between
Blacks & Jews in the United States.*

*"C. L. R. James has arguably had a greater influence on the underlying thinking of
independence movements in the West Indies and Africa than any living man."*
— *Sunday Times*

"It remains remarkable how far ahead of his time he was on so many issues."
—New Society

State Capitalism and World Revolution

C.L.R. James, Raya Dunayevskaya,
and Grace Lee Boggs
with an Introduction by Paul Buhle and a
Preface by Martin Glaberman

ISBN: 978-1-60486-092-4
$16.95   160 pages

Over sixty years ago, C.L.R. James and a small circle
of collaborators making up the radical left Johnson-Forest Tendency reached the
conclusion that there was no true socialist society existing anywhere in the world.
Written in collaboration with Raya Dunayevskaya and Grace Lee Boggs, this is
another pioneering critique of Lenin and Trotsky, and reclamation of Marx, from
the West Indian scholar and activist, C.L.R. James. Originally published in 1950,
this definitive edition includes the original preface from Martin Glaberman to the
third edition, C.L.R. James' original introductions to three previous editions and a
new introduction from James' biographer Paul Buhle.

*"When one looks back over the last twenty years to those men who were most far-
sighted, who first began to tease out the muddle of ideology in our times, who were
at the same time Marxists with a hard theoretical basis, and close students of society,
humanists with a tremendous response to and understanding of human culture,
Comrade James is one of the first one thinks of."*
—E.P. Thompson

"C.L.R. James is one of those rare individuals whom history proves right."
—Race Today

"It remains remarkable how far ahead of his time he was on so many issues."
—New Society

Modern Politics

C.L.R. James with an Introduction
by Noel Ignatiev

ISBN: 978-1-60486-311-6
$16.95   176 pages

"Marxists envisage a total change in the basic structure
of human relations. With that change our problems
will not be solved overnight, but we will be able to
tackle them with confidence. Such are the difficulties,
contradictions, and antagonisms; and in the solution
of them society moves forward and men and women feel they have a role in the
development of their social surroundings. It is in this movement that we have the
possibility of a good life." —C.L.R. James, from *Modern Politics*

This volume provides a brilliant and accessible summation of the ideas of left
Marxist giant C.L.R. James. Originally delivered in 1960 as a series of lectures in his
native Trinidad, these writings powerfully display his wide-ranging erudition and
enduring relevance. From his analysis of revolutionary history (from the Athenian
City-States through the English Revolution, Russian Revolution, and the Hungarian
Revolution of 1956), to the role of literature, art, and culture in society (from
Charlie Chaplin to Pablo Picasso, via Camus and Eisenstein), to an interrogation
of the ideas and philosophy of such thinkers as Rousseau, Lenin, and Trotsky, this
is a magnificent tour de force from a critically engaged thinker at the height of his
powers. An essential introduction to a body of work as necessary and illuminating
for this century as it proved for the last.

*"When one looks back over the last twenty years to those men who were most far-
sighted, who first began to tease out the muddle of ideology in our times, who were
at the same time Marxists with a hard theoretical basis, and close students of society,
humanists with a tremendous response to and understanding of human culture,
Comrade James is one of the first one thinks of."*
—E.P. Thompson

*"C.L.R. James has a special place in the history of Third World revolutionary movements.
He combines Caribbean nationalism, Black radicalism, a once Trotskyist blend of
revolutionary anti-imperialism, and the European classic tradition in an individual and
potent mix. A mine of richness and variety."*
—*Times Educational Supplement*

"C.L.R. James is one of those rare individuals whom history proves right."
—*Race Today*

A History of Pan-African Revolt

C.L.R. James with an Introduction
by Robin D.G. Kelley

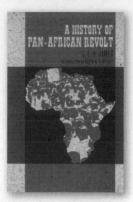

ISBN: 978-1-60486-095-5
$16.95   160 pages

Originally published in England in 1938 (the same year
as his magnum opus *The Black Jacobins*) and expanded
in 1969, this work remains the classic account of
global black resistance. Robin D.G. Kelley's substantial
introduction contextualizes the work in the history and
ferment of the times, and explores its ongoing relevance today.

"*A History of Pan-African Revolt* is one of those rare books that continues to strike
a chord of urgency, even half a century after it was first published. Time and
time again, its lessons have proven to be valuable and relevant for understanding
liberation movements in Africa and the diaspora. Each generation who has had the
opportunity to read this small book finds new insights, new lessons, new visions for
their own age . . . . No piece of literature can substitute for a crystal ball, and only
religious fundamentalists believe that a book can provide comprehensive answers
to all questions. But if nothing else, *A History of Pan-African Revolt* leaves us with
two incontrovertible facts. First, as long as black people are denied freedom,
humanity and a decent standard of living, they will continue to revolt. Second,
unless these revolts involve the ordinary masses and take place on their own terms,
they have no hope of succeeding." —Robin D.G. Kelley, from the Introduction

"I wish my readers to understand the history of Pan-African Revolt. They fought,
they suffered—they are still fighting. Once we understand that, we can tackle our
problems with the necessary mental equilibrium." —C.L.R. James

"*Kudos for reissuing C.L.R. James's pioneering work on black resistance. Many brilliant
embryonic ideas articulated in* A History of Pan-African Revolt *twenty years later
became the way to study black social movements. Robin Kelley's introduction superbly
situates James and his thought in the world of Pan-African and Marxist intellectuals.*"
—Sundiata Cha-Jua, Penn State University

"*A mine of ideas advancing far ahead of its time.*"
—Walter Rodney

The Young C.L.R. James: A Graphic Novelette

Illustrated by Milton Knight.
Edited by Paul Buhle and Lawrence Ware

ISBN: 978-1-62963-514-9
$6.95   48 pages

This unique comic by Milton Knight illuminates the early years of C.L.R. James (1901–1989), known in much later years as the "last great Pan-Africanist." The son of a provincial school administrator in British-governed Trinidad, James disappointed his family by embracing the culture and passions of the colonial underclass, Carnival and cricket. He joined the literary avant-garde of the island before leaving for Britain. In the UK, James swiftly became a beloved cricket journalist, playwright for his close friend Paul Robeson, and a pathbreaking scholar of black history with *The Black Jacobins* (1938), the first history of the Haitian revolt.

The artistic skills of Milton Knight, at once acute and provocative, bring out James's unique personality, how it arose, and how he became a world figure.

Resistance Behind Bars: The Struggles of Incarcerated Women, 2nd Edition

Victoria Law with an Introduction
by Laura Whitehorn

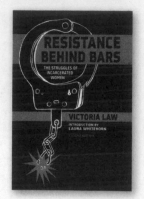

ISBN: 978-1-60486-583-7
$20.00   320 pages

In 1974, women imprisoned at New York's maximum-security prison at Bedford Hills staged what is known as the August Rebellion. Protesting the brutal beating of a fellow prisoner, the women fought off guards, holding seven of them hostage, and took over sections of the prison.

While many have heard of the 1971 Attica prison uprising, the August Rebellion remains relatively unknown even in activist circles. *Resistance Behind Bars* is determined to challenge and change such oversights. As it examines daily struggles against appalling prison conditions and injustices, *Resistance* documents both collective organizing and individual resistance among women incarcerated in the U.S. Emphasizing women's agency in resisting the conditions of their confinement through forming peer education groups, clandestinely arranging ways for children to visit mothers in distant prisons and raising public awareness about their lives, *Resistance* seeks to spark further discussion and research into the lives of incarcerated women and galvanize much-needed outside support for their struggles.

This updated and revised edition of the 2009 PASS Award winning book includes a new chapter about transgender, transsexual, intersex, and gender-variant people in prison.

"Victoria Law's eight years of research and writing, inspired by her unflinching commitment to listen to and support women prisoners, has resulted in an illuminating effort to document the dynamic resistance of incarcerated women in the United States."
—Roxanne Dunbar-Ortiz

"Written in regular English, rather than academese, this is an impressive work of research and reportage"
—Mumia Abu-Jamal, death row political prisoner and author of *Live From Death Row*